William L. Davidson

Theism as Grounded in Human Nature

historically and critically handled - Being the Burnett Lectures for 1892 and 1893

William L. Davidson

Theism as Grounded in Human Nature
historically and critically handled - Being the Burnett Lectures for 1892 and 1893

ISBN/EAN: 9783337190897

Printed in Europe, USA, Canada, Australia, Japan

Cover: Foto ©Andreas Hilbeck / pixelio.de

More available books at **www.hansebooks.com**

BEING

THE BURNETT LECTURES

FOR 1892 AND 1893

BY

WILLIAM L. DAVIDSON, M.A., LL.D.

AUTHOR OF "THE LOGIC OF DEFINITION," ETC.

LONDON

LONGMANS, GREEN AND CO.

AND NEW YORK: 15 EAST 16th STREET

1893

" With busy hammers closing rivets up."
—*Shakespeare.*

Ἡμεῖς δὲ οὐκ ἐσμὲν ὑποστολῆς . . . ἀλλὰ πίστεως.
—*Hebrews.*

" The philosophy that one chooses depends on the kind of man one is."
—*Fichte.*

" Hæc summa delicti, nolle agnoscere, quem ignorare non possis."
—*Tertullian.*

THE FIRST COURSE OF LECTURES,
1892.

WORKS BY THE SAME AUTHOR.

THE LOGIC OF DEFINITION : EXPLAINED AND APPLIED.

Price 6s.

" There is manifested throughout the book sound scholarship, wide general and philosophical reading, and practical acquaintance with the several branches of natural science ; then, with these attainments, there is everywhere combined rare analytical power and a broad independent method of looking at difficult questions. The result is a work that deserves to take a high place in the philosophical literature of the day. It is admirably calculated to assist students in all departments of inquiry : but it is especially fitted to be useful to students of philosophy."—*The Scotsman.*

" Faithful, thorough work. . . . The illustrative examples of this chapter are in themselves studies. . . . The remaining chapters are, taken *per se*, studies of uncommon excellence. . . . A debt of gratitude is due to the author, who brings a logical training to bear on natural science definition."—*The Daily Free Press.*

" The book is one that marks a stage in the development of logical method. . . . It is the product of a vigorous mind, and no one can read such a chapter as that on ' The separation of questions in Philosophy ' —truly a *multum in parvo*—without finding in a few pages more help towards the solution of some of the knottiest problems in metaphysics and morals than is to be found in many other octavo volumes. The style is terse and strong, and the book so abounds in illustrations and examples as to make a subject naturally difficult and uninteresting to many, easy and instructive to all."—*The Banffshire Journal.*

" To clear away logomachies, the smoke and dust which hides the real battles of metaphysics, is certainly a material service to those who have to take a part in those ever-raging contests. And this service Mr. DAVIDSON most patiently and faithfully performs for those who will read and mark *The Logic of Definition.*"—*The Oxford Review.*

"This is one of that useful class of works which apply the principles of formal logic to interesting and important examples. The discipline of the parade is directed to the requirements of actual service."—*The Academy.*

"We cannot here follow Mr. DAVIDSON through his masterly, and we must repeat, entertaining and instructive pages. We can only add that his definitions and principles are laid down with precision and clearness, that his illustrations and examples are well chosen, and that to those who wish to write or think correctly, or to thread their way through the perplexities which many modern writers prepare for them, his volume will prove invaluable."—*Scottish Quarterly Review.*

"This is an able and useful book, and one that treats of a subject of urgent importance."—*British Quarterly Review.*

"The peculiar merit of Mr. DAVIDSON'S work lies in the original and suggestive application of the first principles of logic to the four departments of Dictionaries, School Books, Philosophical Vocabulary, and Biology."—*The Journal of Education.*

"Mr. DAVIDSON'S style is direct and forcible. He writes with fulness of knowledge, and often gives interest to somewhat abstruse themes by means of well chosen examples."—*Daily Review.*

"This work is a valuable contribution to clearness of thought and expression. . . . The arrangement of the work is clear and methodical, the style lucid, and the examples are, as a rule, admirable."—*The Guardian.*

ENGLISH WORDS EXPLAINED.

Price 3s. 6d.

"This little work, intended for schools, and sure to find an entrance where the master is intelligent enough, is a most useful yet simple piece of applied logic—in the way of 'synonymous discrimination'."—*Mind.*

"The book seems to be accurate as far as it goes, and with its object we are in thorough sympathy."—*The Saturday Review.*

"To those who are engaged in teaching, this new work of Mr. DAVIDSON's can scarcely fail to prove exceedingly acceptable. It will be of value also to all who are desirous of speaking or writing with accuracy."—*The Scottish Quarterly Review.*

"A useful little book this . . . carefully executed." *The Spectator.*

"On the whole, Mr. DAVIDSON has done his work well, and a clever teacher might make the book very useful in his lessons on English composition."—*The Athenæum.*

"A very praiseworthy effort to illumine the path of the aspirant to the art of writing the English language with propriety."—*The Guardian.*

"This book, which is intended to be 'An Aid to Teaching,' seems thoroughly well fitted to serve its purpose. . . . Students of the English language, and writers ambitious to attain exactness and accuracy in the use of English words, will find it an invaluable guide."—*The Educational News.*

"The little book named above is one we can heartily welcome. . . . The author as a logician treats his subject with admirable clearness, and at the same time makes it interesting by his wealth of illustrations and examples." *The Practical Teacher.*

"The work is very useful and suggestive, and, what is more, of an accuracy unusual in English school books on the English language."—*The Journal of Education.*

"Mr. DAVIDSON has certainly provided a book which, if studied by teacher and pupil, will do much towards correcting the looseness of style prevalent alike in lectures, conversation, and even in educational text-books. The volume, moreover, forms a convenient little hand-book which is an acquisition to every writing table."—*The Educational Times.*

CONTENTS.

FIRST COURSE OF LECTURES.

LECTURE I.

THEISTIC DOUBT: ITS NATURE, POSSIBILITY, AND LIMITS.

LECTURE II.

ANALYSIS OF HUMAN NATURE : EXPOSITORY AND HISTORICAL.

I.

II.

1. *Plato.*

2. *Aristotle.*

3. *The Bible.*

Contents.

4. Confucius, Buddha, the Stoics.

5. The Neo-platonists.

6. The Schoolmen.

7. From Descartes to Hegel.

8. *Recent Advance.*

III.

LECTURE III.

AGNOSTIC OBJECTIONS.

I.

II.

Contents.

I. Philosophical Agnosticism.

1. Xenophanes.

2. Hume.

3. Kant.

Contents.

LECTURE V.

GOD A NECESSITY OF HUMAN NATURE.

LECTURE VI.

THE IDEA OF GOD, AS PSYCHOLOGICALLY DETERMINED.

II.

III.

SECOND COURSE OF LECTURES.

LECTURE VII.

EMOTIONAL THEISM.

I.

II.

III.

IV.

LECTURE VIII.

ETHICAL THEISM: IDEALITY AND THE ETHICAL SELF.

I.

II.

Contents. xxiii

LECTURE X.

ETHICAL THEISM: CONSCIENCE—METAPHYSICAL.

VII. *Rational Implicates of Conscience.*

VIII. *Ontological or Theistic Implications.*

IX. *Objections.*

X. *Historical.*

LECTURE XI.

INTELLECTUAL THEISM: LOGICAL AND ANALYTIC.

LECTURE XII.

INTELLECTUAL THEISM: PHILOSOPHICAL AND SYNTHETIC.

THEISM,

AS GROUNDED IN HUMAN NATURE:

HISTORICALLY AND CRITICALLY HANDLED.

LECTURE I.

THEISTIC DOUBT: ITS NATURE, POSSIBILITY, AND LIMITS.

THERE is probably no one who has turned his mind seriously to the consideration of Theism who has not felt somewhat as Simonides of old did, when the theistic problem was set him for solution by his royal master. Of Simonides it is recorded that, when Hiero proposed to him the question, "What is God?" he desired a day to consider it. When next day his answer was required, he begged two days more; and as, time after time, he went on doubling the number of days, Hiero at last, in astonishment, asked him the reason for his strange procedure. "Because," replied he, "the longer I meditate upon it, the more obscure does it seem to me to be."

1

What exactly were the difficulties that Simonides encountered, we are not told. Perhaps it was, as Cotta, in the *De Natura Deorum* (i. 22), suggests, that Simonides, "being not only a delightful poet, but also in other respects a wise and learned man, found so many acute and subtle arguments occurring to him that he had doubt which of them was the truest, and so despaired of attaining any truth". Or, perhaps it was, as Caecilius, in the *Octavius* of Marcus Minutius Felix, seems to suppose, that he exercised a wise delay "for fear either of introducing doting superstition or of destroying all religion". But, either way, he should not have finally despaired. For even though, from the very nature of the case, the treatment of such a subject must, at the very best, be imperfect, there is no necessity that, so far as it goes, it should be utterly inadequate; and, allowing that the introduction of "doting superstition" would unquestionably be an evil, it might yet be a greater good than the creation and cherishing of the false impression that Religion has no rational foundation. There is a pithy sentence in Bacon somewhere, which runs: "When the human mind finally despairs of truth, or begins to languish, weakness of mind is as much shown in sceptical despair as it is in unquestioning prejudice or dogma".

We need not, then, be terrified by difficulties;

at any rate, we need not allow them to paralyze
us. Difficulties beset all great questions: shall
we expect them to be absent from the greatest?
There is difficulty in the famous metaphysical problems of External Perception and the Freedom of
the Will; the biologist has difficulty with the conception and proper definition of Life; and if, with
the modern physicist, we permit ourselves to
speculate on the nature and ultimate constitution
of Atoms, we shall soon discover that we have
penetrated into a region where neither sun nor
stars in many days appear. It must never be
forgotten that we may carry our scepticism too
far,—we may be over-cautious as well as over-
bold; and once let us refuse to move because of
obscurity, and we thereby put a stop to progress
altogether, not only in religion, but also in every
field of physical and intellectual research. Difficulties should stimulate rather than deter. "He
that wrestles with us strengthens our nerves, and
sharpens our skill. Our antagonist is our helper."
And so, when I now propose to follow out one
great line of theistic exposition. I hope that I shall
not be accused of attempting the impossible, or be
taunted with too great presumption in essaying a
task in which Simonides seems to have failed.

There are countless ways in which people may

look at theism, and the modes of handling it are
manifold; but three in particular are very prominent, and require to be specialized. In the first
place: starting from the idea of God, given in
experience and duly analyzed, we may set ourselves to trace its origin; using for this purpose
philology or the testimony of language, document-
ary evidence from a period as far back as one can
go, investigation into the thoughts, manners, and
customs of existing races—these, one or more,
according to the individual investigator's particular leanings or his special acquirements. In the
next place: starting still from the idea of God,
given in experience and duly analyzed, we may
investigate its roots in human nature, and, giving
it a philosophical explanation, employ it as a
rational interpretation of the universe. In the
third place: eliminating the idea of God altogether,
we may try to see how the universe looks when
stript of theistic implications, and, if satisfied with
the result, stop short of theism, or cast it aside as
illusion or chimæra.

It is the second of these three attitudes that is
taken here. I do not, indeed, ignore the other two,
I shall have much to say, one way or other, of
each of them; but I regard Theism essentially
from the side of the philosophy of human nature.
It is a doctrine psychologically grounded, and

rationally defensible ; and I venture to defend it.
In doing so, I hope to be able to show that Theism
is logically valid ; meeting a distinct want of man,
and making imperative demands upon him. Or,
if you refuse me this, I hope at any rate to be able
to gain the negative merit of refuting certain for-
midable-looking arguments that are frequently
launched against Theism in the name of Philosophy, but which have really no true philosophical
value. Even this negative merit is of vast importance, and goes a long way towards answering those
who accuse the theist of indulging in the worthless
chase of an *ignis fatuus*, rather than in the sober
quest of a great Reality justified by reason. For
if, as Berkeley maintains, the main end of discussion is, not simply to persuade, but to discover
and defend the truth, then " truth may be justified,
not only by persuading its adversaries, but, where
that cannot be done, by showing them to be unreasonable " (*Alciphron ; or, The Minute Philosopher*, iv. § 2).

The subject of Theism is a very great one, and
needs both patient and reverent handling. But
this need for reverence and patience is only what
we find in every department of knowledge. Not
here alone but elsewhere is it true, that the
pondering gaze of reverence sees farthest into the

secrets of the universe. The reverent spirit is
the earnest spirit and the open spirit ; and to it,
necessarily, revelations are emphatically made. It
is, also, the tolerant and sympathetic spirit. Implying as it does entire loyalty to Truth and a
desire to be guided by it,—a desire to practise
it and live by it, and not simply to know it,
implying, in other words, a certain attitude of
will, as well as of intellect, it spurns, of necessity, the notion of arguing merely for victory's
sake, and it strives to throw itself sympathetically
into the point of view of opponents.

I do not think that Truth has ever been
attained by any man who did not strenuously
cultivate it, nor do I think that it has ever been
attained by any man who looked contemptuously
on those who differ from him in opinion. Scorn,
unless it be in the shape of moral indignation
against insincerity and hypocrisy, is weakness and
disease, and blinds the eye to clear perception and
the light. Very easy is it to assume that oneself
is always in the right and one's adversary always
in the wrong, and, if very easy, so too very gratifying. But is it not too gratifying and too easy
for the attainment of any solid result ? Cromwell
spoke words of deepest wisdom when he gave the
famous advice to the General Assembly : "I
beseech you in the bowels of Christ, think it

possible you may be mistaken". We may take it as a fundamental axiom, that truth is not the exclusive property of an individual, nor of any one class of individuals; and, wherever the earnest inquirer is, *there* is the man on the way to light. Truth, indeed, is infinite, and the roads that lead to it are numberless. We can attain it, apparently, only piecemeal and by degrees. But, however diverse the approaches and however numerous the paths, the ultimate result can only be unity. Whatever else we lose, never let us lose our faith that "Truth is catholic, and Nature one".

All this granted, it may, nevertheless, be maintained that neither reverence nor tolerance solves difficulties; neither of them is even an antidote to Doubt. Doubts assail the earnest seeker after truth, and it is impossible to allay them.

Doubts, indeed, assail the earnest seeker after truth: but I cannot admit that it is impossible to allay them. A great authority has told us to "prove all things". This just means that we are to believe only as we see reason, that we must not pretend more than we actually feel, that we are not to *force* conviction. But, while we are not to force conviction, we are at the same time to see that we do not consciously retard it. There is a twofold duty in connexion with the matter, and

one part of that duty is equally necessary with
the other. All philosophy, and, therefore, all
rational religion, must pass through the ordeal of
Doubt: their validity must be tested by every
method applicable to the subject-matter. But
we must take care that our tests are of the appropriate kind. We do not weigh our thoughts
in literal scales, nor measure our ideas with the
actual foot-rule. The ponderable is simply irrelevant in the one case, and the mensurable in
the other. We do not gauge the capacity of the
eye by instruments suited only for the ear; nor
are the phenomena of life subject to the same
treatment as those of inorganic matter. So, to
demand that spiritual facts shall conform to
material manipulation is unreasonable. Lalande
might sweep the heavens with his telescope, and
yet find no God; but had he seriously asked himself the reason why, he would have soon discovered that a God so found would be no God
at all. It is possible that God may be seen,
though not with the fleshly organ. The telescope
is suitable for the stars, and the microscope for
the lower living organisms; but, fine though these
instruments are, and marvellous in their revelations,
they are all too coarse for the perception and discovery of spiritual things. The world is not exhausted by what we see and taste and handle.

Remembering this, we may be able to perceive a way of removing Doubt. There may be methods of investigation that we do not always sufficiently respect, but which, nevertheless, carry in them the means of satisfying earnest inquiry.

The method that I adopt is a very simple one. It consists in a statement and analysis of Theistic Experience, together with an explicit reference to its psychological grounds and logical implications. This, and nothing more. Yet it will be found to be very much. I take my stand firmly on experienced fact, on the psychological and historical data on which religion is based, and argue from that in accordance with the acknowledged canons of dialectic. This I hold to be the true method of Philosophy: for philosophy may be defined as the systematic and sustained attempt to turn spontaneous into reflective thought, and, in doing so, to give explicit expression to the rational presuppositions of human experience.

Observe, then, the two parts of the method: Experience, and the Interpretation of experience. On this latter, of course, I place distinct stress. It is the deductive and inferential side of the process, without which the other would be incomplete. But, just because it is deductive and inferential, many people distrust it. They think that inference is a dangerous thing, and they will not allow that anything that needs to be reasoned out, anything that is supported by argument or demonstration, has that degree of validity about it which would justify them in giving it an unreserved acceptance. *That* is a strange notion, and somewhat ludicrous, if it were not also painful. If human nature is to be trusted at all, it must be trusted as much on its intellectual as on its sensational side; and, though reasoning may undoubtedly err, so too may the senses, and the cure of both is found in Reason itself, whose laws and constitution we know. It is a doubtful compliment to Aristotle and the logicians of the past two thousand years, to suppose that they have been working all that time and yet have been unable to discover any valid tests of truth and falsehood, of error and correctness; and ill has Evolution been doing its duty these many æons if it has been evolving us all in the wrong direction, if it has been propagating and continuing life and consciousness and thought by an unceasing *mal*-adjustment of organism and environment. The notion is laughable, were it not that it has been a source of much pain to many timid souls. They have been harassed and distressed by it, not perceiving that it is a spectre of their own raising—a fear that has its origin solely in their own weakness.

What, then, is it that timid souls would like in place of this rational procedure? They would like to be able to apprehend the Deity by an intuition, just as they have (so they express it) an intuitive perception of the external world. Is that reasonable? Would it answer the purpose, supposing it were given them?

An intuition![1] The external world itself does not stand so secure in this respect as at first sight it seems to do. Philosophy has little difficulty in shaking our faith in the plain man's crude intuition; and Science, with its many incontestable facts about the fallaciousness of sight and the other senses,[2] leaves us very uncomfortable. Descartes, when he wishes to give expression, in geometrical form, to the reasons that establish the existence of God, has to begin with the postulate: " I request that my readers consider how feeble are the reasons that have hitherto led them to repose faith in their senses, and how uncertain are all the judgments which they afterwards founded on them; and that they will revolve this consideration in their mind so long and so frequently, that, in fine, they may acquire the habit of no longer trusting so confidently in their senses; for I hold that this is necessary to

[1] For an historical account of the meanings of Intuition in philosophy, see *The Logic of Definition.* pp. 176-189.

[2] See, for instance, Professor Sully's *Illusions.*

render one capable of apprehending metaphysical truths" (Professor Veitch's *Descartes*, p. 268). To this we must add, that "every assertion of an external world, being an assertion of something beyond the present data of consciousness, must spring from an activity of judgment that does more than merely reduce present data to order. Such an assertion must be an active construction of non-data. We do not receive in our senses, but we posit through our judgment, whatever external world there may for us be" (Dr. Josiah Royce, in *Mind*, 1st series, vol. vii. p. 43).

X But intuition in religion is pre-eminently precarious. It has been tried, and it has failed. Let us note its nature and its characteristics.

By intuition in religion is meant a direct or immediate apprehension of the Divine Being, self-evidencing and unimpeachable,—such a close contact of the finite with the Infinite as to forbid in the former all doubt or hesitation as to the existence of the latter: in other words, it is such a clear revelation of God to the individual soul as to assure him absolutely of God's existence and to free him from all harassing or disturbing questionings or fears regarding it. But, philosophically interpreted, this just means that God is a dictum of consciousness. Now, what do we understand by

God's being a dictum of consciousness? We understand that the individual has simply to interrogate his own mind, and there he will find the assurance either (1) that God is, or (2) that He is a God of such and such a character. But mark, now, what this signifies. If the deliverance of consciousness be simply that "God is," this can only mean, that *"something not-ourselves is"*; for the God whose existence is asserted is altogether undefined, He lacks all characterization. He is, therefore, a bare abstraction ; and the deliverance of consciousness, even supposing it to be given, would be practically valueless. But the fact of such a deliverance will, I presume, be generally denied, if not contemptuously set aside. Whoever claims the testimony of consciousness to God's existence is sure to claim it as declaring a God of such and such attributes or qualities,—a living concrete God, not a lifeless, useless abstraction. Let us accept, then, this form of the intuitive utterance, and note the implications. A man's consciousness assures him that God is as he conceives Him to be ; in other words, that *his* idea of God exactly corresponds with the reality. But men of different ages and of different countries have had very different, and even diametrically opposed, ideas of the Deity. Polytheists, pantheists, monotheists are in irreconcilable disagreement. If then people are to be

allowed, under the plea of intuition, to identify
their idea of God with His existence, the Mahom-
etan will interrogate his consciousness and find
his God there; the savage will do the same with
a similar result, and so on all along the line; and,
as each is positively assured in the matter, and,
ex hypothesi, has a right to be positively assured,
we shall have as the outcome "gods many and
lords many." each established on the surest foundation, yet some moral, others immoral—some embodying a lofty conception, and others representing
what is base and ignoble. Intuition; then, lands
us in an awkward dilemma. If it merely testify
that "*something* not-ourselves is," and allow us to
call this undefined something God, the whole of
experience rises up against it and says, "No such
testimony does consciousness give": or if it testify
to God as possessing particular characteristics,
then, in the face of the great diversity of religious
opinion in the world, *Whose* consciousness is to be
accepted as authoritative, the Gentile's or the
Jew's? and on what ground, from within intuition
itself, can you decide this question?

But, it may be said, there is another meaning
of intuition,—*viz.*, that claimed by the Mystic. We
reach God by a special exaltation of spirit, produced by self-abasement and by a process of pious

meditation, passive contemplation, prolonged con-
centration of the thoughts on the One Great Being;
and, having reached God, we find that all distinctions are removed and we ourselves become
one with Him in nature, being, and substance.
May not this avail us? No! Philosophically
regarded, this method is equally futile with the
other. For, the process here referred to is sentimental and individualistic solely ; and it lands us
in pantheism, not theism. The God of the mystic
is an undefined object,—He is simply a permeating
essence, or an overshadowing presence ; and the
individual when absorbed in Him abnegates his
rationality. Mysticism is sickly and wanting in
robustness ; and, being ecstatic and inactive, rests
satisfied in impressions that are wholly subjective.
It appeals essentially to the passive side of our
nature, that side of it which craves for rest and
placid repose ; but is ineffective in satisfying the
intellectual and active side. It is dreamy, and,
therefore, obscure ; suited at the most for a
" cloister'd vertue," but incompetent to bear the
stress and pressure of our robuster needs.

In vain, then, do we trust to mystical intuition.
If God comes to the soul, it must be through the
mediation of reason ; and mysticism cannot help
us as a philosophical principle. On the contrary,
when philosophy becomes mystical it thereby

acknowledges its own impotence. It is only when
effort seems to be useless that "the mind idealizes
Inaction, and seeks a metaphysical basis for it".
Mysticism and scepticism are alike confessions of
despair. Both "flourish in the same atmosphere,
though in different soils, both, though in different
ways, implying the abandonment of the rational
problem. The sceptic, the agnostic or positivist
of to-day, declares it insoluble, and settles down
content to take things as they are; the mystic re-
tires into himself, and dreams of a state of being
which is the obverse of the world of fact" (Aubrey
L. Moore, *Essays Scientific and Philosophical*, p.
198).

But, although thus denying that Intuition is of
avail as a philosophical faculty for apprehending
the Divinity, I quite grant, of course, that familiarity with divine things produces an alacrity or
readiness to discern them and to perceive their
exact nature and import, which is altogether
wanting in the absence of such familiarity. This
you may, if you care, denominate intuition; but it
is, obviously, the result of discipline and practice.
None the less important, however, is it on that
account: and its virtue needs to be emphatically
recognized. It is only "those who, by reason of
use, have their senses exercised" that can be

accepted as authorities in spiritual things. But this is only saying, in the spiritual sphere, what we say and insist upon in other spheres—in all spheres, indeed, without exception. In the matter of mere seeing, it is the trained eye that best takes in the character and beauty of a landscape, or that, perhaps, alone takes cognizance of an object which is equally within the range of the untrained eye but is unobserved by it. It needs an education to be able to discriminate shades of colour with anything like precision, or exactly to distinguish between certain sounds or tastes or touches. The fallacy in an argument that has entire plausibility about it for the untutored intellect is instantly detected by the disciplined logician; and the sensitive conscience is alone alive to fine moral distinctions. So, practice in Religion produces a wonderful effect in the matter of clearness of apprehension and justness of appreciation of divine objects; and the question whether, on any given occasion, we shall see or not see, is, in great measure, the question whether we are occupying the right standpoint and are practised in the art of seeing.

And this is really what we mean when we say that some men are distinguished by deep spiritual insight, or that they have pre-eminently a genius for religion. Religion is so inwoven into their

character, they are so perpetually alert on the
spiritual side, that they seize at a glance the truth
that less-practised and lower-toned people are
labouring to reach but fail to achieve. Here, as
everywhere, faculty increases by exercise. and,
with faculty, facility. With every advance in
spiritual growth, there come greater distinctness
of vision, finer susceptibility to spiritual sugges-
tions, an increased power of reading spiritual signs
or indications, and a firmer hold of spiritual
realities.

Thus we can distinctly see the true place of
authority in things religious. Men, jealous of
dogmatism and eager for the rights of private
judgment, sometimes speak as though it were
irrational, were servile or slavish, to acknowledge
dependence on the religious teaching, views, and
experiences of others. But, surely, it is rational
to submit ourselves for instruction, in any sphere,
to men who, we have every reason to believe, have
greater insight or fuller knowledge in that sphere
than we ourselves possess. A leader in Science
commands our assent, just because he is a leader
in science—a man who has made science his
special study, and has, therefore, a special right
to be heard on his own subject. A Prophet or an
Apostle is authoritative, just because he is a
prophet or an apostle—because he has a deeper

experience and a closer familiarity with the divine than the majority of men have. The irrationality is all the other way. "To submit to authority," as Marheineke says, "is not unworthy of a free intelligence ; but what it ought to reserve to itself, is the right to recognize its necessity." "He who excels," says Dr. Johnson, speaking of Dryden, "has a right to teach, and he whose judgment is incontestable may without usurpation examine and decide."

"But still," it may be urged, "we cannot give over Intuition ; for a man *may* hold intercourse with God, may have communion with Him, may speak to Him 'face to face, as a man speaketh unto his friend'."

Ah yes! no doubt he may : *that* is the very essence of piety and devotion : and this close fellowship and communion is, in the deepest sense, what we mean by Prayer. But note exactly what this communion is. You have just said, "as a man speaketh unto his friend". *That* gives you precisely the nature of the act, and points you to the philosophical interpretation. While we are engaged speaking with a friend, self-consciousness is in abeyance : we do not then ask, How comes all this about? what does it all mean ? It is only when critical reflection sets in, that we come to see

its exact character and import. So, while engaged
in close communion with God, no one stops to
analyze the process. Critical reflection then is
not ; and, likely enough, critical reflection is never
exercised by many religious persons at all. They
simply rest in their devotional experience, and
push inquiry no further. As Principal Caird puts
it : "In the attitude of devotion, in simple faith
and communion with God, the spiritual mind
seems to be in immediate converse with its objects.
and to have the same assurance of their reality
which the ordinary consciousness has of the reality
of the external world. The certainty of that
which it knows is bound up with the certainty
which it has of itself. It seems to know God and
divine things, not by the intermediation of any
process of proof, but because in its own consciousness there is a revelation of their presence which is
beyond the reach of doubt. It does not ask how
it comes to know God, or how it is possible for
the individual mind to transcend its own limitations
and attain to a knowledge of objective realities ?
It does not ask how it can verify their existence or
justify its own conceptions of them ? They are
there, and the sense of their reality comes to it
with a force of conviction which it feels no need to
define or defend " (*Introduction to the Philosophy
of Religion*, pp. 41. 42). But once let critical

reflection supervene, once let us be driven to think, either by our descent from the Pisgah-height or by the upstarting of doubt in the mind, and immediately it is seen that the Object of devotion, with whom in prayer we hold intercourse, is assured to us just as the existence of a friend or of a brother is assured to us—*not by intuition, but by inference.* We have no intuition of a fellow-man's existence. We do not *see* his soul, even as we see his body; he simply makes his existence and his presence felt by certain outward signs and manifestations and by his producing certain effects, and these we regard as infallibly demonstrative. Each one's own being alone is known to him directly; and yet no sane man would think of maintaining that he himself is the sole existence in the universe, or that all other living beings are illusions.

Devotion, then, remains, and the facts of the religious life remain; and, in denying Intuition as the organ of perceiving the divine, I simply deny that God is known to us in any other way than kindred human souls are known to us, or that His presence is discoverable save through its effects.

And here may be the place to say a word on the *language* of devotion. To some, this language seems extravagant and reprehensible, and bespeaks the visionary. But devotion, be it remembered, is

not simply rational,—it is deeply touched with
emotion : it is the attachment of the heart, as well
as the assent of the understanding,—it is union
with God through the medium of feeling. That
being so, it would surely be the very height of un- ✓
reason to expect the impassioned soul to restrict
itself to the unimpassioned utterances of reason.
All strong feeling expresses itself strongly, and
why should religious feeling be an exception ?
Affection, indeed, when it runs deep, is often
undemonstrative. But times come when the
flood-gates are opened, and the streams pour forth.
Where affection is real, it is ever *intense;* and
intensity is not incompatible with permanence.
Intensity is only incompatible with permanence
when it is a mere play upon the nerves, an
unhealthy physical excitement. But religious love
is not of this description ; and, as the Object of it
is unique, the advice of the Son of Sirach is only
soberest reason : " When ye glorify the Lord, exalt
Him as much as ye can ; for even yet will He far
exceed : and when ye exalt Him, put forth all your
strength, and be not weary ; for ye can never go
far enough ".

Moreover, devotion is the pouring forth of the
grateful and adoring heart to the Great Being
in whom alone it finds rest and satisfaction :
and when the pious man represents the Object

of his worship as being his all in all, as *dwelling* in him and working in him and transforming him, he gives no greater signs of being a visionary than does one friend deeply attached to another when he represents that other as constantly occupying his thoughts and guiding his conduct. The results of true friendship are, indeed, marvellous : yet, *there* they are. A being not myself can so lay hold of me, so attract me by the purity of his character or by the superiority of his wisdom or by the strength of his will, as to become my loadstar ; and he can so seat himself in my affections as to be, in more than a metaphor, " a second self " to me. The manner, indeed, that spirit can thus act on spirit is in the last result inexplicable : but the fact of such action is itself beyond dispute. So, the pious man finds God to be his Loadstar. He enthrones Him in his heart, he submits to Him with his will, and accepts His law as his rule of conduct. Is it visionary, then, to say that God *dwells* in him ? Is it visionary to represent himself as being in God ? If this were all that mysticism meant, then are we all mystics : every man who really loves the God whom he avows, and allows himself to be guided by His word,—every man who has a vivid conviction of the reality of God and of his own personal relations with Him.

Note, now, another point. Earnest seekers after truth, and religiously minded men, disturbed by doubt, yet tenacious of faith, are apt to complain (inwardly to groan) that God's existence should be capable of doubt at all; and non-theists make it an argument against Theism that the evidence is not so plain as to put it beyond all possibility of dispute. "God, if He existed," they say, "would so reveal Himself to man that no one could deny Him."

Now, the nature of the demand here made is perfectly intelligible; and, in the form of a longing or desire, I daresay, we are all acquainted with it. It is the "cry out of the depths," which every earnest soul can understand.

But, though intelligible, is this demand just? Observe, in the first place, regarding it, that the longing or the sigh that prompts it is only a part of a much wider sigh or longing: it is only a part of that more general desire to be freed from uncertainty or hesitation of *every* kind that one experiences when tired out with the problems and perplexities of life. Difficulties have to be unravelled, not only in religion, but in ethics and psychology and metaphysics, in politics, society, and art; and every student, in whatever sphere, is apt to grow disheartened sometimes, and, in his gloomier moods, to curse or to bewail his fate.

But then, observe next, the demand for absolute certainty is really at bottom irrational. The ground of all progress here is, unquestionably, *activity:* activity is the very condition of life. Man is essentially an active being, in soul as well as in body; and his intellectual and his spiritual nature can only thrive through exercise. Remove, then, all possibility of doubt with regard to the supersensible, and you remove the very condition of our spiritual health and growth; you atrophy the spiritual organ, and replace life and vigour by stagnation and death.

Then, lastly, man's very nature—the very constitution of his being—implies two things: it implies the possibility of ignorance, and it implies the possibility of sin. Such is his make, and you cannot help it: you can only work with the material that you have. It is not, therefore, of man but of another being that you are thinking, when you demand that knowledge shall be perfect —shall be full, and thoroughly adequate, and at all points beyond the range of question: and *that* would not be man, but a creature of your own imagination, a mental fiction, in whom the fact of spiritual corruption made no difference to his power of spiritual perception.

If absolute certainty, then, may not be had,

what kind of certainty may? The answer we shall
see, after a moment's consideration.

I have already said that we know nothing
immediately save our own selves;[1] all other objects
are, in comparison, mediately cognized. But,
amongst these other objects, there are some of
whose existence we have much greater assurance
than of others,—some of whose existence we can
hardly doubt, any more than we can doubt of our
own existence. How comes this about? How
comes it, for example, that we think it almost
irrational to dispute the existence of the external
material world, or of our friends and comrades, or
of other human beings in general? The reasons
are—(1) First, that these external objects, or
these fellow-men, are constantly present with us
and palpable to the senses; (2) secondly, that it is
by things external that we are first impressed, and,
through them, first become aware of our own self-
activity, and (as Berkeley says) "what first seizes
holds fast" (*Siris*, § 294); and (3), thirdly, that
things external are perpetually making their
presence felt by us. Wherever we turn we are, as
it were, stumbling up against them; and the vividness with which they affect us very much prevents

---

[1] There is no need, for our present purpose, to obtrude at this
point the distinction between the immediate consciousness of mental
states and the relatively indirect cognition of the unity of the Ego.

our entertaining doubts as to their reality or being. Hence, when away from friends or absent from well-known objects or places, we try to keep alive our remembrance of them, and, therefore, to stimulate our sense of their reality, by photographs or pictures of them, or, it may be, by keeping in our possession relics, or mementoes of them,—a friend's staff, a lock of hair, a stone from a mountain, a piece of wood from a forest, a flower from a hill-side, a shell or pebble from the sea-shore. The presence of these brings up memories of the person or the places or the objects wherewith they are associated, and the absent and the departed are thereby brought nearer to us, and we feel their power.

"How comes it, then," it may be asked, "that we have not the same undoubting belief in the reality and existence of God as we have of these? Does not the want of this belief tell against the theistic position?"

This is, undoubtedly, a very proper question to ask : and it may, I think, be satisfactorily answered. It really resolves itself into this : How come things that appeal to the senses—external objects to have an apparently greater certainty to us than spiritual things, especially than the Supreme Being Himself? To this. I answer :—

(1) First, that we need not suppose it to be because the Supreme Being is absent from us, while these are always present with us; for, mere presence of an object does not necessarily ensure our cognizance of it. Many objects may be about us and within our ken which, nevertheless, *from want of having the attention turned to them,* remain unknown to us. It is only what we attend to that we can know; an unobserved thing and a thing non-existent are for us practically the same. Moreover, constant familiarity with a thing may blunt our apprehension of its presence and its existence :—

"That is the truly secret which lies ever open before us; And the least seen is that which the eye constantly sees".

The difference, therefore, (2) secondly, seems to lie in the superior power that external material objects have of drawing our attention to them, of exciting our interest in them, or of compelling us to concentrate our mind upon them. Is this actually the case? I think not. External objects have no power of attracting the attention, if we voluntarily exclude them from our view. The trees and sky and fields, the flowers and grass, the lovely scenery, outside the room in which I am now writing, are impotent to impress me if I close my eyes or draw down the blind. By fiercely concentrating my attention on a single object, I shut out the consciousness of all other objects, even of those in the immediate neighbourhood, which would otherwise lie within my range. There are conditions of objective perception; and, unless these conditions be conformed to, the external object cannot make its power felt. So, God may be present with us, and His presence may be indubitably realized, if we conform to the conditions. But mark that qualification " if we conform to the conditions "; for therein, I think, lies the whole explanation. If we erect a barrier between ourselves and Him, if we interpose a concealing object, if we voluntarily turn away our attention, or preoccupy ourselves with other objects, we thereby necessarily shut out God from our view. And, unfortunately, the temptation to such preoccupation, or such voluntary withdrawing of the attention, is very great. It is so easy to lay hold of a material object, and the presence of such an object so frequently ministers to our self-indulgence and appeals to that indolent and languid side of our nature which is so strong in most of us, that we rest content in this lower plane and refuse to rise into the higher, which it would take trouble, effort, and self-sacrifice to reach, and where the lower indulgences are not. But once let us rise into this higher plane, once let us open the soul's eye to the heavenly prospect, and divine things will be found to be not less impressive, and our conviction of their reality equally strong, yea, stronger. Yet, because of the constant pressure of external things, with our inevitable practical interest in them, and for many other reasons, the chief of them being *moral*, it will be difficult for us to maintain ourselves in the right attitude for perceiving spiritual reality: and so helps, memorials, symbols will be needed. We shall require, in this sphere, something corresponding to the staff of an absent friend or the pebble of a once-traversed but now distant shore. These are fasts and feasts, the sacraments and ordinances, the rites and ceremonies, practised, with more or less detail, by every religion.

But I have just said that, if we conform to certain conditions, our conviction of the Divine will become as strong as, yea *stronger than*, our conviction of material realities. Is this so? Yes: because God, the Divine Being, stands to us in the relation of a living person; and we all know how intercourse and communion with a living person, when heart goes forth to heart, and spirit touches spirit, is a more intimate thing than converse with external nature. And if it be so, as I believe, that external nature itself has its perennial charm and interest for us mainly through the fact of its being supported by the

Divine, then we can see, intellectually, how God's existence should be held with even a higher assurance, by those who keep their hearts and minds open, than even the existence of objective reality.

You see, then, the answer to our question. Our question was, How comes it that external material objects— things that we can see and taste and handle—affect us more strongly than spiritual objects? And the answer is, That, *in themselves*, they do not: the difference, where it exists, lies, not in the object, but in the subject. It is the man himself that makes all the difference. He has the power of voluntary attention; and there are many reasons, well known and thoroughly understood, why he should be averse to exercise this power in the spiritual sphere. It is a fact of experience thoroughly attested, apart altogether from Scripture revelation, that "blessed are the *pure in heart*, for *they* shall see God". "What," says Schiller, "no intellect of the intellectual sees, is practised in simplicity by a childlike heart." And finely has our own poet sung :—

Dark is the world to thee: thyself art the reason why;
For is He not all but thou, that hast power to feel "I
    am I"?
Glory about Thee, without thee; and thou fulfillest thy
    doom
Making Him broken gleams, and a stifled splendour and
    gloom.

Speak to Him thou for He hears, and Spirit with Spirit
can meet—

Closer is He than breathing, and nearer than hands and
feet

And the ear of man cannot hear, and the eye of man
cannot see :

But if we could see and hear, this Vision—were it not He?

(TENNYSON, *The Higher Pantheism.*)

LECTURE II.

I.

NOTHING at first sight seems simpler, as nothing in the history of thought may appear older, than knowledge of human nature. Such knowledge, in a rough and ready way, must have begun with the first man who turned his thoughts inwards and reflected upon his own acts and motives, or who watched the actions of other men and compared them with his own. But nothing is really more difficult, as nothing is more complex; and the wisest counsel of the ancient Greek sages, to which also has been assigned a divine origin, was "Know thyself".[1] Self-knowledge, or knowledge of man in the workings of his mind and in the hidden springs of his conduct, is, and must neces-

---

[1] See Juvenal, *Satires*, XI 27: "E caelo descendit γνῶθι σεαυτόν". The advice has been attributed to each of the seven wise men, as well as to the Delphic Oracle; but the latter, impressed by the difficulty of self-knowledge, toils over the expression of it in lumbering spondees (Xenophon, *Cyropædia*, vii. 2):—Σαυτὸν γιγνώσκων εὐδαίμων, Κροῖσε, περάσεις (Thyself knowing, Croesus, thou shalt happily live then).

3 (33)

sarily be, a progressive thing. Implying as it does
accurate observation and clear steady insight, together with analytical power of a very high order,
it could not have been a thing of very early development; and, before it could assume anything
like a scientific or philosophical aspect, it needed
the co-operation of many thinkers and many
analysts, and a wide experience, involving the
study not only of the individual human being, but
of social manners, ways, and institutions, and
the comparison of different peoples and different
races of mankind.

No wonder, then, that the science of human
nature should really be one of late, rather than
of early, origin; and no wonder that, even at the
present day, there should remain a vast deal to
be done.

The difficulties attaching to it are of the following kind. The individual mind can be reached
directly only by the individual himself. Nobody but
myself knows exactly what the contents of my own
consciousness at any particular moment are, or
what the inward springs or motives of my actions.
But even I myself, when I turn my attention
inwards, am met by seemingly insuperable difficulties. When I withdraw within myself and try
to note and analyze and classify my conscious ex-

periences; when I set myself to watch my own
thoughts and feelings and volitions—to mark
their nature, their strength, their sequence, their
combinations, the conflicts among them and the
coalitions; when I study them at one time, as
far as may be, in isolation, and endeavour at
another time to obtain a distinct view of their
mutual dependence and *tout ensemble,*—I am
apparently upon the safe ground of inner observation, where everything seen is a present fact,
carrying its own meaning and the evidence of
its existence within itself. But, in reality, I am
here dependent on memory and reflection : *introspection is in great measure retrospection.* The
mental phenomena that I mark and examine are
fleeting states or passing moods, and ere ever I
can combine them, or reflect upon them, I have
to unite the present with the memory of the
past ; and what security have I that Memory
is exact?—Again, I run the risk, more particularly in the case of motives, of inaccurate observation, taking the complex for the simple : over
and above the circumstance that, in dealing with my
motives, I am apt to deceive myself, to substitute the
counterfeit for the real.—Again, my inner nature, in
order to be studied accurately, must be studied in
a calm, philosophic mood, free alike from prejudice
and from passion. But, long before I reach the

stage of self-reflection, I have acquired a mass of
preconceived opinion, resting for the most part on
authority ; and, when I approach the work of
deliberate introspection, I bring with me partialities and prejudices as to what I am to find and
what not to find, and my eye is fain to see only
what it brings the power to see.—Then, lastly,
the very act of inward observation is an analytic
one. We must discriminate and classify—separ-
ating feelings from cognition, and cognition from
will. But the mind is in reality a unity,—an
organic unity,—whose operations are in most
intimate connexion with each other, and with
the whole. There is no such thing as pure
thought, or pure will, or pure feeling. What
we find is simply that, in every mental state,
there is a predominating element— feeling, volition, thought ; and from this predominating factor
the particular state takes its distinctive designation.

There are difficulties, then, in the study of
human nature from the side of individual consciousness. But the individual is not the sole
reality in the universe ; and help may be got from
studying other individuals, by carefully noting and
examining the effects of mind as shown in human
language, customs, institutions, as also by com-

paring man's work and actions with those of the
lower animals. Helpful, however, as this is, it is
not absolutely infallible. On the contrary, in
dealing with others, we are necessarily thrown
upon inference; and how can we be certain that
our grounds of inference are secure? Our starting-
point is necessarily ourselves; and, unless we
know ourselves, how can we know others? Moreover, men may dissemble; and we ourselves may
err in the interpretation of signs, or in the understanding of speech. And, as for analogy between
man and the brutes,—it may be only a seeming
one, or, at least, may be much less reliable, as a
ground of evidence, than is frequently supposed.

All this I mention, not with any design to prove
that knowledge of human nature is impossible, but
simply with the view of pointing out the difficulties
of the subject, and of showing reason why we
should be prepared for the late origin and slow
progress of scientific anthropology. So far am I
from believing that knowledge of human nature is
impossible, that I have a very firm conviction that
such knowledge is at this moment very full and
has reached a high degree of accuracy. And what
the nature and extent of it are, will best be brought
out, I think, if we take a rapid historical survey
of it.

II.

1. *Plato.*

I naturally begin with Plato.

Man, according to Plato, consists of two parts
—a body and a soul. His soul is of a triple
nature, partly rational and immortal, partly irrational and mortal; the irrational being again
divided into two—the spirited or courageous and
the appetitive or lustful. Each of these three
divisions of the soul has a separate habitation in
the body. The head is the seat of the rational
soul (τὸ λογιστικὸν); the spirited soul (τὸ θυμοειδὲς)
is located in the breast, and the appetitive soul (τὸ
ἐπιθυμητικὸν) in the lower regions. It is of the
nature of passion, much more of lust, to be lawless and rebellious; Reason's function is to bring
both under due control, to harmonize and to
restrain them. Hence, in the *Phædrus,* the soul is
represented as a charioteer, riding in a chariot
drawn by two winged steeds; fiercely struggling
often to curb and guide the dark and vicious horse,
which is ever wont to be troublesome and re-
fractory. Hence, too, in the *Republic* (ix. 12),
man is represented as a compound of a hydra-
headed monster, a lion and a man; and his great
aim should be to tame the lion and subdue the
monster, and gain for "the inner man (ὁ ἐντὸς

ἄνθρωπος)[1] the entire mastery of the man". This ordering and controlling power of reason is obviously ethical; for, it is in the placing of rational restraint on the lower nature that morality emerges.

But, besides this guiding and order-giving function of Reason, there is another, and, in some respects, a higher function. For man, besides being a bundle of impulses which need to be rationalized, is also an intellectual being, with definite perceptive relations to the world around him, and with the power of understanding and interpreting the meaning of things. As thus conceived, he is in part a creature of sense, passively receiving the impressions that are made upon him from without, but in part also an active thinker with divine insight, penetrating below the mere sense-impressions, and grasping the reality that underlies phenomena. He is the member of an intelligible world, and, as such, has the power of freeing himself from the limitations and the deceptions of the senses, and of bringing himself into contact with the eternal Ideas, which are the sole true existence, all else being but shadow and appearance. These supersensible Ideas have objective being; they are both paradeigmata or patterns, supersensible counterparts of the sensible.

---

[1] Compare with St. Paul's τὸν ἔσω ἄνθρωπον of Romans vii. 22.

and efficient causes (though how these two things can be reconciled, Plato does not say): they constitute a graduated system, at the top of which stands the Good —comprehending all, harmonizing all,—and this highest of all, this *summum genus*, designated the Good, is God. This "idea of the Good" is, according to the famous allegory of the Cave, given at the opening of the seventh book of the *Republic*,—"the last object of vision, as respects human knowledge, and hard to be seen; but, when seen, it must be inferred to be the cause of all that is right and beautiful in all things, begetting in what is seen light and light's sovereign (the sun), and being itself, in what is intelligible, the sovereign producing truth and intelligence".

Man's kinship to God is to be found both in his rational and in his moral nature. It is by the speculative reason, together with moral conduct founded on reason, that he attains to knowledge of the divine; and, through the persistent exercise of philosophic contemplation and upright living. he is rendered more and more like to God.

A leading distinction with Plato is that between man's body and his soul. Except in the *Timæus*, the body. though mortal, is not regarded as essentially vile: it is not (as Plotinus, later on, held) the origin and source of sin (sin is a disease, and arises either from ignorance or from madness).

It is simply the prison of the soul—a clog or hindrance, therefore, to the highest perfection, and the occasion or condition of moral evil ; and, until man is freed from it, he has not full scope for the development of his higher self. Death, then, is to be welcomed, not feared—it is a blessing, not a curse ; and our present life is a season of probation in preparation for that great event.

The soul, on the other hand, is immortal. But, if immortal, then also pre-existent. Immortality and pre-existence stood or fell together in the mind of Plato. And this for various reasons. In the first place, the metaphysical arguments, or arguments based on the nature of the soul, on which Plato laid such stress (seen, *e.g.*, in the *Phædo*), proved both or neither. If it be so that the very essence of the soul implies Life, then the life that is implicated must have an eternal past as well as a never-ending future. In the next place, Plato taught the doctrine (adopted, no doubt, from Pythagorean sources), of the transmigration of souls,—which was simply *his* way, as it was also Origen's and Lessing's way, of expressing what has come to be known in these later ages as the necessity for a progressive purification of the sinner, and the need of a cleanzing process, if not actually a probationary period, hereafter as well as here. Judgment full and minute follows death, and reward is proportioned to merit.[1]   Lastly, the doctrine of pre-existence was needed to explain the fact that truth is attainable by man at all, and that Virtue can be taught: the theory of Heredity had not yet occurred to the philosophic mind as suggestive of a satisfactory solution. In the *Meno*, the question is distinctly raised,—" How, then, can you search for that of which you know nothing: and how, even if you find it, can you be sure that you have got it?"   And the answer is returned— the same that we find in many other Dialogues of Plato,- " Reminiscence ": *i.e.*, truth is latent in the mind: and, in learning here, we only revive what we have known elsewhere.

> Our birth is but a sleep and a forgetting:
> The soul that rises with us, our life's star,
>   Hath had elsewhere its setting,
>   And cometh from afar;
>   Not in entire forgetfulness,
>   And not in utter nakedness,
> But trailing clouds of glory do we come
>   From God, who is our home.

Two other points remain to be noticed.   First, man, in the *Timæus*, is viewed as a microcosm, of which the universe is the macrocosm.   The same

---

[1] The doctrine of metempsychosis may have a twofold ground.   It may be based either (*a*) on the metaphysical consideration of the nature of the soul, or (*b*) on the demands of Conscience for the due punishment of the transgressor.

elements that are found in the one are discoverable also in the other,—only, on a larger scale. The world has a soul, no less than man ; and in this soul-inspired world mass, as in man, we can discern a nous or mind, a psyche or soul, and a soma or body. Secondly, man is essentially a social being. and he has necessarily relations to the State. Hence, in the Ideal Republic, man's threefold soul finds its concrete counterparts in the grades or classes of the citizens. The highest class or rulers represent the rational element ; the spirited or courageous factor is embodied in the soldiers ; and the artizans, agriculturists, and tradesmen stand for the appetitive soul.

Such, in brief, is Plato's analysis of Human Nature and his doctrine of Man. Note now. about it, various things.

(1) First, on the ethical side, Plato draws a clear distinction between reason and the passions : ascribing law and order to the former, and lawlessness and licence to the latter, and laying upon reason the duty of restraining or controlling the unruly impulses. In this way, he bears testimony to the fact of disorder or a rupture in man's nature. and lends the weight of his authority to the teaching that the real truth of morality lies in the ideal.

(2) Next, this rupture is more deeply seated than in the mere antagonism of the body to the soul. That the body is frail and liable to disease, and that it is even in itself an impediment to the soul, Plato indeed emphasizes: he even calls it, in due Orphic fashion, "our sepulchre" and "prison," and wonders, in one place, whether the earthly life of soul united to body does not give the proper meaning of Death: "for, indeed, I should not wonder if Euripides speaks the truth when he says, 'Who knows whether to live is not death, and to die, life?'" (*Gorgias*, 104). But he does not regard the body as the cause of sin,—only its instrument and occasion; nor does he admit that we have a right to cut the thread and hasten the consummation of the separation of soul from body. On the contrary, Suicide is strictly condemned by him: we are not our own (he tells us), but belong to God, and must await the summons hence at His good pleasure.

(3) Thirdly, he is very explicit in his teaching that man can rise above mere sense: and that, if he does not, he remains simply in the region of shadows and delusions. Through his intellectual nature, through his speculative power, he is akin to God.

(4) Lastly, man is akin to God also through holy living; for, holiness and justice are Divine

attributes, and Plato's philosophy is supremely ethical.

2. *Aristotle.*

As with Plato, so with Aristotle: human nature is characterized by the attribute of Reason. On the side of speculative reason ($\sigma o \phi \iota a$), man can attain to truth; on the side of practical reason ($\phi \rho \acute{o} \nu \eta \sigma \iota s$), he is possessed of the consciousness of right and has the power of forming character. On both sides, he sets himself an ideal; an ideal of knowledge, on the one hand, of character and conduct, on the other. It is only, however, in intellectual or speculative reason that he approximates to God: this is the "divine element" in his nature, constituting his "true self" (*Ethics*, X., vii. 8, 9). The Deity, therefore, is simply Self-consciousness: Aristotle defines His life, in a classical passage (*Metaphysics*, XI., ix. 4), as "the thinking upon thought". He has not moral qualities; indeed, ethical attributes are (see *Ethics*, X., viii. 7) distinctly denied Him, and His life, "which surpasses all others in blessedness," is declared to consist in contemplation. The proof of His existence may, as Socrates maintained, be found in the marks of Design so visible in the universe; but Aristotle's great demonstration was cosmological. Observing in ordinary experience that things move only when set in motion, he concluded that the world, as an ordered system of things in motion, needed for its existence a moving cause; and so he posited the Deity as the prime mover or first cause of motion, " Himself unmoved the while ". This, however, must not be confounded with the conception of God as the Creator of the universe. Such a conception was quite alien to Aristotle's thought. The universe, no less than God, existed from eternity; and the prime mover was simply the immanent principle of Reason in the world,—reason pervading the universe, not outside it, and the object to the universe of desire. Once, indeed, in the eleventh book of the *Metaphysics*, the idea of God as distinct from and independent of the universe seems to have dawned upon Aristotle; but it did not rise into clear light of day. He there represents the Deity as standing to the world in the relation of a general to his army,—which seems to imply the notion of a personal overruling Providence. But this is a solitary passage, and not much can be built upon it: although it seemed quite enough to justify the Schoolmen in claiming Aristotle as a pure theist, at the time when the Stagirite reigned supreme in the schools.

Man, while a rational being, is also an animal; and, alone of animals, is endowed with speech. In

many points, he resembles the brutes. Like them,
he has appetites and desires; but while, with the
brutes, these are simply instinctive wants and
appetencies, with man they are brought under the
control of will—that is, are associated with a wish for
the good, with a desire for welfare (εὐδαιμονία),—and
thereby are rationalized. This rationalizing is
nothing else than imposing law and order (for
reason is law) upon elements that would otherwise be lawless and indeterminate.

Man is further social, and the individual is
practically subordinated to the State: for, the
chief good of the one is the chief good of the
other, and the state, as being the greater of the
two, has the paramount interest. Now, the chief
good of the state is the cultivation and development of speculative thought; and that is the chief
good of the individual too. As Sir Alexander
Grant pithily puts it, "Aristotle thought that the
highest aim for a State was to turn out philosophers, and that the highest aim for an individual was to be a philosopher" (*Aristotle*,
p. 101).[1]

Man's soul is in the closest connexion with his
body; the union is even so intimate that the former
cannot be defined at all except in terms expressive

[1] See also Grote's *Fragments on Ethical Subjects*, Essays v. and vi.;
or Chapters xiii. and xiv. of the second edition of his *Aristotle*.

of its relation to the latter.[1] Nevertheless, the soul is not wholly mortal. Those functions of it that are concerned with nutrition, sentience, and the like, perish; but the Intellect is immortal. Not the whole intellect, however, but only the active and creative portion of it; for, Aristotle draws a distinction between the passive and the active intellect (at least, he does so in the *De Animâ*, although not in any other of his treatises), and the latter alone survives death. Here is the leading passage on the subject, as translated by Edwin Wallace :-

" The same differences, however, as are found in nature as a whole must be characteristic also of the soul. Now in nature there is on the one hand that which acts as material substratum to each class of objects, this being that which is potentially all of them : on the other hand, there is the element which is causal and creative in virtue of its producing all things, and which stands towards the other in the same relation as that in which art stands towards the materials on which it operates. Thus reason is, on the one hand, of such a character as to *become* all things, on the other hand of such a

---

[1] Aristotle's famous definition of the Soul is, " The first entelechy (or perfect realization) of a natural organized body, having life potentially ". For explanation, see, in particular, Edwin Wallace's *Aristotle's Psychology*, Introduction, pp. xii., etc. See, also, Sir A. Grant's *Ethics of Aristotle*.

nature as to *create* all things, acting then much
in the same way as some positive quality, such as
for instance light: for light also in a way creates
actual out of potential colour. This phase of
reason is separate from and uncompounded with
material conditions, and, being in its essential
character fully and actually realized, it is not subject to impressions from without: for the creative
is in every case more honourable than the passive,
just as the originating principle is superior to the
matter which it forms. And thus, though knowledge as an actually realized condition is identical
with its object, this knowledge as a potential
capacity is in time prior in the individual, though
in universal existence it is not even in time thus
prior to actual thought. Further, this creative
reason does not at one time think, at another time
not think: [it thinks eternally:] and when separated from the body it remains nothing but what it
essentially is: and thus it is alone immortal and
eternal. Of this unceasing work of thought, however, we retain no memory, because this reason is
unaffected by its objects; whereas the receptive
passive intellect (which is affected) is perishable,
and can really think nothing without the support
of the creative intellect " (*De Anima*, iii. 5).

This at once raises the question, What precisely
was the kind of immortality that Aristotle per-

mitted to the soul, or, rather, to that part of it
denominated the Active Intellect? Was it personal or was it impersonal? If left simply to
logical inference, we should distinctly say "impersonal," for future existence *without memory*
would be the same thing as absorption into the
Deity, and Averroës had unquestionably good
ground for maintaining that, according to Aristotle,
men exist after death but not as individuals, only
as constituents of the universal intellect common
to mankind. Yet, Aristotle himself drew no such
inference. In the *Ethics* (i. 11), he even inclines
to the contrary opinion. When discussing the
question, whether the fortunes of survivors affect the
dead, he pronounces the negative answer to be "too
cold and too much opposed to popular opinion";
but, at the same time, he is not at all strong on the
affirmative side. He is cautious and hesitative
to a degree, and his final conclusion is simply this:
"It seems then to conclude that the prosperity,
and likewise the adversity, of friends does affect
the dead, but not in such a way or to such an
extent as to make the happy unhappy, or to
do anything of the kind" (Mr. F. H. Peters's
transl.).

It is not, however, in the question of immortality that Aristotle's interest centres, but in mental
processes and the analysis of the soul's functions.

It is to Aristotle, therefore, that we trace the
beginning of scientific Psychology; and from him
was derived the first great impulse to psychological investigation, the effects of which are discernible
at the present day.

3. *The Bible.*

From what has now been said, it will be seen
that both to Plato and to Aristotle, and (as these
are typical in this respect) to the ancient Greek
philosophers generally, man is first and chiefly an
intellectual being, and his affinity to the Divine is
mainly, if not wholly, on the side of the theoretical
or speculative reason. Neither Plato nor Aristotle
based Theism in the emotions, and the latter distinctly disowned theistic ethics. The reason is not
far to seek. As the Greek philosophers naturally
waged an uncompromising war against the baseness
and degradation of the popular mythology, their
zeal was apt to carry them into the extreme of
denying that there was any truth whatever in the
popular conceptions; and Plato cuts God thus far
off from man at one point that, in the *Republic* (ii.
20, 21), he maintains that a Divine theophany, or
a Divine incarnation, or a Divine revelation to
man by dreams, visions, and the like, would be a
subversion of the Divine nature; it would be
equivalent to saying that God could change from

a better state to a worse, and could associate Himself with falsehood and deceit.

But it is entirely different when we pass from
the Greeks to the Hebrews. To the ancient Jew,
man is pre-eminently an ethical being, and his
speculative ability is quite secondary. Indeed,
accentuation of man's moral nature, carrying with
it the teaching that man is a spirit, a free ego, and
as such has a unique personal worth and dignity,
is the leading distinctive contribution of the Jews
to the analysis of human nature : he is both "but
little lower than God (*Elohim*)," being "crowned
with glory and honour," and has natural lord-
ship, deputed authority, dominion over the lower
animals. Hebraism is further unique in this
respect that it clearly sees that the disorder in
man's nature is deeper than any intellectual
impotence, deeper too than the opposition of the
Appetites and the Reason ; that it is a breach in
his being, caused by his own self-will and having
connexion with his relation to the Supreme. Remove this disorder, and all will be well. But the
removal of this disorder means help from without,
help from a higher source than himself. The
great cause of human misery is *guilt*, and the
highest human happiness is ethical fellowship with
God, union and communion with the Divine.
Here the Jewish ethics joins on to theology.

But the theology itself is essentially ethical.
While, on the one hand, the Jew regarded man as
eminently a moral being, he no less regarded God
as the Moral Counterpart of man. God is the
Creator and Sustainer, indeed, but He is, above
all, the giver of the Decalogue; and, in enjoining
the Ten Commandments direct from heaven, He
shows that morality is both heaven's great concern
and man's chief need. Human nature, in other
words, is to the Jew a coin struck in the celestial
mint : the reverse representing man in his ethical
aspirations, and the obverse representing God as
their source, fulfilment, and completion. Hence
the further contribution to psychological theism in
the idea of God's pardoning guilt. The Emotions,
no less than the moral sense, have now a place
in theism. A vast advance is made when it
is seen that "mercy and truth are met together ; righteousness and peace have kissed each
other".

And what is true of the Hebrew faith is no
less true of Christianity. All that was distinctive
of the former, in anthropology and theology alike,
was taken up and vitalized and purified and
deepened by the latter. Regenerate man is man
still,—only, his powers and the capacities of his
being acquire a fresh energy, and a new direction
is given to his aims and his affections.

Now, the Bible doctrine of Man came early into contact with Greek philosophy, and was a potent factor in moulding philosophical conceptions. There were action and reaction, no doubt: but the distinctive Hebrew mark was indelibly impressed, and it is unambiguously apparent in Western philosophy at the present day. It becomes necessary, then, to consider briefly this Bible doctrine, and to give it its rightful place in the current of theistic thought.

The Hebrew teaching about Man all circles round three psychological terms. These three terms are,—*Spirit, Soul,* and *Heart* (ruach, nephesh, lebab or leb; translated into Greek by pneuma, psyche, kardia). Each of these terms is used both in an exceedingly loose and general fashion, and also in a more accurate and restricted manner. Thus, Spirit (ruach) designates (*a*) breath, (*b*) wind, (*c*) life or vital principle, (*d*) animus or mind. Soul (nephesh), in like manner, is (*a*) breath or breath of life, (*b*) soul or vital principle, (*c*) mind. While heart (lebab) is either a synonym for soul, or else does duty with equal impartiality, in the expression of mental phenomena and states, as an intellectual, an emotive, and a volitional term. Yet, in the midst of all this confusion, there can be traced a central conception characteristic of each term, and to which that term (and no other) is most properly applied. What, then, are the characteristic conceptions of the three words? They are these.

The one great idea attaching to Spirit (ruach or pneuma) is given quite early in the Old Testament. It is unfolded at the very commencement of the book of *Genesis;* where creative energy of a particular kind is ascribed to the Spirit of God, and where the action of this Spirit is represented as a *brooding over* the face of the waters, vivifying and cherishing, as a hen does in the process of incubation. The chief product of Divine creative power is, immediately after, declared to be Man; and while one part of man (his body) is simply "dust of the ground," the other and higher part is expressed as "the breath of life, breathed into his nostrils," whereby he became "a living soul". Now, what is meant by this "breath of life," and what by this special act of "breathing"? There can be little doubt that the meaning underlying both is, that man is himself a *spirit,* having drawn his life from the formative Spirit, and that to this formative Spirit he stands in a special personal and close relationship. It is what Elihu, later on, interprets, " But there is a spirit (ruach, pneuma) in man, and the inspiration of the Almighty giveth them understanding"; or what Job distinctly characterizes when, speaking of himself, he says,

"All the while my breath is in me, and the Spirit of God (not the Holy Spirit, but the πνεῦμα θεῖον, as the Septuagint has it) is in my nostrils": or what the *Proverbs* (as interpreted by St. Paul in 1 *Corinth.* ii. 11) indicates in the sentence,— "The spirit (literally, *breath*) of man is the lamp of the Lord, searching all the innermost parts of the belly". In other words, according to the Creation narratives, Man is a heaven-descended God-related being, he bears in himself the image of the Deity; and this Divine relationship (derived from the " Father of spirits," from "the God of the spirits of all flesh ") constitutes him a spirit : because of his heavenly origin, he is himself a ruach or pneuma.[1]

What, then, of Soul (nephesh or psyche)? On its physiological side, it is simply life or vital principle : but, on its psychological side, it is the emotive and volitional part of man,— his "glory," as several of the *Psalms* express it. If man is a " spirit " because he shares in the image of the Deity, he is a " soul " both because he lives and because he is possessed of feeling and of will.

Next, Heart (leb or lebab) : what is designated

[1] Whether the narrative of the Creation of man be regarded as the literal account of an historical fact, or simply as the literary presentation in pictorial language of Man in his *ideal* character, the doctrine of the Pneuma is sufficiently suggestive. But, perhaps, its meaning is best brought out under the second interpretation.

by this? Not, in the main, what *we* understand by the term, not pre-eminently the æsthetic and emotional side of our being (although the word sometimes bears this signification, just as it is also the Biblical synonym for *conscience*): rather, it is intellect or thought, or, it may be self-consciousness. Lebab comes nearer to our word "mind" than perhaps any other Hebrew term does. To the *heart*, according to the Jewish conception, belong "thought," "imagination," "wisdom," and other mental functions. Job, referring to his controversial friends as "men of understanding," denominates them literally, "men of heart": while, in reference to himself, in the famous ironical passage beginning, "No doubt but ye are the people, and wisdom shall die with you," he says, "But I have understanding (literally, *I have heart*) as well as you". On the other hand, when Ahasuerus asks Haman the question, "What shall be done unto the man whom the king delighteth to honour?" Haman "thought in *his heart*, To whom would the king delight to do honour more than to myself?"— where "thought in his heart" is rightly translated by the Septuagint by ἐν ἑαυτῷ, *in himself*.

Where then, let us ask, is there any special psychological significance here? Do these distinctions enable us in any way to grasp mental

facts. and to understand human nature, better than
we could have done without them? I think they
do. And we shall best see how, if we take them
in connexion with their Hebrew contrasts.

The opposite of Spirit (ruach, pneuma), in the
Old Testament, is *body;* but body in its aspect of
"dust of the ground"—the earthy, in antithesis
to the heaven-derived. There is here, therefore,
no question raised as to the materiality or im-
materiality of the higher part of man—that question never came before the ancient Hebrews at all.
The sole truth meant to be conveyed by the antithesis is. that man is to be viewed in two distinct
relations,— as a heaven-born being and as a son of
the earth. And this discrimination is perfectly
clear and intelligible, having both a psychological
and a religious value.

A different view is taken of man when he is
regarded as Soul (nephesh or psyche). The contrast still is body; but body as a lifeless and
insensate thing, but, when animated, the instrument of sensation and volition. To the soul.
psychologically considered, belong "hope," "fear,"
"courage," "disquietude," "thanksgiving," "praise,"
etc. : in other words, the soul is characteristically
the seat of emotion and of will.

The opposite of Heart (lebab, kardia), on the
other hand, is still body; but body under its

denomination "flesh" (basar, σάρξ): not flesh, however, in the sense of vitiosity or carnal desire (the ethical signification is not found in the Old Testament), but in the sense of physical, as distinguished from mental, existence,--frequently with the superadded notion of mortality, frailty or weakness, "dust and ashes," "earth and ashes". The body, indeed, according to the Apocrypha (see *Ecclus.* xiv. 18, etc.), and according to rabbinical analysis, consisted of "blood and flesh" or "flesh and blood".

In these three terms, then, taken in conjunction with their contrasts, we have a tolerably complete account of the leading phenomena of man's nature: and it can easily be seen that an important step was gained, towards spiritualistic philosophy, when Hebrew distinctions began to exert an influence outside the Jewish community.

But the influence was not all on one side. On the contrary, whenever Hebrew conceptions began, as they did in Alexandria, to act on Greek thought, Greek thought began to react on Hebrew conceptions. This is best seen when we turn to the Hebrew Scriptures as embodied in the Greek terminology of the Septuagint. Not only is Hebrew anthropomorphism now purified—Enoch, for instance, no longer "walks with God," but

simply "pleases" Him;[1] but a richness of synonymous rendering of mental facts is introduced that
is sometimes even bewildering. In Philo, too, we
find Greek thought wedded to Hebrew feeling,
with marvellous results as to subtlety and refinement. And when we turn to the later books
of the Apocrypha, we feel at once what has
been effected by contact with Hellenism and
Greek philosophy. Many of the sharp-cut psychological distinctions that we are accustomed to
associate with other sources entered Hebrew religion from that quarter, and became, by and by,
current phrases in the New Testament. Such,
for instance, is the antithesis of "mind and body"
or "soul and body". In the ancient Jewish
Scriptures, we have simply "heart and flesh" or
"flesh[2] and soul"; but now the very name, as well
as the thing, has come to light, and it is at once
accepted as the fit expression of the Jewish notion.
So, the cosmogony of the Apocryphal books shows
us Hebrew doctrine influenced by Greek ideas.
The main lines are still, of course, Hebrew; but
such touches and variations as are perceptible in

---

[1] This is the Septuagint rendering of Genesis v. 24, and is the
basis of the argument in Hebrews xi. 5, 6.

[2] That *basar* means "flesh" in this antithesis (as, *e.g.*, in Is. x. 18,
and Job xiv. 22), both the Septuagint and the Vulgate clearly see.
What, again, our Revised Version translates by "my soul and my
body," in Ps. xxxi. 9, should be "my soul and my belly".

the *Wisdom of Solomon* are eminently Hellenic: Plato mingles here with Moses. Plato, too, has now affected the Hebrew conception of Body: "For the corruptible body," so says *Wisdom* (ix. 15), "presseth down the soul, and the earthly tabernacle weigheth down the mind that museth upon many things". Plato is also in great measure responsible for the clear and full teaching on immortality, discernible in *Wisdom* and other similar writings. So, the doctrine of Resurrection, as taught in 2 *Macc.* vi. and vii., though in itself anti-Hellenic, has strong psychological implications evidently of a Greek cast.

This reference to Resurrection suggests two questions: (1) What of Immortality in the Old Testament? (2) What of Resurrection?

That Immortality did come within the ancient Hebrew's range of vision, seems to me unquestionable. It is implied in the Creation narratives the doctrine of Spirit (ruach) would be unintelligible without it: though how far the notion grew in vividness as time went on, and how far the doctrinal belief influenced the Jew's practice, are questions for the scientific theologian. Again, the belief in Sheol, the doctrine of Hades, sombre though it was, embodied the conception of life as *persistent*;[1] and

---

[1] It has been said that the Jews, in their doctrine of Sheol, meant to express the fact that the departed *exist* but do not *live*. To this

the Hebrew's intense realization of personal communion with the Deity (as expressed, for instance,
in *Ps.* xvi.) seemed to give indication of life as *full.*
So that, the words of *Wisdom* (ii. 23), late though
they be, may be taken as faithfully reflecting the
Jewish opinion : " God created man to be immortal,
and made him to be an image of His own eternity".

Resurrection, on the other hand, we may confidently enough pronounce to be of late origin ;
and although there are glimpses of it in the
ancient Scriptures, and types of it, which the
rabbis came by and by to lay stress upon, it can
hardly be said to have assumed a definite dogmatic
form till the second century B.C. If we cannot
positively affirm that it actually originated in the
Maccabean period, we can say, with little fear of
contradiction, that it " became then for the first
time an article of the popular creed," and gave rise
to the practice of prayer for the dead. Yet, *there*
it was in Maccabean times—men's solace under
persecution, suffering, martyrdom,— to be handed
on to Christianity, and, thence, to affect all future
faith and speculation.

We come, then, to Christianity. The psycho-

---

distinction between mere personal existence and life, I object on two
separate grounds : first, because it is in itself untenable—a personal
existence that is not living is inconceivable ; secondly, because it is a
touch of *metaphysics* that is alien to Jewish thought.

logical matter that the New Testament writers
found ready to their hand was this :— (1) The
doctrine of a divine principle in man (ruach or
pneuma); (2) the doctrine of man as an active,
intellectual, and emotive being (nephesh *plus*
lebab, or psyche *plus* kardia); (3) the doctrine of
a lower and earthly part of man—his body (basar,
σάρξ and σῶμα); (4) the doctrines of Immortality
and Resurrection. How did they operate on
these? In what light did they consider them?

It is quite unnecessary to say that they
accepted them: but, while accepting them, they
deepened and transformed them. The pneuma
or spirit became now the *regenerated* nature of
man, the divine life-principle in him *renewed*,
and that through the operation of, and in connexion
with, the Holy Spirit, and resting on faith in the
atonement of Christ. Man's psyche became his
unregenerated nature: and his body (σῶμα, in
contradistinction now to σάρξ or "flesh") contracted a sanctified and sacred character: it
became, in a sense that the Hebrew "dust of the
ground" did not attain to, a part of the human
being absolutely necessary and indispensable to
his complete existence—it became the "temple of
the Holy Ghost," the "tent" that God Himself
inhabited, and, in the form of the resurrection-
body, it had immortality secured to it. The

advance over previous interpretations is obvious ; and we shall see it most clearly by attending to the psychology of the New Testament as it confronts us in the writings of St. Paul.

With St. Paul, man is still (as in the Apocrypha) a compound being, consisting of soul and body ; but the soul, in its unrenewed state, is at war with itself : the pneuma strives with the psyche, not as a battle of the reason against the appetites (that contest is also represented in St. Paul, but under the form of the "flesh" or σάρξ, contending with the "mind" or νοῦς, and overcoming it), but as the struggle of the psychical or "natural" man with the "spiritual" man ; and so great and vehement is this warfare that it seems as if there were in man two distinct souls. A threefold partition of the human being, therefore, becomes desirable, if we would adequately express the fact ; and St. Paul announces it (reproducing the Apocrypha, perhaps [1]) as "spirit, soul, and body" (πνεῦμα, ψυχή, σῶμα). Much has been made of this trichotomy, as though the Apostle teaches in it a literal threefold division of the human being, implying a tripartite nature ; just as Plato has sometimes been interpreted as teaching that man has three distinct souls (the rational, the spirited, and the appetitive), because he locates

---

[1] See *Song of the Three Children*, 64. Also, *Wisdom of Solomon* (xv. 11).

each of its three functions in a particular part of the
body. But, without arguing the point here, nothing
seems to me clearer than that St. Paul is simply
endeavouring to express his own vivid realization
of the spiritual warfare that went on in himself
(so passionately portrayed in *Romans*), and which
he believed other Christians experienced, and is
trying to bring into strong relief the central point of
his religious teaching—the need, namely, for fallen
man to have his *entire* being, (soul and body
equally) *spiritualized*, in order to perfection. It is
no more a literal trichotomy than the ancient
threefold Jewish enumeration of mental facts as
ruach, nephesh, and lebab (spirit, soul, and heart)
was a literal trichotomy; or the modern threefold
classification of the mind's states into feelings,
cognitions, and volitions implies the possession by
man of three separate and distinct minds; or than
the fourfold division of man's being, in the Epistle
to the Hebrews, into "soul and spirit, joints and
marrow" (where "joints" seem to stand for the
organs of motion, and "marrow" for those of sensation), is to be taken as a literal tetrachotomy.
It is simply the Christianized form of Old Testament teaching; the additions and changes being
necessitated by the advance that religious experience had made in the interval. The underlying
truth is: That man, originally formed in the

Divine Image, is fallen and needs to be restored;
as fallen he is at best but "psychical," as restored
he is "spiritual," and while this spiritual restora-
tion, like the original creation, is of Divine
origin,[1] it is also accomplished by a Divine
Person, and is inexplicable unless on the supposition of the agency and indwelling of the Holy
Spirit.

The Apostle's meaning is still further brought
out by his famous antithesis of Flesh and Spirit.
Flesh, to him, signified something entirely different
from what that term in its Hebrew form, *basar*,
did to the Old Testament Jews. To them, it was
simply one of three or four synonyms for man's
body; to him, it stands for the whole *corrupt*
nature of man, represented by, but not exhausted
in, the sensual lusts and passions.[2] It is the
unruly belligerent principle in human nature;
warring against the mind ($\nu o \hat{v} s$) and subduing it,
warred against by the spirit ($\pi \nu \epsilon \hat{v} \mu a$) and subdued.
This view went far beyond, though it is clearly on
the same line as, that of the Stoics, which represents man's great struggle towards right as being

---

[1] Hence the meaning of designating Jesus a "*life-giving* spirit."
$\pi \nu \epsilon \hat{v} \mu a$ $\zeta \omega \pi o \iota o \hat{v} \nu$ (1 Cor. xv. 45).

[2] Nevertheless, there seems to be a trace of this meaning in
Genesis vi. 3, where it is said, "My Spirit (*i.e.,* the Divine breath)
shall not always strive with (properly, *abide in*) man, because he also
is flesh (*i.e.,* is fallen or corrupted)".

"with the flesh"—where "flesh" stands for the carnal appetites and desires.

Here, then, we have a distinct addition to anything that has gone before; and it has been brought about by the religious fact of redemption and regeneration. In the interests of this fact, the ancient Hebrew terminology, as well as the ancient psychical conceptions, has been in measure changed. But it is a transformation, not an actual reversal, that is made. There is not even an actual reversal of old Greek psychical teaching, save in one point. That one point is the doctrine of a future "glorified" body, taught by St. Paul and endorsed by other New Testament writers. This is something that neither Plato nor Aristotle ever conceived, which they would have summarily rejected, and which even later Greek thought in post-Christian times failed to appreciate. Yet, modern philosophy has come to see that mind is not opposed to body in the absolute antithesis set forth in ancient Greek philosophy.[1] But the part that Christian teaching

---

[1] Hence, Hegel denominates the view that looks on man as a compound of soul and body as "the mechanical theory," and rightly objects to it that, according to this conception, "the two things (soul and body) stand each self-subsistent, and associated only from without. Similarly we find the soul regarded as a mere group of forces and faculties, subsisting independently side by side" (*The Logic of Hegel*, Wallace, p. 291).

has played in bringing about this result has yet
to be explicitly acknowledged.

4. *Confucius, Buddha, the Stoics.*

I said, a short way back, that the Bible's
conception of God is essentially ethical, and that
man is, in the eye of Scripture, first and mainly
a moral being. It becomes of interest, then, to
compare the conception of human nature that is
here given with other similar conceptions that are
famous in the history of human speculation.

One such conception is that of Confucius.

With Confucius, Morality is everything, and
his system is a series of practical rules designed to
educate and guide the individual in his efforts to
discharge his duty towards his neighbour and to
act the part of a good citizen. We are here very
much on the level, though prior to Aristotle's
time, of Aristotle's *Ethics*. The great thing is to
strike the mean, and the teacher's chief endeavour
is to point the path of respectability in living.
"Heaven," indeed, is regarded as the source of
Confucius's wise counsels: but this Heaven is
simply a word connoting superior authority,—such
authority as truths and customs coming down to
us from a venerable antiquity possess, or such as
have stood the test of experience, and must not

be regarded as equivalent to God. To Confucius, God, in any Western meaning of the term, is not ; and investigations about the Deity, about what awaits man in the future, about the immortality of the soul, and all attempts to deal with the problems that are distinctly known as metaphysical—such problems as Lao-tsze exercised himself with, are distinctly discouraged: "You do not yet understand life, how then can you profess to understand death?" It is enough, according to Confucius, if a man knows what are the rules whereby he should guide himself in his conduct and in his daily dealings with his fellow-men: Speculative problems are not for him.

The contrast here is very evident. The Hebrew, like Confucius, had a distinct dislike to speculative inquiry; but, on the side of Ethics, his creed is in the highest degree stimulating and ennobling. This it is, because he does not dissociate man from God, but, on the contrary, sets God forth as the necessary ethical correlate of man's nature, and makes the Deity Himself the inspiring Agent in the Moral Law. The distance is simply immeasurable between, "The master said, 'Perfect is the state of equilibrium and harmony! Few have they ever been who could attain to it.'" "The master said, 'I know how it is that the Path is not walked in. The cunning go beyond it, and

the stupid fall short of it,'"—and, "Hear, O Israel:
The Lord our God is one Lord: And thou shalt
love the Lord thy God with all thine heart, and
with all thy soul, and with all thy might," "I call
heaven and earth to record this day against you,
that I have set before you life and death, blessing
and cursing: therefore choose life, that both thou
and thy seed may live: That thou mayest love the
Lord thy God, and that thou mayest obey His
voice, and that thou mayest cleave unto Him: for
He is thy life, and the length of thy days".

Another moral system that has played the part
of a religion in the world is Buddhism. Contemporaneous with Confucianism in its origin, although
belonging to India, not China, it is vastly higher in
its tone, and approaches the distinctly spiritual
and ideal standpoint with which we are now-a-
days accustomed to associate Ethics. Its aim is
tersely expressed in the celebrated verse :—

> To cease from all sin,
> To get virtue,
> To cleanze one's own heart :
> This is the religion of the Buddhas.

The high tone that characterizes Buddhism, as
contrasted with Confucianism, arose from two
causes: first, from the pantheistic Hindu atmosphere in which Buddhistic ethics was generated:

secondly, from the fact that Buddhism, at its origin, was essentially anti-sacerdotal and ascetic. A morality based on self-denial and set forth as within the reach of all men without regard to caste, can never be low; and thus far it bears resemblance to Christianity. But Buddhism, as it faced theology, was weak. Being non-theistic in its groundwork, it could not rise to the height of the Jewish ethics; and, regarding life as an evil and human desire to live as the great source of man's misery, it was too unnatural to be really effective in regenerating the race. With no personal God to believe in, with annihilation or Nirvâna as its goal, and pessimism as its foundation, Buddhism could only be a maimed, albeit impressive, creed; and no wonder that, in its propagandist efforts in the world, it found it necessary to ally itself with polytheism. It was only thus that it could be galvanized into life and gain a hold on the affections of mankind.

A third ethical system was ancient Stoicism. Here, too, as in early Buddhism, elevation of view was reached by fixing on the stern and heroic side of morality; and here, too, Character became the one leading concern. The advantage, however, lay with Stoicism: and this was owing to its doctrine of Conscience, and to its stimulating

cosmopolitanism or teaching of the universal
brotherhood of men—where the approach to
Christianity is apparent. Founding on Plato's
analysis of human nature, the Stoics laid firm hold
on Reason, and made this the ruling principle (τὸ
ἡγεμονικόν). They went beyond Plato, however,
in the stress they put on the ethical and practical
side of our being. They despised pleasure and
crucified the passions, and set philosophic indifference to the ills of life before them as their
aim. This is their far-famed doctrine of Apathy
(ἀπάθεια). Pleasure they held to be no good, and
pain to be no evil. Character was the great thing
that interested the ideal wise man, and character
alone had intrinsic value. Hence Stoicism, like
early Buddhism, overshot the mark: but, unlike
Buddhism (although not unlike Talmudic Pal-
estinian philosophy), it was fatalistic. Because
events in life are fated, therefore (argued the
Stoic) it is the mark of the wise man to accept
with composure whatever happens to him by
ungrudging submission to the inevitable he shows
his wisdom; or, if untoward circumstances
circumstances brought about by no fault of the
man himself— should render life unendurable, then
moral freedom and true independence is best
shown by suicide. No (said the philosophic
Buddhist), not fate rules in life, but the necessity

of cause and consequence. This is the doctrine of
Karma. Evil is evil, and is no good; pain is pain,
and should be got rid of. But it arises from man's
own acts; it is the result of his yielding to Desire.
Let him renounce desire, then, and he will free
himself from pain. Self-annihilation is the end,
mysticism the means; and through mystic contemplation, aided by asceticism, Nirvâna may be
reached.

5. *The Neo-platonists.*

We have now, practically, obtained all the elements of human nature. Once the Greek analysis
had become welded with the Scripture teaching,
there was little further, in the way of actual discovery of elements, to be done. Many old problems, indeed, had to be faced anew; and many
fresh problems presented themselves, from time
to time, for solution, as experience deepened and
knowledge increased. The nature of the Soul,
with all the train of allied questions, became a
subject of engrossing interest to some: "fix'd
fate, free will, foreknowledge absolute" taxed the
energies of others. Boëthius stands conspicuous,
among the Latin writers of the early Christian
times, for his wrestling with the last of these
subjects; and, in many respects, no greater work
on the problem of evil and its theistic bearings has

ever been produced than his treatise *On the Con-
solation of Philosophy.* But human nature, in its
essentials, was now known; for, though subsequent
attempts have been made to add to them, they have
been without success. Two of these attempts,
however, demand our consideration.

The first is the attempt to give a supreme place
to Mysticism, as a normal element of man's being.
The Neo-platonists of the third and fourth centuries
of our era may stand as our example.

Regarding the Absolute as entirely characterless, and refusing to admit that God could in any
way be known by man, they, nevertheless, taught
the possibility of ecstatic union with Him, implying
the abnegation of self on man's part and all that
constitutes individuality. Such ecstatic union and
self-effacement was a new thing, so far as pure
Greek philosophy was concerned; and it was alien
also to ancient Hebrew thought. Pantheism, indeed, was native to the Greek—yet pantheism, not
as a religious mood, but as an intellectual explanation of the universe. Pantheism, too, was not quite
foreign to the Jew, with his deep emotional theism
and his vivid consciousness of God as the all-
comprehending presence, in whom men lived and
moved and had their being. But mysticism was
Oriental in its origin; and came into Greek and

Jewish philosophy only about the time of Philo Judaeus, and commended itself first to the schools of Alexandria. Its value we shall consider more particularly in a future lecture;[1] but, meanwhile, note the thing itself, and the fact that it was an element additional to any that we have yet had in the analysis of human nature, and an element which, when accepted either by philosophy or by theology, has produced disastrous consequences.

6. *The Schoolmen.*

The other retrograde doctrine— also very fatal to philosophy and to theology alike - is of Mediæval origin. We are now dealing with a time when Philosophy was regarded as the handmaid of the Church. Its help was sought, not for the independent truth that it might disclose, but for the defence that it might be able to give to ecclesiastical dogmas, and for its utility in formulating and systematizing these. Hence, the great point over which the Schoolmen argued for centuries, beginning at the tenth, was the nature and meaning of Universals. The dogmas of the Church, and more especially the doctrine of the Trinity, seemed at stake: and Philosophy was here of value, when it supported Realism. But it was different when Philosophy presumed to show life of its own, and

---

[1] Lecture IV.

to speculate in independence of Church control.
The cases of Roscelin and Abaelard, in the eleventh
and twelfth centuries, are typical. Let philosophy
show originality, and it must be suppressed; convinced or unconvinced, the offending thinker must
bow to ecclesiastical authority, and recant. By
and by, however, freedom of speculation was to
assert itself, -though sometimes by means rather
dubious. First came the partial emancipation of
philosophy, under the sanction of the Church,
by the two celebrated Latin Doctors of the thirteenth century Albertus Magnus and St. Thomas
Aquinas. A sphere of theistic doctrine was now
distinctly assigned to Reason, and another sphere
was strictly reserved for Revelation. This was
the famous distinction between truths "competent
to reason" and truths "beyond" or "above
reason," though not "contrary" to it, between
Natural and Revealed Theology: a distinction
destined to play such a conspicuous part in the
philosophy of Bruno, and, later on, in the dogmatic rationalism of Leibniz, Wolff, and the
German Illuminism (*Aufklärung*). It was but a
step to the further doctrine that what is true in
philosophy may be false in theology, and inversely;
and the less orthodox Churchmen eagerly seized
at it. It came, no doubt, from the Arabian Averroës. But, surely, if it originated with the dis-

tinguished Mussulman, whose name was a thing
to conjure with in the learned world, it might well
be accepted by perturbed philosophers in Latin
Christendom. Only one more refinement was
necessary: and this was made by Pomponatius,
about the opening of the sixteenth century, when
Reason itself was divided into an intellectual
and a practical reason—the one speculative and
the other regulative, the first dealing with the
truths of philosophy and the second assigned to
theology and to the guidance of morality and
conduct.

Now this distinction, in each of its two forms
as an opposition between Faith and Reason and as
an opposition between speculative and regulative
Reason, is an entirely vicious one, and has been
productive of much harm. Sunder Faith from
Thought, and truth is rent in twain, and the parts
remain in helpless separation. Affirm with Tertullian, " I believe, because it is impossible " (*certum
est, quia impossibile est*), and Theology becomes the
embodiment of irrationality, and Revelation is
degraded to the level of nonsense. " The human
spirit," says Principal Caird (*Introduction to the
Philosophy of Religion*, pp. 69, etc.), " is not a thing
divided against itself so that faith and reason can
subsist side by side in the same mind, each assert-

ing as absolute principles which are contradicted by the other. If it were so, then either there must be a higher umpire than both to decide between them, or thought and knowledge are reduced to chaos. For, in the first place, we must have rational grounds for the acceptance of a supernatural revelation. It must verify its right to teach authoritatively. Reason must be competent to judge, if not of the content, at least of the credentials, of revelation. But an authority proving by reason its right to teach irrationally is an impossible conception. The authority which appeals to reason in proof of its rights commits itself, so to speak, to be essentially rational. To prove to reason a right to set reason at defiance is self-contradictory, inasmuch as the proof itself must be one of the things to which that right extends. . . . In the second place, reason itself lies nearer to us than any external authority, and no other or outward evidence can be sufficient to overturn its testimony. . . . The attempt therefore to maintain an unreal equilibrium between faith and reason—between a reverence which accepts, and an intelligence which rejects, the same things—can only issue in one of two results, practical unbelief or the violent suppression of doubt. No adjustment of the difference can be satisfactory save an adjustment *in thought.*"

7. From Descartes to Hegel.

Modern philosophy is usually regarded as beginning with Descartes. Be it so, if the meaning is that the greatest impulse to philosophizing in post-Reformation times came from him, and that subsequent schools looked to him as to a master. But neither Descartes's standpoint nor his ontology, nay nor even his method, is original. When Descartes lays the basis of philosophy in self-consciousness (*Cogito, ergo sum*), he is simply reverting to a position long ago taken up by St. Augustine, and expressed with all the clearness and vigour of that great thinker. When, again, he prescribes Doubt as the one leading philosophic method, and bids us build only on what stands the test of doubt, he is but repeating St. Augustine: and when he argues for the existence of God from the concept of the Deity in the human mind, he attaches himself to St. Anselm. Ontology, however, was Descartes's special province. He was no psychologist—he did not even greatly interest himself in Theory of *Knowledge*; his supreme concern was Theory of *Being*. But here he has left an indelible mark on philosophy, and has done much to vindicate for human nature its right to a rational theism.

Ontology, in like manner, was the great concern of his continental successors, down to the time of

Kant: including the two greatest of them all—Spinoza and Leibniz.

This cannot be said of Britain, however. British ontologists, it is true, were not wanting, not even eminent ones: it is enough to mention Berkeley. But Bacon ruled in science, and Locke gave the impulse in philosophy: and Locke's philosophy was no ontology,—although God, the World, and the Soul find their place in it. It was not even, strictly speaking, a psychology or analysis of the human mind, notwithstanding that Locke is usually cited as an English psychologist. We have, of course, a good deal of psychology in it, and we have also the important enunciation that philosophy, if it is to have real value, must start from psychological inquiry; but it was itself distinctively a Theory of Cognition,—an attempt (1) first, to trace the origin, and (2) secondly, to determine the extent and validity, of human knowledge. The very title of the famous Essay proves this. Locke calls it *An Essay Concerning Human Understanding*; and, in the opening paragraph, he lays down his object. "This, therefore, being my purpose," he says (I., 1, § 2), "to inquire into the original, certainty, and extent of human knowledge, together with the grounds and degrees of belief, opinion, and assent, I shall not at present meddle with the physical consideration of the mind, or

trouble myself to examine wherein its essence
consists, or by what motions of our spirits or
alterations of our bodies we come to have any
sensation by our organs, or any ideas in our understandings. . . . It shall suffice to my present
purpose, to consider the discerning faculties of
a man, as they are employed about the objects
which they have to do with. And I shall imagine
I have not wholly misemployed myself in the
thoughts I shall have on this occasion, if, in this
historical, plain method, I can give any account
of the ways whereby our understandings come
to attain those notions of things we have, and
can set down any measures of the certainty
of our knowledge, or the grounds of those
persuasions which are to be found amongst
men."

The same is true of Hume. Hume's great
interest lay, not in psychology nor in ontology, but
in the theory of knowledge. There is this difference, however. Locke never allowed his doctrine
of the *genesis* of knowledge to shake the validity
of knowledge; with Hume, the theory of *origin*
reacted unfavourably on that of validity. Nevertheless, in morals, Hume distinctly upheld the
dignity of human nature and maintained "that the
sentiments of those who are inclined to think
favourably of mankind are much more advan-

tageous to virtue than the contrary principles, which give us a mean opinion of our nature".

Hume's position brought out Kant. Theory of knowledge became Kant's great problem too. Conversant with psychology, but not starting from it, nay rather, deliberately setting it aside and "giving it a little attention only upon sufferance," [1] Kant set himself to analyze human experience, and thereby to secure a foundation for human knowledge. For, in experience, when duly analyzed, he found the mental elements that gave the validity that he desiderated; and, through reason, he claimed to overthrow the scepticism that aimed at impugning reason.

On the high speculative side, however, Kant's philosophy was clearly defective (this we shall see later on). Knowing and Being he left standing apart; and it was the problem of Hegel to show the power of Philosophy in bringing the two into union.

8. *Recent Advance.*

But what now of more recent advance? It has lain in a threefold direction.

(1) First, in the region of Psychology.

By Psychology is meant the science of the

---

[1] See this very clearly brought out in the late Professor Croom Robertson's striking article on "Psychology and Philosophy," in vol. viii. of the first series of *Mind*.

phenomena of consciousness, of the states and
operations of the mind, their nature and their
origin, together with the laws that determine their
combination and interaction, without, however,
raising the question whether these manifestations
do or do not imply a distinct spiritual self as their
groundwork. It asks, What are the actual contents of our minds; what feelings, ideas, thoughts,
volitions do we consciously experience? Also,
How do these various elements in our mental
furniture arise, coalesce, and continue to be? Its
character and scope will be clearly seen by
referring to such works as those of Professor Bain,
Professor Sully, Dr. James Ward, Professor
Höffding.

Now, clearly, all progress in other spheres of
mental science is dependent upon accuracy and
fulness here. And what we have to credit modern
psychological investigation with, is—(1) a luminous
classification of mental phenomena (originated by
Tetens, a contemporary of Kant) into Feeling,
Intellect, and Will; (2) a just appreciation of the
physiological side of mind, and an admirable
analysis of each of the various groups of mental
phenomena (Dr. Bain leading the way); and (3) a
clear perception of the fact that no mental element
stands isolated or alone, but that, in every one
element, the others are implicated too. A soul

divided into parts (as with Plato), or even a mind working through separate and distinct "faculties" (as with psychologists of last generation), is now happily an anachronism, and cannot again, we may hope, be resuscitated to retard mental science and confuse clear thinking.

But we must not forget to include in the recent psychological advance Comparative Psychology, or "the psychology of peoples or races,"—_i.e._, of mind acting in the aggregate under diversity of time, place, and circumstance, and manifesting itself in collective works. This is a study quite modern, and of great promise. The good effects of it are already discernible in many quarters.

In the advance, we ought, too, to include Animal Psychology.

(2) Secondly, in the region of Epistemology.

This is Theory of Knowledge; which, taking up the facts of consciousness as given by psychology, proceeds to inquire into their _worth_. It does not dispute their existence, it accepts them as subjective facts; but goes on to ask whether they are valid on the side of truth—whether they are, in whole or in part, as they _ought_ to be.

Now this is, obviously, a most important operation, and one fraught with momentous consequences. Psychology, suppose, approaches the subject of human Belief. All that it can do is, to tell us *what* men actually believe and *how* they have come to believe it, or how they *will* believe under given circumstances; but whether their beliefs are true or false, valid or not, it cannot say. Here Epistemology steps in, and declares that the mere fact of a man's having a particular belief is no sufficient assurance of its truth, but that the criterion of truth must be determined outside mere psychology; and this determination Epistemology itself undertakes.

If psychology gives us the *fact* and the *genesis* or process of belief, epistemology supplies us with its *justification*. Clearly, therefore, Epistemology presupposes that not only do men have experience, not only are they aware of mental facts or of things happening, but they are also in possession of a power of appraising these facts; and this again implies that Mind or Reason has within itself, as part of its nature, a standard of criticism. Epistemology, therefore, may be regarded as a section of Metaphysics (for metaphysics is the science of first principles as well as of supersensible essence); but it is metaphysics on its *normative* side.

If now it be asked, " What is the advance that recent Epistemology has made?"— I answer, in the words of the late Professor Croom Robertson,

" Let us . . . note but two points in the philosophical theory of knowledge which, since the
time of Kant, may be regarded as placed beyond
reasonable question : (1) that we know Space,
abstractly, as a ' form ' inclusive of sensation, and,
actually, as one great *continuum* (percept, not
concept) within which all sensible objects are
ordered ; (2) that anything to be definitely called
Object, as a sensible reality for all men alike, is
a complex product of thought-activity working
under common conditions in all " (*Mind*, first
series, vol. viii. p. 21).

(3) Lastly, in the region of Ontology.

This is Theory of *Being* ; or Metaphysics as it
deals with the three great entities— God, the Soul,
the World. Take, as example, the case of the
Perception of an External World. There are
three questions here that must be kept separate.
(1) First, What, as given in consciousness, is
the nature of external sense-perception ? This
question may again be broken up into two : (*a*)
What is the *psychological analysis* of Subject and
Object in external perception ? (*b*) What is the
genesis of our notion of Subject and Object in
external perception ? (2) Secondly, What is the
value of our knowledge in external perception ? Is
it valid ; and, if so, in what sense ? (3) Thirdly,

What is *Being*, as distinguished from knowing, in external perception? Or, what is meant by saying that there is an (independent) external world?

The first of these questions, in both its aspects, is purely psychological. The second belongs to Epistemology or theory of knowledge. The third alone is Ontological.

Now, as to Ontology, the obvious advance (speaking generally) is, that it has become more and more clear that, if we are to achieve a rational interpretation of the universe we must work outwards from our experience of our own inward selves, and upwards from psychology through epistemology, and that the unity of things is, not a mere mechanical union, as of part in external contact with part, but an *organic* unity, after the type of the living Ego.

III.

From our hasty review of the various conceptions of human nature, as represented in the history of philosophic thought, we are now in a position to see what different standpoints may be taken as to the Theistic aspirations.

1. First of all, it may be argued that Theism is founded in the rational, speculative, or intellectual side of our being, but is excluded from the emotional and the ethical sides. This was the

view of Aristotle, and of many other ancient
Greeks.

2. Secondly, it may be held that Theism is
grounded in emotion. This, according to Hume
and to modern anthropologists, is the view of
primitive man. But it is the view also, as we shall
see later on, of many men (Schleiermacher, for
instance) that cannot be denominated "primitive".

3. Thirdly, it may be said that Theism is a
postulate of ethics. This was Kant's position,
and it is popular at the present moment. Fichte
at one time accepted it—only, he identified the
Deity with the moral order of the Universe : and
Matthew Arnold did the same. It is curious to
observe how it actually reverses the Aristotelian
point of view. Aristotle shut out morality from
Theism altogether ; Kant shut out cognition.

4. Fourthly, it may be maintained that Theism
is grounded in some two of the provinces of human
nature say, intellect and morality, as with Plato ;
or in all the three provinces – in intellect, emotion, and ethics. This last is the view of many
of the most recent theistic writers in Germany, in
France, and in Britain. It is substantially the
view that shall be taken here ; the working out
of which, in the way that commends itself to
my acceptance, is the task that lies before us
in succeeding lectures.

LECTURE III.

In entering on the reasoned exposition of Theism, it will scarcely be permitted us, at the present moment, quietly to take for granted even the possibility on man's part of attaining a knowledge of the Deity. Time was when, even if the existence of God were called in question, the possibility of knowing Him, on the supposition that He actually existed, was generally admitted. But such a time is past and gone; and the rational theist has now, not only to make clear the being and nature of the Object with whom his speculations profess to deal, but also his own and his fellow-man's capacity to rise to an apprehension of that Object. In modern philosophical language, he has to present his subject both as epistemology and as ontology.

Before proceeding, therefore, with our argument, it becomes incumbent upon us to meet certain current objections *in limine*. Not only are we confronted with the difficulty, as old as Job, that man cannot find out the Almighty "unto perfection," but we are further told that our con-

ceptions of the Deity are and must be magnified
or transformed pictures of ourselves, and, consequently, untrue ; or that they are pure fabrications
of the mind, to which we illegitimately attach an
objective value. In other words, it is objected to
us that, being men, we necessarily ascribe to God
human qualities and human feelings, which are in
reality inapplicable to Him ; or that, although
finite, we delude ourselves into the belief that we
are able to rise to and grasp the Infinite.

This is the argument from Anthropomorphism
and anthropopathy. Stated generally, it runs :
That man, being what he is, finds it impossible to
conceive of the Deity as other than a kind of man :
even when he does not clothe Him in the human
form, he assigns Him human attributes and passions that are not in place. Says Matthew Arnold:
" Man, however, as Goethe says, *never knows how
anthropomorphic he is.* Israel described his Eternal
in the language of poetry and emotion, and could
not thus describe him but with the character of a
man " (*Literature and Dogma*, p. 123). But, put
more specifically, the argument assumes a twofold
aspect according as the objector occupies the position of one considering the religious history of the
human race, or sets himself forth as a theorist
reasoning from the limitations of man's faculties,
or *a priori* from the bare ideas " man " and " God".

In the first case, he argues that God is not discoverable by us, for, as matter of fact, He has never yet been found—on the contrary, man's gods are all demonstrably false. In the second case, he argues that God is not discoverable by us, for, if He were (ignoring for the moment the contradiction in terms), that would be to reduce Him to a man.

I.

Taken in the first of these two aspects, the objection may be stated in this way :—

Looking to the history of mankind, we find as a simple fact that different men in different ages, and different races of men in different countries, have elaborated very different conceptions of the Deity. And, when we closely examine it, we discover that this diversity in conception arises from difference in habits, circumstances, and cast of mind: so that a man's deity, or a community's deity, may be briefly stated as a transferring to an imaginary power, in an intensified form, of the properties and attributes that are held in highest estimation, or that are most dreaded, by that man or that community. Thus, we take the warlike heathen, those wild and barbarous races that have delighted in bloodshed and in slaughter: and what we find is that they have uniformly thought of God as a mighty warrior like themselves: they

have endowed Him with all the fierceness and
cruelty of their own natures, and have paid
Him homage because they believed Him to be
merciless and revengeful, never weary in pursuing
the war-path, and always strong to deal destruction
to His foes. Take, again, the less warlike, but
more lustful heathen—those who, through the
more favourable natural circumstances in which
they have been placed, have had less need of fight-
ing enemies, and more time for gratifying their
own baser appetites; who have been too volup-
tuous or too slothful to bestir themselves to active
aggression,—and we find that their religious ideal
has been of a wholly different kind: they have
clothed their God with the same base appetites
and slothful nature as themselves, and His unbridled
lust has been to them His highest glory. Again,
take those savages whose lot has been cast in lands
of frequent storms and earthquakes, who have been
brought up from the beginning amid Nature's
frights and terrors; and these have made God a
stern and terrifying Deity, too wrathful or too
powerful to be approached, or to be approached
only with sacrifices and offerings—"thousands of
rams and ten thousands of rivers of oil," "my first-
born for my transgression, the fruit of my body for
the sin of my soul," and their worship of Him has
always been directed towards this one end of

appeasing Him, and so has ever been degraded—
sometimes to the very lowest depths. Once again,
take races of a more refined and philosophic
temperament—races who, through one cause or another, have in great measure risen above the base,
the sensual, and the devilish, who have not been
paralyzed by fear, and whose own lives have been
marked by contemplation and reflection, and by
comparative purity on the side of morals: these
have endowed God with thought, reflection, contemplation too, and, in keeping with the advanced
purity of their own lives, they have robed Him in
moral attributes of a really high order. It is a
pure God here, it is a cruel God there; in one
place it is a mighty warrior, in another place an
unrelenting tyrant. But everywhere the tendency
is one and the same: a people's God, or, for that
matter, an individual's God, has largely been the
expression of that people's or individual's own
peculiar characteristics. Our proneness is to
humanize God; and, reversing the Scripture teaching that man is formed in the Divine image, we
are apt to conceive the Divinity as formed in
man's image, and to think Him "altogether such
an one as ourselves". Hence, it is maintained,
our error: hence, our very great and grievous mistake. Rousseau has put it in a single sentence.
"As a rule," says he, "believers make God like

themselves: the good make Him good; the wicked make Him wicked; the bigots, bitter and bilious, see nothing but hell, because they would damn all the world; loving and sweet souls think differently."

Now, the facts on which this argument is based are unquestionably true. It is true that people have shown and do show a tendency to colour their theistic notions with anthropomorphism even in its worst signification. It is true that some nations have had, or do have, a miserably inadequate, or a miserably low, view of the Deity. We may, further, admit that the main cause of this has been or is the particular stage in intelligence and morality that the individual or the tribe has reached at the particular moment. And yet we need not be driven to maintain that all theistic reasoning is thereby vitiated, and man is cut off entirely from God. For, (1) in the first place, even base notions of the Deity may have a grain of truth in them: they, at any rate, bear witness to man's sense of a being or beings higher or greater than himself. Although the greatness conceived be merely of the kind that the individual or the nation prizes most, it is regarded as supereminent; and this alone places the fact of false gods, so far, on the theistic line. But, (2)

secondly, base or degraded notions of the Supreme
Being have not, in any age, been absolutely universal. In every age, and somewhere, it has been
possible to point to individuals, if not to nations,
whose conceptions of God have always surpassed
the highest moral attainments of the people of
the time, and which have even been condemnatory
of many of the qualities and practices that, in
the eyes of the masses, were looked upon as the
highest excellences or virtues. No age has been
without its prophets, philosophers, and reformers
– without men who have been in moral and in
intellectual advance of their day. And this proves,
at least, that there is no absolute necessity, that,
as the man's age or nation is, so precisely will
his own ideas of God be. It may also prove much
more than that ; for, the *exceptional* men in an age,
or in a nation, may turn out to be the men who
are giving for the first time explicit utterance to
what has all along been implicit in reason. They
are the "elect" because of their superior insight :
and to them, after-ages look back as to the
beacons of the past, the lights that are most worth
regarding in our efforts to retrace the progressive
path of Reason in its historical development.
Then, (3) thirdly, it is possible that cases of degraded notions regarding the Deity may be susceptible of an explanation that shall not be wholly

derogatory to human nature. Two facts have to
be borne in mind. First, there is such a thing
as deterioration, or lapse from a higher plane to
a lower in religion, according to the law of Degeneration, so pregnant and so well known in
biology. Secondly, there is evidence to show that
much of the immorality and baseness ascribed to
the gods in heathen mythologies is only myth-
forming man's way of expressing the observed
workings of the great forces of nature : natural
phenomena are readily transformed into the personal adventures of superhuman beings when per-
sonification is the accepted explanation of all that
is striking or mysterious in life. Is it not, also,
possible that the reputation of the gods may sometimes have been compromised by the bad behaviour
of their official representatives—the priests ? Then,
(4) fourthly, History clearly shows a progress in
mankind's idea of the Supreme—a marked advance
of one age over another, the idea growing with
man's growing experience and ever increasing in
richness of content as time went on. And this
very fact forbids our putting the worst possible
interpretation on man's anthropomorphic tendencies, and may be even used to prove the existence
of an overruling Providence, guiding men on, slowly
yet surely, to a true knowledge of Himself. But,
(5) fifthly, theistic progress is discernible, not only

in mankind generally, but in distinct peoples confined to particular areas of the earth, or belonging to particular nationalities. We find a striking example in the writings of Homer. "It has been observed," I am quoting Canon Taylor, "that in the *Iliad* the men are nobler and better than the gods, while in the *Odyssey* the gods have the higher moral status. In the *Iliad* the gods deceive men for their own purposes; in the *Odyssey* they are the avengers of crime, and interfere with human affairs, not from spite, favouritism, or mere caprice, but only for some high moral purpose. In the *Iliad* Zeus exhibits what Mr. Gladstone calls 'cynical selfishness and lust'; in the *Odyssey* he has developed into the supreme moral ruler of the world. In the *Iliad* we have the turbulent Olympian court--- spiteful, immoral, intriguing, brawling and lascivious, with its petty jealousies and everlasting quarrels, and dwelling locally on the summit of Mount Olympus. In the *Odyssey* all this has disappeared, the gods are lofty intelligences, inhabiting the expanse of the empyrean, with no local terrestrial abode. It might almost be said that in the *Iliad* they are subject to the law of gravitation, from which in the *Odyssey* they have been emancipated" (*Academy,* 8th Nov., 1890, p. 412). Then, (6) lastly, something must be allowed to the exigencies of lan-

guage. If it be impossible to speak of the Deity
without applying to Him anthropopathic terms,
this is only of a piece with the impossibility of
speaking of mental phenomena without employing
language drawn from the material world. Although the words in either case are charged with
metaphor, they, nevertheless, contain a distinct
adumbration of the truth, and need not be so
grossly misleading as to be utterly unsafe.

We need not, then, lay much stress on the first
form of the anthropomorphic objection. The facts
on which it claims to be grounded are interesting
and important, but they do not bear out the
conclusion drawn. All that they prove is that man
at a particular stage of his development, or man in
particular circumstances, forms his God in the
likeness of himself; but they do not prove either
(*a*) that man may not at some time, or under
certain circumstances, reach true notions of the
Deity, or (*b*) that he may not, in the course of the
progress of the race, himself become so changed in
nature as to be, to a certain extent, an accurate
reflection of the Divine. The progressive clearing
of man's conceptions, as experience deepens and
time goes on, is a very common phenomenon, and
is not confined to Theism. There is no branch of
Truth that does not show a similar development.

Wrong notions, false notions, inadequate notions of the leading ideas in science, philosophy, and art alike, have been entertained in some age. In all departments of knowledge, men have groped their way towards light erringly and stumblingly, and, frequently, themselves creating the darkness that enveloped them. Yet, no one thinks of maintaining that there is no such thing as truth, or that there were no glimpses of what we clearly see to-day in the dim anticipations of the past. Copernicus did not originate Astronomy, though he revolutionized it; nor is the Uniformity of Nature an absolutely new discovery of these later days. Man's knowledge advances, and his character improves; and, with advancing knowledge and improved character, great things are achieved. But the light at the beginning, and throughout all the struggles at self-revelation—sometimes sadly baffled, at other times obscurely asserting itself,—was light still; and we must not despise the beginnings because they were weak and humble, nor must we exaggerate the early darkness so as to make believe that darkness alone existed then.

What the struggling towards pure Theism (as shown in history) proves, is precisely what is proved by the continual struggle towards clearer and ever clearer knowledge of the nature and capability of human reason. I do not suppose that Reason's laws were unknown, or were not acted upon, before the time of Aristotle; yet it was Aristotle who clearly formulated them, and developed, on their basis, the science of Logic. I do not suppose that Aristotle was the first to set himself to a persistent and systematic study of the human mind; yet he was the first to give scientific form to Psychology, and to inaugurate that close and careful investigation into mind and mind's phenomena that is only to-day approaching a satisfactory position. I do not suppose that the earliest philosopher, or the man who first gave himself to speculation, was altogether devoid of some notion of the criterion of truth and the theory of knowledge; yet it is only now that we are awaking to the true nature of Epistemology. In each and all of these cases, there has been a gradual advance, often through conspicuous retrogressions; but the germ of truth was never wanting. Wherever, indeed, man's curiosity is really awakened, *there* is Truth beginning to make a revelation; and we are not to refuse to call it truth because the earliest form of the revelation may be something entirely different in appearance from the latest.

II.

We turn, then, to the second form of the anthropomorphic objection; and this is a much

more serious affair. Man and God, it is maintained, are direct opposites; they have, in their
essence, nothing in common. It is impossible,
therefore, that there should be any communication
between the two. Not only do man's feelings,
thoughts, and volitions differ in degree from those
of the Deity, they differ also in kind: the finite
and the Infinite, the relative and the Absolute, are
separated *toto cœlo*.

This is what is usually denominated by pre-
eminence the *agnostic* position, although it is an
agnosticism of a very positive kind. It does not
simply profess that it does not know whether
God exists (*that* was the position of the ancient
Pyrrhonists and Academics generally,—it is the
position that we usually associate with the term
sceptic); but it clearly maintains that God, though
existent, cannot be known. It is the second limb
of Gorgias's threefold nescience: (1) Nothing is;
(2) if anything is, it cannot be known; (3) if it
can be known, it cannot be communicated.

Agnosticism: what, then, is it ? One has
defined it as " Doubt emptied of Faith, and turning its face towards Denial". And this, unfortunately, is only too true of much of the secularist
agnosticism of the present moment. There are
many so-called agnostics who rejoice in being

"atheists". But atheism and agnosticism are by no means synonymous terms, and I am not surprised when high-toned agnostics indignantly disclaim the imputation of atheism. Absolute denial is not of the essence of agnosticism, and there is such a thing as agnostic *faith*. Even Professor Huxley admits that "a man may be an agnostic, in the sense of admitting he has no positive knowledge, and yet consider that he has more or less probable ground for accepting any given hypothesis about the spiritual world. Just as a man may frankly declare that he has no means of knowing whether the planets generally are inhabited or not, and yet may think one of the two possible hypotheses more likely than the other, so he may admit that he has no means of knowing anything about the spiritual world, and yet may think one or other of the current views on the subject, to some extent probable" (*Essays upon Some Controverted Questions*, p. 466). On the other hand, we must never forget, as Dr. Martineau reminds us ("Preface" to *A Study of Religion*, p. xi.), that "for much of the Agnosticism of the age, the Gnosticism of theologians is undeniably responsible".

Sometimes, Agnosticism has been prompted by the highest and deepest religious feeling: the individual agnostic having such an overpowering consciousness of the majesty and greatness of God and of his own intellectual and moral impotence as to be driven to refuse to ascribe to the Deity any qualities which his own weak nature possessed, and to conceive Him (if that word may be permitted) simply as the negation of all that is finite. At other times, agnosticism has been prompted by a baffled intellect; as when Kant, through his metaphysical distinction of things-in-themselves and their mere manifestation, shut the door against a speculative knowledge of the Divinity, but opened it again to the ethical aspirations of man, and based the theistic argument in the Practical Reason; or when Democritus, feeling keenly the limits of the human mind, declared that "Truth lies buried in the deep". Once more, baffled intellect has given rise to an agnosticism more thorough-going than Kant's. Mr. Herbert Spencer's is a case in point; but it was substantially in existence long before Mr. Spencer's time. Says Hobbes, for instance: " Forasmuch as God Almighty is incomprehensible, it followeth, that we can have no conception or image of the Deity: and, consequently, all his attributes signify our inability and defect of power to conceive anything concerning his nature, and not any conception of the same, excepting only this, that there is a God.

For the effects we acknowledge naturally, do include a power of their producing, before they were produced; and that power presupposeth something existent that hath such a power: and the thing so existing with power to produce, if it were not eternal, must needs have been produced by something before it, and that again by something else before that, till we come to an eternal (that is to say the first) Power of all powers, and first Cause of all causes: and this it is which all men conceive by the name of God, implying eternity, incomprehensibility, and omnipotency. And thus all that will consider may know that God is, though not *what* he is: even a man born blind, though it be not possible for him to have any imagination what kind of thing fire is, yet he cannot but know that something there is that men call fire, because it warmeth him" (*Human Nature*, c. xi. § 2).

Now, of all the forms of this philosophical agnosticism it may be said that they do contain an important truth, but they press it to the point where it becomes grievous error. They all testify to the surpassing greatness of God, and to the impossibility of our ever exhausting His perfections—they warn us, and warn us properly, with *Ecclesiasticus*. "without eyes thou shalt want

light : profess not the knowledge, therefore, that
thou hast not ". But they err in supposing that
we ourselves have no greatness, or that our faculties are simply defects, and so have nothing in
common with the Divine. Hobbes's example of
the man born blind very well shows the weakness
of the position. All that this case proves is, not
that a man born blind is devoid of *all* knowledge of
fire, but that he lacks only such knowledge of fire
as is derived from sight. He still has touch and
the sense of temperature and other means to give
him a conception of fire ; and, so long as he has
these, he cannot be said to be ignorant of what
fire is. On the contrary, he knows it ; only his
knowledge is *more limited* than that of the normal
man, who, to the other avenues of knowledge,
adds sight. But, though more limited, it may be
equally accurate, and very probably, in some
respects, more accurate : for, deprivation of one
sense, particularly sight, has often been found to
be the condition of revealing marvellous powers
in some of the other senses. So, man may want
this means and that means of knowing God —
means which we may suppose higher intelligences
to possess ; but, so far as his means carry him, he
knows more than the mere fact of God's existence
—he knows, to some considerable extent, the
nature of God.

In pursuing our subject, it will be necessary to go with some minuteness into Agnosticism; and, as my plan is historical, it will be best to present Agnostic systems in selected types.

One representative form is that founded on purely philosophical considerations, trusting merely to the dry light of reason. This I may call, distinctively, *Philosophical* agnosticism. Xenophanes is the leading example in the days of old: and Hume and Kant may be taken as examples in modern times. Another form, also philosophical, but with deep religious feeling entering into it, is what I may call *Philosophico-devout* agnosticism. It manifests itself in mysticism, on the one side, and in emotional monotheism, on the other: represented respectively by the Neo-platonists and by Mansel. The third form is permeated by the scientific spirit, still under the guidance of philosophy, and may be denominated *Philosophico-Scientific* agnosticism. As being supremely scientific, it is pre-eminently modern: and may best be seen in such writers as Mr. Herbert Spencer and Professor Huxley.

These groups, of course, are not mutually exclusive: I lay no claim to a logical division. They merely give us a very simple and convenient classification,—such as it may be well to follow, with a view to definite presentation and clear exposition.

I. Philosophical Agnosticism.

I begin, then, with Philosophical agnosticism ; making the start with Xenophanes.

1. *Xenophanes.*

Xenophanes, who lived in the sixth century, B.C., was the founder of the Eleatic school of philosophy, and his teaching, which has come down to us only in poetic fragments, was as nearly monotheistic as anything in ancient Greece could be, but eminently agnostic. He preached the doctrine of one God —"There is one God," he said, "highest among gods and men"; but in the same breath he maintained that " He is like to mortals neither in body nor in mind". Nevertheless, he cannot help speaking of Him metaphorically in the language of men : for, he says that " He is all eye, all mind, all ear," and, in expressing His causal relation to the universe, he declares that "without effort He rules all things by the power of thought (νόου φρενί)," or, as some render it. "by mind and will," or, as we might say, "by intelligent volition". Xenophanes's position, however, cannot be understood unless we take it in connexion with the doctrine that it directly opposes. Polytheism is the conscious antithesis in the philosopher's own mind to monotheism ; and against the grossness of the Greek mythology, and the current religious belief of his countrymen, his whole soul revolts. On the one hand, he assails it with intellectual sarcasm — believing, apparently, with Shaftesbury, that ridicule is a good criterion of truth ; and, on the other hand, he showers upon it moral indignation. On the ethical side, he ridicules the notion of the birth and genealogy of the gods, holding it to be equally impious (so Aristotle tells us) to maintain that the gods are born as to maintain that they die ; and he complains with warmth of Homer and of Hesiod for ascribing to the gods such base acts as " theft, adultery, and mutual deceit," which are the reproach and disgrace of men. In the sarcastic vein, he declares : " If oxen or lions had hands, and could draw and fashion things as men do, they too would make the gods after their own likeness, each ascribing to them such form and body as they themselves possessed, horses making them like horses, and oxen like oxen ". He is, also, represented by Cicero as having inveighed against divination.

Now, regarding this doctrine, we may remark :—

(1) First, that, as an attack on Greek polytheism and the popular religion, it is unassailable. Such anthropomorphism and anthropopathy as we find in Greek mythology—gods revelling in cruelties and jealousies and lust, in petty quarrels and

incessant intrigue, in the basest passions and the grossest means of gratifying them, in hatreds and partialities and unrighteousness and injustice—is utterly revolting, alike to reason and to conscience. A great and memorable step was taken, fraught with good no less to philosophy than to religion, when it was clearly shown and driven home to men by the shafts of wit that such anthropomorphism as this is altogether derogatory and unworthy. God is one, and, as such, is far removed from human mutability and frailty and sin.

(2) But, next, Xenophanes's monotheism was, intellectually, too unbending. For, while he teaches the unity of God, and bases it on the idea of His supremacy ("there is one God, *highest*—μέγιστος—among gods and men"), he, at the same time, refuses to allow us to ascribe to this supreme Deity either physical form or spiritual qualities ("like to mortals *neither in body nor in mind*, οὔτε δέμας οὔτε νόημα"). But a Deity without attributes, of whom no qualities can be predicated, a mere characterless Deity, is simply a nonentity. Bodily attributes are, indeed, inapplicable to God, because God is a Spirit; or they are allowable only in a figurative sense, in compliance with the exigencies of human speech. But mental and moral attributes stand on a different footing. These are essentially spiritual; and, although they

may not be, by any means, the whole of what Spirit designates, they are at least a part of it. Xenophanes was too much afraid, and many people at the present day are too much afraid, of anthropomorphism: it seems to them, mistakenly, a breach of the Second commandment. Our starting-point in Theism is, and must be, self; and this it may rightfully be, if man is formed in the image of God. No doubt, human reason may err; but this does not invalidate it wholly. If it may err, it has within itself the power of detecting error and of correcting mental aberrations.

And this gives us the answer to Xenophanes's objection (in so far as it is an objection to our really knowing God, and not simply an argument against Greek polytheism) that, if horses and oxen could fashion things as men do, they would make their gods like themselves: as it equally gives us the answer to the similar objection—urged, however, from the side of pantheism—made in later days by Spinoza. Said Spinoza: "It is as little fit to ascribe to God the properties that make a man perfect as if one should ascribe to man such as belong to the perfection of the elephant or the ass"; and, again—"I believe that a triangle, if it could speak, would in like manner say that God is eminently triangular, and a circle that the divine nature is in an eminent manner circular; and thus

should every one ascribe his own attributes to
God, and make himself like God, counting everything else as misshapen" (Sir F. Pollock's *Spinoza*,
pp. 54, 63). Obviously, horses and oxen and
asses, if they possessed Thought, would cease to
be horses and oxen and asses; and a conscious
triangle or a conscious circle would be something
considerably more than a triangle or a circle.
Moreover, if horses and oxen and asses and the geometrical triangle and circle possessed thought, they
would possess also, implicitly at least, the power of
rectifying the errors into which the mistaken use of
thought might lead them. This is implied in the
very meaning of thought, according to any conception we can form of it, or to any experience
that we have of it. The whole system of Logic is
a product of thought, and the doctrine of the
fallacies is a standing witness that man has within
himself a rational norm, by which he can test truth
and distinguish falsehood. This rational norm
(which comes out in another way in Epistemology
or theory of knowledge) is, *ex hypothesi*, ascribed
to the conscious brute creatures by Xenophanes,
and to the thinking triangle and circle also by
Spinoza; and, in ascribing to them this much,
they ascribe to them more. They suppose them
to know, or to be able to discover (laboriously, it
may be, and after a lapse of time, yet none the less

really), what truth there is in their thoughts about God, how far their own attributes either serve to express the Divine nature or to symbolize it, and what the rational limits of equine or bovine or asinine or circular or triangular thought are : in other words, possession of thought means possession also of a criterion of truth.

This first form of Agnosticism, then, need not appal us. Nevertheless, it is very interesting and most important. Xenophanes is more than a name in the history of natural theology ; he was a real power in guiding the stream of philosophical theism into the agnostic channel. Although himself a monotheist (or as nearly so as a Greek could be), his principles, if consistently carried out, end in pantheism—all the more so as he himself emphasized the *immanence* of Deity, and, along with the unity of God, held also the unity of the world. And this his famous disciple Parmenides distinctly saw, and he did not hesitate to push on to the logical conclusion. This, too, later pantheists have perceived ; and, when we read in Spinoza such a sentence as this,- "That neither intellect nor will pertains to the nature of God, for such intellect and will as would constitute the essence of God ought to differ from our intellect and will *toto cœlo*, nor could the two have

anything but the name in common; there is no
other agreement, indeed, between them than there
is between the constellation Dog and the animal
that barks" (*Ethics*, Part i., scholium to prop.
xvii.),—we seem to hear but an echo of Xenophanes's sentence, "There is one God, highest
among gods and men, like to mortals neither in
body nor in mind". Xenophanes stood to Parmenides very much in the relation that Descartes
stood to Spinoza. Both Xenophanes and Descartes gave their disciples a great philosophic
impulse, and both were theists after the monotheistic type. Parmenides and Spinoza, men of far
greater intellectual power, carried out the teaching
of their respective masters with unflinching fear-
lessness to the ultimate issue; and both were
pantheists of the purely metaphysical stamp.

2. *Hume.*

Passing now at a bound from ancient, we come
to modern times.

Hume has been called "the father of modern
agnosticism". This designation may be very readily
allowed him, if we do not rigidly mean by it that
he was positively the first among the philosophers
of the past three hundred years to use agnostic
arguments and to manifest the agnostic spirit.
That, we know, remembering Hobbes, Pascal,

and others, would not be true. But Hume is "the father of modern agnosticism" as being, what Professor Huxley terms him, the "prince of agnostics," and as being also the greatest influence in recent days in the stimulating and directing of agnostic tendencies. Not only did he undermine Theistic dogmatism, he struck equally at dogmatic assertion as to the reality of the individual Self and of the External Material World. In depriving us of "matter," he simply followed in the footsteps of Berkeley; but, in turning Berkeley's reasoning against the Ego (which he did, however, only in his youthful *Treatise on Human Nature*, yet never retracted), he made the new departure that may be taken as the commencement of modern scepticism.

Given the sensational standpoint of Locke, such as Hume conceived it to be, and given the critical weapons of Berkeley, and Hume undertakes to show that, while Locke was largely inconsistent in the working out of his system, and Berkeley only half thorough in his attack, the logical outcome of both Lockian and Berkeleyan principles is pure agnosticism. That was his intention: and that the execution of it was crowned with a great measure of success, cannot be disputed. For if, as Locke (not quite meaning it) supposed, the mind be originally an entire blank, and if the ultimate origin of all our ideas be sense-impressions, then indeed our mental beliefs may be mere illusions, useful for practical purposes, but philosophically incompetent. In sense units, as thus conceived, units isolated and unconnected, there could be no true causality: and of them there is nothing that we can predicate as certain apart from experience, and Experience (so Hume argued) is here the same thing as Custom or association, and this is an unstable ground of truth. If, moreover, as Hume insisted, the ultimate test of every idea is turning it into the original impression, there can, obviously, be no such test of Theism at all, and God, being no object of the senses, must remain unknown.

This agnosticism of Hume's, if you grant the principles from which it starts, is irrefragable. If sensation, in the form he conceived it, be the sole origin of ideas, nothing but sensation can be the final court of appeal, and all that modern philosophy regards as spiritualistic must go.

But sensation, it may be rejoined, is not the sole origin of ideas: and, indeed, in mere sense units as presented to us by Hume, knowledge could never originate at all. Sensations existing in isolation and unrelated are mere logical fictions, pure abstractions of the mind. An unrelated entity would be no entity ; and, if by possibility it could exist, there is no means of bringing it into relation, or of making it a part of an intelligible world. Not Hume's reasoning is vicious, but the preliminary starting-point which he believed to be Locke's, and the presupposition that to add a mental element to sense-given fact is to introduce illusion.

But, apart from his general philosophical position, let us see what precisely Hume says of Theism. This we find in numerous passages of his writings, but more particularly in two distinct treatises devoted to the subject. One of these is *The Natural History of Religion*, and the other is *Dialogues Concerning Natural Religion*.

In his *Natural History of Religion* (first published in 1755), he starts with the announcement : ".As every enquiry, which regards religion, is of the utmost importance, there are two questions in particular, which challenge our attention. to wit, that concerning its foundation in reason, and that concerning its origin in human nature. Happily, the first question, which is the most important, admits of the most obvious, at least, the clearest solution. the whole frame of nature bespeaks an intelligent author; and no rational enquirer can, after serious reflection, suspend his belief a moment with regard to the primary principles of genuine Theism and Religion. But the other question, concerning the origin of religion in human nature, is exposed to some more difficulty. The belief of invisible, intelligent power has been very generally diffused over the human race, in all places and in all ages; but it has neither perhaps been so universal as to admit of no exception, nor has it been, in any degree, uniform in the ideas, which it has suggested. Some nations have been discovered, who entertained no sentiments of Religion, if travellers and historians may be credited; and no two nations, and scarce any two men, have ever agreed precisely in the same sentiments. It would appear, therefore, that this preconception springs not from an original instinct or primary impression of nature, such as gives rise to self-love, affection between the sexes, love of progeny, gratitude, resentment; since every instinct of this kind has been found absolutely universal in all nations and ages, and has always a precise determinate object, which it inflexibly pursues. The first religious principles must be secondary; such as may easily be perverted by various accidents and causes, and whose operation too, in some cases, may, by an extraordinary concurrence of circumstances, be altogether prevented. What those principles are, which give rise to the original belief, and what those accidents and causes are, which direct its operation, is the subject of our present enquiry."

Here, then, we have a very clear and concise statement of the plan and purpose of the treatise. One point is distinctly and entirely excluded : the *rational* basis of theism—*that* is, meanwhile, taken as unimpeachable, and it is frequently referred to throughout the writing in strong terms of assent. The point that is here to be considered and sifted is the origin of theism *in human nature;* and what creates difficulty is the want of universality among men, and the fact of endless diversity of religious opinion in the nations and ages of the world.

What, then, has Hume to say on this matter? Put briefly, his theory is :—

That theism is not original to man : that it is not a primary or instinctive principle of his nature, like love of offspring, or self-love, but a derivative principle - a principle originating in man's attitude of fear and hope towards the unknown causes of the natural events (favourable and unfavourable, beneficent and maleficent) that befall him in life.[1]

---

[1] It is interesting to compare Hume's view with Renan's. Renan, too, thinks that Religion arose in feeling (*Dialogues philosophiques*, pp. 38, 39), but he "compares man's religious impulses to the instinct that makes the hen-bird 'sit,' which instinct spontaneously declares itself as soon as the appropriate stage is reached" (Count Goblet d'Alviella's *Hibbert Lectures*, p. 48).

In other words, Religion takes its rise, not in thinking or in reason, but in emotion,—*i.e.*, in the play of the fancy or imagination around the invisible and secret causes of natural events—more particularly *future* or *expected* events,—in which man's self-interest is bound up. Given, on the one hand, man's dependence upon Nature, and his powerlessness to control Nature, and, on the other hand, the working of terror and of hope in him at the prospect of what Nature, through her various processes, may effect,—and you have the datum of the psychological basis of religion in man. Hence, polytheism is man's primary religion the deification and worship of a variety of beings or powers under the promptings of human fear, on the one side, and of human gratitude, on the other. Out of this primary polytheism, monotheism was gradually evolved. The process of evolution is peculiar. It is owing to man's native propensity to overpraise or flatter beings on whom he is dependent, motived either by love begotten of self-interest or by terror. "It may readily happen," says Hume (section vi.). " in an idolatrous nation, that though men admit the existence of several limited deities, yet is there some one God, whom, in a particular manner, they make the object of their worship and adoration. They may either suppose, that, in the distribution of power and territory among the gods, their nation

was subjected to the jurisdiction of that particular
deity; or reducing heavenly objects to the model
of things below, they may represent one god as
the prince or supreme magistrate of the rest, who,
though of the same nature, rules them with an
authority, like that which an earthly sovereign
exercises over his subjects or vassals. Whether
this god, therefore, be considered as their peculiar
patron, or as the general sovereign of heaven, his
votaries will endeavour, by every art, to insinuate
themselves into his favour; and supposing him
to be pleased, like themselves, with praise and
flattery, there is no eulogy or exaggeration, which
will be spared in their addresses to him. In
proportion as men's fears or distresses become
more urgent, they still invent new strains of
adulation; and even he who outdoes his prede-
cessor in swelling up the titles of his divinity, is
sure to be outdone by his successor in newer and
more pompous epithets of praise. Thus they proceed; till at last they arrive at infinity itself,
beyond which there is no further progress."

Such, in summary, is Hume's theory. Into its
historical accuracy, it is not necessary to enter.
Our Darwins and our Tylors, our M'Lennans,
our Spencers and our Lubbocks, our Hibbert
Lecturers and others, have brought much to light

since Hume's day, partly corroborating, partly modifying, Hume's positions. Totemism,[1] henotheism,[2] and many similar ethnographical notions, were practically unknown to Hume; and the whole doctrine of physiolatry transforming itself into polytheism (as seen in India, in the sacred writings of that country) is, of necessity, quite modern. But what it concerns us to observe is, that Hume is here exercised directly with the *origin*, and only indirectly with the nature, of Religion. When, therefore, he maintains that Religion arose in such and such a way, we need only answer,—" Be it so: what then? No theory of the historical origin of theism can really affect the validity of theism itself, nor do you prove that religion is illusory because it is derived from certain principles and tendencies of the human mind. All that you prove is that man's theistic notions are, like his other knowledge, subject to the law of progress; and that they are not, any more than his other notions, at any time complete." Yet Hume wishes us to go farther than this. He

---

[1] Totemism may be generally defined as the worship by a tribe of some species of plant or animal (the wolf, the bear, the serpent), regarded as the progenitor and special protector of the tribe.

[2] Henotheism is Professor Max Müller's name for the tendency on the part of the worshipper to ascribe to each god, at the moment of invocation, all the attributes of supreme power, as if he alone were God. Specialized meanings have been given to the term by E. von Hartmann, Professor Otto Pfleiderer, and others.

does not, certainly, deny God's existence; but he desires us to assume an agnostic attitude as to His attributes. "The whole," he says (in the *General Corollary*, at the conclusion of the treatise), "is a riddle, an aenigma, an inexplicable mystery. Doubt, uncertainty, suspence of judgment appear the only result of our most accurate scrutiny, concerning this subject. But such is the frailty of human reason, and such the irresistible contagion of opinion, that even this deliberate doubt could scarcely be upheld; did we not enlarge our view, and opposing one species of superstition to another, set them a quarrelling: while we ourselves, during their fury and contention, happily make our escape, into the calm, though obscure, regions of philosophy."

Here, then, he goes beyond mere Academic doubt, or conclusion of probability, such as we find in Cicero's *De Natura Deorum*. In the last sentence, he refers in an oracular way to betaking oneself to the calm of philosophy. This I interpret as equivalent to saying:—The philosophical attitude is the true one, and the philosophical attitude is that of entire indifference towards Theism; it is the simple refusal to go on exercising oneself in the search for the supersensible, which evermore eludes our grasp. Such knowledge (it says) is too high for me, I cannot attain unto it; therefore, I will leave it alone.

But, surely, this agnostic indifferentism is too easy a solution of the problem to be really effective. To summarily dismiss the difficulty is not to solve it. You may, indeed, get rid of a pain by administering a soporific; but the experiment has cost you too dear, if the soporific produce in you a permanent anaesthesia.

The agnostic conclusion which is here reached is reached, also, in the *Dialogues Concerning Natural Religion* (not published till after Hume's death, although composed as early as 1751), but in an entirely different way. In the *Natural History of Religion*, Hume deliberately set on one side the rational evidence for theism; representing it as so strong and conclusive as to be practically irresistible. This very evidence, however, is now in the *Dialogues* submitted to a strict and unsparing criticism. This substantially resolves itself into an examination of the nature and value of the Teleological argument, or argument from Design: with the result that, by the end of the examination, the argument is so riddled through and through as to be left with little force remaining. The burden of the indictment is that such a mode of viewing the universe—the teleological mode—is too anthropomorphic to be true: that it is, at many points, imperfect; and that it could not, even at its best, reach pure theism.

Still, even here, Hume continues to assert the Divine existence. He is no atheist, but an agnostic. His difficulties lie simply with the kind and amount of knowledge we can have of God. This knowledge, on the basis of teleology, is found to be very slight; and the close of the *Dialogues* lays down the exact state of the case. The dispute (so Philo and Cleanthes, the two leading interlocutors, agree) has all along been about words. While, on the one side, it is admitted that the original intelligence presupposed in the universe is far removed from human reason, on the other side it is allowed that the principle of order in the universe has some distant resemblance to human reason. And there the matter ends.

Not in any way different is the result of Hume's investigations in the *Enquiry Concerning Human Understanding*. It is not alone the famous attack on miracles that we find here; we find, also, the outline of the argument regarding teleology which is so rigorously and systematically carried out in the *Dialogues*, and we find many distinct formulations of Hume's general agnostic contention. One such formulation is given thus, in section vii. : —
" It seems to me, that this theory of the universal

energy and operation of the Supreme Being, is too
bold ever to carry conviction with it to a man,
sufficiently apprized of the weakness of human
reason, and the narrow limits, to which it is
confined in all its operations. Though the chain
of arguments, which conduct to it, were ever so
logical, there must arise a strong suspicion, if not
an absolute assurance, that it has carried us quite
beyond the reach of our faculties, when it leads us
to conclusions so extraordinary, and so remote
from common life and experience. We are got
into fairy land, long ere we have reached the last
steps of our theory ; and *there* we have no reason
to trust our common methods of argument, or to
think that our usual analogies and probabilities
have any authority. Our line is too short to
fathom such immense abysses. And however we
may flatter ourselves, that we are guided, in every
step which we take, by a kind of verisimilitude
and experience ; we may be assured, that this
fancied experience has no authority, when we thus
apply it to subjects, that lie entirely out of the
sphere of experience."

This reads like a passage from Kant's *Critique
of the Pure Reason.* "The greatest, and perhaps
the sole, use of all philosophy of pure reason," says
Kant, " is, after all, merely negative, since it serves
not as an organon for the enlargement (of know-

ledge), but as a discipline for its delimitation; and, instead of discovering truth, has only the modest merit of preventing error."

A passage that we could almost believe to be taken from Mansel's Bampton Lectures is found in section xi.:—"The great source of our mistake in this subject, and of the unbounded licence of conjecture, which we indulge, is, that we tacitly consider ourselves, as in the place of the Supreme Being, and conclude, that he will, on every occasion, observe the same conduct, which we ourselves, in his situation, would have embraced as reasonable and eligible. But, besides that the ordinary course of nature may convince us, that almost everything is regulated by principles and maxims very different from ours; besides this, I say, it must evidently appear contrary to all rules of analogy to reason, from the intentions and projects of men, to those of a Being so different, and so much superior. In human nature, there is a certain experienced coherence of designs and inclinations; so that when, from any fact, we have discovered one intention of any man, it may often be reasonable, from experience, to infer another, and draw a long chain of conclusions concerning his past or future conduct. But this method of reasoning can never have place with regard to a Being, so remote and incomprehensible, who bears much less analogy to any other being in the universe than the sun to a waxen taper, and who discovers himself only by some faint traces or outlines, beyond which we have no authority to ascribe to him any attribute or perfection. What we imagine to be a superior perfection may really be a defect. Or were it ever so much a perfection, the ascribing of it to the Supreme Being, where it appears not to have been really exerted, to the full, in his works, savours more of flattery and panegyric, than of just reasoning and sound philosophy."

The agnosticism of Hume, then, is evident; and we can readily see its defects. It is not atheism, but what he himself would call a "*mitigated* scepticism". Being prior in order of time to Kant's, it may rightly claim to be the first formulated statement of modern agnosticism; and, both in spirit and in detailed argument, it is the source and precursor of what is rampant on every hand at the present day.

3. *Kant.*

After Hume comes Kant. This is not only the order of time, but the order also of logical sequence. It was Hume, as Kant himself declares, that first awoke him from his dogmatic slumber; and the

Critique of the Pure Reason is Kant's deliberate, but ineffective, attempt to answer Hume.[1]

The leading doctrine of Kant is, that man's knowledge is twofold, according as it has an experiential or a mental origin : it arises (1) from the matter of sensation as given through the senses, and (2) from the *a priori* forms of Intuition (Space and Time) *plus* the Categories of the Understanding. But the forms of Intuition and the Categories of the understanding are in man, not in the object. Hence, man can never know things-in-themselves, but only phenomena. Nevertheless, though things-in-themselves (or noümena) cannot be known, they must be posited as underlying phenomena : otherwise, thinking could never proceed at all. Although we cannot tell *what* they are, we must assume *that* they are : they do not come within our range of thought, but they are the condition of all thought. Our nescience, however, is only partial,—restricted to one sphere. For, noümena, though excluded by the Speculative Reason, are brought back by the Conscience. Neither God, Freedom, nor the Soul is known as a thing-in-itself, yet all three are postulates of the Practical Reason.

---

[1] The ineffectiveness of Kant's reply to Hume is admirably shown by Dr. J. Hutchison Stirling in two articles in the first series of *Mind* (vols. ix., x.), entitled " Kant has *not* answered Hume ".

The realities that intellectual philosophy cannot attain to are secured by man's ethical nature. Thus, in Kant, Reality is saved ; but only by creating a breach between the speculative and the regulative side of our mental being.

Now, obviously, there is here a deep-seated agnosticism, inherent in the doctrine of noümena, although Kant confined it to the speculative reason. For if, as Kant maintained, man can know only phenomena, while, at the same time, in order to explain this phenomenal knowledge, it is necessary to assume the existence of underlying things-in-themselves or noümena, unrelated to phenomena in any way conceivable by us, then of necessity agnosticism follows. For noümena are, by the supposition, altogether unrelated to phenomena : and so they must for ever escape our cognizance. But there is a fallacy here. Kant starts with the erroneous conception that reality is something apart from real things,—that we can take it by itself and examine it, and then bring it into connexion with phenomena and watch the result, just as the chemist can take an acid and an alkali in separation and then bring them together as a definite product. But the acid and the alkali are real things within the realm of intelligence : whereas Kant's reality is nothing, being outside the realm of intelligence—it is a bare abstraction having no real existence, which can, therefore, legitimately be put to no use.

The step from this phenomenism, which confines us to knowledge of relations, to the position that relations are all that exist, is not a great one; and it has been taken. The doctrine of phenomenism has sometimes been put in this way: - We know nothing of objects save in relation, and, as relation is something purely mental, there is nothing in existence but relations. This, clearly, is invalid. For, although we know nothing of objects save as related, although objects are nothing apart from their relations, although, in other words, an unrelated object is a mere name expressive of nothing, —this is quite a different thing from saying that objects are only relations. So far, indeed, are objects from being only relations, that relations without something to relate would be an absurdity. The confusion, I presume, arises from not distinguishing between "objects as related" and "our knowledge of the relations of objects," or "our perception of objects in their relations". But this is a distinction that is paramount and fundamental, and cannot be neglected except at great risk.

But, if Kant's doctrine of noümena be untenable, it is scarcely to be supposed that he himself should

not at times have been at least half conscious of it.
And so he was; for his caution and vacillation in
expressing the doctrine are patent to every student,
and his inconsistency in casting it aside at critical
points is notorious. Although beyond the sphere
of the categories, and therefore not expressible in
quantity or quality or relation, noümena are yet
represented by him as *causes* of sense-impressions,
and, in the region of ethics, they are identified
with *worth*. But Cause is a relation, and so is
applicable only to phenomena; and "cause" and
"worth" are by no means identical conceptions.
If noümena and phenomena be absolute opposites,
they must for ever remain in isolation—no philosophy can bridge the gulf between them: and the
sole legitimate function of the former is, as Jacobi
long ago remarked, to "enjoy a position of *otium
cum dignitate*".

But now let us turn from Kant's general philosophical position to his Ethical theism in particular, and see of what kind it is. God, says Kant,
is a postulate of the Practical Reason: in other
words, His existence is demanded by the conscience. But how so? The Moral law comes to
us as an unconditional command: its injunction is,
"Act as if the maxim of thy will were to become,
by thy adopting it, an universal law of nature,"

"Act according to that maxim which thou couldst at the same time will an universal law," "Act as if thy maxim were to become law universal," "Act agreeably to the maxims of a person ordaining law universal in the realm of ends" (Kant's *Metaphysic of Ethics*, Semple's transl., pp. 36, 54, 56, 57). But this peremptory and unconditional command: what does it imply? It implies (1) that there is in man a tendency or disposition to transgress the command; and (2) that, nevertheless, perfect obedience is both due and possible. But perfect obedience means the realization of the highest good, and, as this cannot be achieved within a limited time, such as the three-score years and ten of man's earthly existence, the implication is that there is a future life or that man is immortal. But even the idea of a future life is not sufficient: for, if the highest good is to be realized, account must be taken of *all* the elements of moral character, and all must be harmonized. This involves Happiness as well as Virtue; and as happiness and virtue are not coincident here, but quite otherwise, the further implication is that there must be not only a future life, but also a Being capable of harmonizing happiness and virtue in that life—a Being of holy will, possessed of full knowledge of men's hearts and inmost thoughts, powerful to reward according to desert: and this

Being is God. God, therefore, is a postulate of
our moral nature; and both His existence and His
character are thereby established.

Now, this reasoning, although quite open to
philosophers holding different views regarding the
nature and sanctions of morality from Kant's, is
not open to Kant himself. For (1), first of all,
Kant's Categorical Imperative is a purely *formal*
principle. He tells us very plainly in his *Metaphysic of Ethics* that it is the issuing of an unconditional command; it is an injunction demanding
our obedience, not with a view to happiness, nor
even from love of obeying, but simply out of regard to duty. If feeling of any kind enters into
our obedience, the moral act is thereby vitiated:
"there is nothing in the world which can be
termed absolutely and altogether good, *a good
will* alone excepted," and a "good will" is one
constantly set on duty. But here, in establishing
God's existence, Happiness is made to play an
important part. In other words, the very thing
that Ethics, in Kant's strict notions, forbids, is
here made to be the turning-point and indispensable condition of the theistic proof. This is the
little rift within the lute that is as fatal to Kant
in ethics as his phenomenalism was to him in pure
speculation.

But (2), secondly, the God that the moral consciousness postulates is an efficient cause—a cause competent to bring about there and hereafter what is impossible here and now. But the idea of Cause, we have been taught, is valid only subjectively: it is applicable to phenomena, but not to noümena. And thus we are brought back to the fundamental inconsistency of Kant's philosophy—the entire separation of the theoretical and the practical reason, with the impossibility of maintaining this distinction if philosophy is to move on at all.

Neither, then, in his metaphysical agnosticism nor in his ethical theistic proof is Kant satisfactory. It is not possible, on the one hand, to divide our being—to shut out God from one part of it, and to affirm Him on the testimony of another. Our being is whole and indivisible; and God is a datum, if at all, of our entire nature. It is not legitimate, on the other hand, to insist on the absolutely non-emotive or non-eudæmonistic character of Ethics, and yet to bring in Happiness, which stern Duty discountenances as an end, as the determining factor in the proof of a future life and of God's existence. Either the Categorical Imperative is, or it is not, purely formal; and if it *be* purely formal, the Happiness-argument is thereby rigorously excluded.

LECTURE IV.

II. Philosophico-devout Agnosticism.

4. *The Neo-platonists.*

WE turn now to types of Agnostics of the second group—to those whose nescience is coloured by strong religious veneration : and we begin with the Neo-platonists.

The central position of the Neo-platonic system was :—To man knowledge of God is impossible ; for, man's thoughts of God, being the thoughts of a finite and limited creature, are altogether inadequate for the object, and to suppose them adequate would be to reduce the Deity to the limited and finite. Hence, the Neo-platonists defined God as absolute Unity, as the absolutely Indeterminate One, and regarded Him as the inexpressible and the incomprehensible. As a necessary corollary, they maintained that He could be spoken of only as the negation of all finite modes—whether of thought, of will, or of feeling. " This primal being,"

(135)

says Schwegler (*Handbook of the History of Philosophy*, Dr. J. Hutchison Stirling's transl., p. 140), "is now variously named by Plotinus; he calls it the first, the one, the good. . . . Thought and will he allows it not, because it is in want of nothing, can require nothing; it is not energy but above energy; life is not a predicate of it; nothing beënt, no thing and no being, none of the most universal categories of being can be attributed to it: all other negative determinations are incompetent in its regard: in short, it is something unspeakable, unthinkable." [1]

This very position had been laid down by other Platonists long before Plotinus, and it was accepted by monotheistic Platonizers of the early centuries of our era, both Jewish and Christian. It was precisely that, for instance, of Philo Judaeus: and we find it in Justin Martyr clearly expressed in his *Dialogue with Trypho the Jew*.

Nevertheless, though the Neo-platonists thus regarded God as the Unknowable, they emphasized man's craving for a union with the Infinite and the Absolute One,[2] in whom there is no determinate-

[1] This is also, substantially, the doctrine of Brahmanism in India and of Taoism in China; and the criticism of the one is applicable, *mutatis mutandis*, to the others.

[2] The latest Neo-platonists, however, regarded God as *inaccessible*, as well as incognizable.

ness and no difference, and whom they put forth
as the "unutterable and inexplicable," and as
"beyond being". And, in order to provide for this
craving, they had recourse to a special spiritual process and a special spiritual faculty. They taught the
necessity of non-rational *ecstatic* communion with
the Deity, of high spiritual intuition and exaltation
(μανία and ἕνωσις), and insisted on prayer and sym-
bolic rites (which ultimately degenerated into gross
superstition) as the means of its attainment. In
the state of spiritual ecstasy or trance (to which
even Plotinus himself attained only four times
during six years), the finite is merged in the infinite,
and a man, united to the Source of his being, becomes absorbed in Him.

To the Neo-platonists, however, as philosophers,
an *intellectual* difficulty presented itself. For, if
God was the undifferenced or indeterminate One,
if He was simply Unity, the absolute, τὸ ἕν, how
came the world, how came matter, into existence?
To solve this difficulty, they supposed (very illogi-
cally) a series of Emanations from the Deity,
each emanation losing in divine pureness the
farther removed from Deity it was. First came
Intelligence (νοῦς): which, being the emanation
nearest the Divinity and immediately from Him,
was the purest. Next came an emanation from
Intelligence—less pure than intelligence, as being

more remote from the primal source. This emanation was ψυχή or Soul. Then, from soul proceed other souls; and, as souls must have a house to dwell in, soul produces matter and the world.

Now, three characteristics of this famous system are specially observable:—(1) It was essentially devout in its motive; (2) it was mystical in its method; (3) it was pantheistic in its result.

Two criticisms at least may be ventured. (1) In the first place, we deny, what the Neo-platonists assert.—that knowledge of the Deity by man would be derogatory to the Divine character: there is no sense in saying that it would reduce the Infinite to the finite, and the Absolute One to unworthy determinateness and difference. I consider that philosophy, in its later developments, has made this clear. Neo-platonism takes an altogether erroneous view of the distinction between the Infinite and the finite, regarding the former only as the negation of the latter, and placing the Absolute in such entire opposition to us men that the bringing together of the two extremes would be nothing less than a contradiction in terms. Of course, if you deal with irreconcilable abstractions, no rational power in man can ever unite them; but neither can they be united by ecstasy or any other power that is non-rational. Your emanations even, or series of graded powers, interposed between the Deity and you, whereby the finite ascends in conception as by the steps of a ladder to the Infinite, solve no difficulty : they only serve to bring the primary difficulty into bolder relief. This is an explanation that explains nothing. How can absolute Unity—a Unity, too, which is "beyond being"—give being to emanations? How, if indeterminate and unrelated, can it stand to these (directly or remotely) in the relation of an author or creator? How even, in any way, can they be dependent upon it? The solution of the difficulty thus unsolved lies only in the perception of the truth that the Infinite and the finite are not in irreconcilable antithesis, nor is the Absolute a unity that is incompatible with diversity. On the contrary, this unity, in order to be real, must be the meeting-point of differences, and the finite must, from the beginning, be in relation to the infinite.

Then, (2) secondly, the Pantheism of Neo-platonism does not meet the requirements of the religious nature, nor does its ecstatic method commend itself either to sober reason or to the moral sense. If God is, He must also be a personal God; and the union that the creature claims with the Creator is not one of undifferentiated absorption, but one of rational and ethical fellowship, and personality, as being the highest fact in our experience, cannot be disowned.[1]

5. *Mansel.*

We may leave this form of Agnosticism based on devoutness, and proceed to the second, which is even more important.

Dean Mansel's Agnosticism is also characterized by deep religious feeling ; but, although it has this in common with Neo-platonism, it is neither mystical nor pantheistic. After Sir William Hamilton, it emphasizes the impotence of human reason and exalts the place and function of Faith.

Hamilton had said: To think is to condition ; but God is the unconditioned: therefore. He cannot be the object of thought—He is simply a postulate of Faith.[2] Put in technical language : "The Unconditioned [*i.e.*, the Absolute and the Infinite expressed generically] is incognizable and inconceivable ; its notion being only negative of

---

[1] The temptation here is great to supplement what is said in the text by some account of the Great Christian Neo-platonist of the ninth century Scotus Erigena. But these Lectures are neither a history of philosophy nor a history of theology.

[2] Nevertheless, in the *Logic (Lectures*, vol. iv. pp. 70, 73,. Hamilton maintains that, as to knowledge and belief. "each supposes the other" : not only may the certainty of knowledge be resolved into a certainty of belief, but "the manifestation of this belief necessarily involves knowledge ; for we cannot believe without some consciousness or knowledge of the belief. and, consequently. without some consciousness or knowledge of the object of the belief".

the Conditioned, which last can alone be positively known or conceived " (*Discussions*, 2nd edition, p. 12). He had even, in one place (*Id.*, p. 15 *n.*), gone the length of saying—altogether regardless of the correct translation of the Greek,—" But the last and highest consecration of all true religion must be an altar Ἀγνώστῳ Θεῷ—*To the unknown and unknowable God*". This doctrine Mansel accepted, and proceeded to carry out in a systematic fashion, with much learning and great logical acumen.

His position may be summarized as follows :—

God, according to the metaphysician, is the Absolute and the Infinite. " By the *Absolute* is meant that which exists in and by itself, having no necessary relation to any other Being. By the *Infinite* is meant that which is free from all possible limitation ; that than which a greater is inconceivable ; and which consequently can receive no additional attribute or mode of existence which it had not from all eternity" (*The Limits of Religious Thought*, 4th edition, p. 30). But if so, God is unthinkable ; for, when we try to realize the notions that the words Absolute and Infinite imply and try to put them together, we are landed in a mass of contradictions. " There is a contradiction in supposing such an object to exist, whether alone or in conjunction with others ; and there is a contradiction in supposing it not to exist. There is a contradiction in conceiving it as one; and there is a contradiction in conceiving it as many. There is a contradiction in conceiving it as personal; and there is a contradiction in conceiving it as impersonal. It cannot without contradiction be represented as active; nor, without equal contradiction, be represented as inactive. It cannot be conceived as the sum of all existence; nor yet can it be conceived as a part only of that sum." But if this be so, what becomes of Revelation: for, is it not the very object of Revelation to declare to man the Absolute and the Infinite? No, says Mansel, Revelation does not, any more than Reason, give us the Absolute and the Infinite: by both alike, "God is represented under finite conceptions, adapted to finite minds; and the evidences on which the authority of Revelation rests are finite and comprehensible also" (*Id.*, "Preface," pp. xvi., xvii.). On what grounds, then, one naturally asks, is the existence of the Absolute and the Infinite secured? In the first place, says Mansel, the absolute and the infinite are purely *negative* notions, they are simply the negation of thought, simply names for the absence of those conditions under which thought is possible; and "it is characteristic of all mere negative notions that we cannot possibly say

whether their supposed objects exist or not"
(*Prolegomena Logica*, p. 132), for, "the limits of
possible thought are not the limits of possible
existence" (*Metaphysics*, p. 278). In the next
place, notwithstanding this speculative impotence,
and notwithstanding the "inextricable confusion
and contradiction" into which the attempted
analysis of the ideas suggested to us by the Absolute
and Infinite throws us, "we are compelled, by
the constitution of our minds, to believe in the
existence of an Absolute and Infinite Being, a
belief which appears forced upon us, as the complement of our consciousness of the relative and
the finite" (*Limits of Religious Thought*, p. 45) : that
is to say, the absolute and the infinite is a *regulative*, not a *speculative*, truth "sufficient to guide
our practice, but not to satisfy our intellect": it
is a necessity of human *belief*,—we can believe *that*
it is, but cannot conceive *how* or *what* it is. "we
are compelled to take refuge in Faith". All this
notwithstanding, our "moral and religious consciousness"—our conscience and our sense of
dependence—imperatively demands God, and demands Him as a *person*. What then? "Human
personality cannot be assumed as an exact copy
of the Divine, but only as that which is most nearly
analogous to it among finite things" (*The Philosophy of the Conditioned*, p. 144).

Such is Mansel's teaching, given most fully in
the Bampton Lectures (*The Limits of Religious
Thought*), but found in all his philosophical writings
—the *Prolegomena Logica*, the *Metaphysics*, and *The
Philosophy of the Conditioned*. Let us look at it
somewhat closely.

1. In the first place, observe, Mansel is merciless in his logic against the Absolute and the
Infinite as defined by the metaphysician. In this
he is irresistible. For, these terms, as so used,
represent pure abstractions: they are fictions of
the mind, or, rather, they are words without
any true signification. Possibly enough, in his
criticism here, he had directly in view the philosophy of Spinoza, which (after the manner of
geometry) is based upon definitions, especially the
definition of Substance: but his strictures are
equally applicable to all philosophy that does not
lay a sufficiently stable groundwork in psychology.
He himself regarded the criticism, legitimately or
illegitimately, as specially effective against Schel-
ling and Hegel.

But the remorseless logic that thus shatters
the metaphysician's Absolute and Infinite may be
turned against Mansel himself at the next step.
Not content with demolishing these abstractions,
Mansel proceeds to affirm that, all contradiction

notwithstanding, this very Absolute and Infinite is demanded by human Faith; we cannot conceive it, but we must believe it. Now, what faith demands, what is demanded by human nature, is not this, but the existence of the Absolute and the Infinite as the correlative and ground of the relative and finite. No Spinozistic Substance is demanded—call it substance, the absolute, the unconditioned, or by whatever other metaphysical name you choose,—from which all characterization or determination is absent; but a definitely characterized and completed something. The Absolute, as I understand it, is not that which is wholly unrelated, but that which is the source and positive condition of all relation,—that which gives to relation its very meaning. Relations there must be, though not this or that particular class of relations; and, as man's experience of relations is very limited, there is nothing contradictory in supposing all relations as experienced by man and man himself non-existent, and yet the Absolute not thereby annihilated. The need of relation of *some* kind, is one thing; the need of a particular kind of relation, or of a certain definite number of relations, is quite another thing; and we may very well affirm the former of the Absolute, while we deny the latter. The Infinite, on the other hand, is not the mere negation of the finite; on the

10

contrary, it is its completion and perfection. We call spiritual qualities—such as intelligence, wisdom, goodness finite, because they do not reach in us the full perfection of which they are in themselves capable; in God, this perfection is reached, and hence, as predicated of Him, we call them infinite. The Infinite is the Unlimited in the sense that to it limits, in the materialistic signification of the term, are inapplicable. It would, indeed, be absurd to suppose that the Deity is limited by the external world in the same way as the human body is limited by it, when, as one object outside another, the human body comes into contact with the external and finds itself resisted. It would also be absurd to suppose that the limit of human ignorance or error, or the impediment of human vice, exists in God. But no true conception of the infinite as applied to God can refuse to recognize that Reason's laws are as much binding on the Divine as they are on the human mind; and to say that, to the Infinite Being, a thing can both be and not be in the same sense and at the same time, or that past events may by Him be undone, is simply to use words at random. These things are not, in any proper meaning, *limits:* the term "limit" is simply irrelevant here. Intelligence is still intelligence, whether it be human or Divine; and man's knowledge, though imperfect, is, to the extent of its perfection, real.

The truth is, that, in his doctrine of the Conditioned, Mansel (like Hamilton) overstrained the principle of the Relativity of human knowledge. Human knowledge, no doubt, is relative in a very genuine sense : it is *I* that know, else that knowledge were not *mine.* No doubt, also, man is to himself "the measure of all things," in the sense that he can understand only what he has the ability to understand. But the very point in question is, *What* has man the ability to understand ? And it will not do summarily to exclude from this ability knowledge of God, or ingeniously to plead that, because it is *I* that know God, it is not God that I know. Such argumentation is worthy of the Sophists in their palmiest days. And, indeed, the Sophists were the originators of it. In their hands, however, it was unanalyzed. To Protagoras is ascribed the saying, " Man is the measure of all things "; and what Protagoras meant by it seems to have been that all knowledge is relative to a knower (which, of course, is true), or that knowledge must start from the subject knowing (which, again, is true). But his disciples used it as a kind of Ockham's razor wherewith to cut the throat of truth, and to produce general scepticism. It was not till Socrates confronted it, that the Protagorean dictum was subjected to a strict critical analysis : and Socrates, still occupying the subjective stand-

point, accepted the formula, but showed that man,
who is indeed the measure of all things, has in himself the power of refuting scepticism and of grasping
truth, and that his speculative tendencies are not
a human weakness but an intellectual strength.
That gave to Plato the ground and basis of his
spiritualistic philosophy ; and it has constituted
the philosophical position, more and more definitely conceived as time passed, in all subsequent
ages.

Indeed, so far is it from being the case that,
because we know reality, it is not reality that we
know, that the very opposite is true. It is only
when we know something about a thing that we
regard it as existent. A thing of which we know
nothing, a thing which never in any way comes
under our cognizance, is to us a nonentity. Our
intelligence gives truth to the extent that it grasps
reality ; and the highest of all intelligences grasps
reality fully. On any other supposition, we are
landed in absurdity and utter inanity.

2. Hence, secondly, it follows that Faith cannot
be dissociated from Reason in the way that Mansel
maintained.

By Faith here is not understood "intuition";
nor is it regarded (like sensation and reflection) as a
distinct source of conviction. On the contrary, it

is the characteristic of a negative notion (so Mansel
tells us) that "it has never been realized in intuition" (*The Philosophy of the Conditioned*, p.
116): and, as for Faith's being a distinct source
of conviction, why, he says, it is conviction itself.
" No man would say that he is convinced of the
truth of a proposition *because* he believes it : his
belief in its truth is the same thing as his conviction of its truth. Belief, then, is not a
source of conviction, but a conviction having
sources of its own. The question is, have we
legitimate sources of conviction, distinct from those
which constitute Knowledge properly so called ? "
(*Id.*, p. 124). Faith, then, is simply belief; and the
distinction between Faith and Reason is not the
distinction between Intuition and Reasoning. But
if so, then we may confidently assert that Mansel's
contention is not true, that " Reason itself requires
us to believe in truths that are beyond reason," in
the sense that these supra-rational truths represent
the entire negation of human thought. What
is true is, that there may be truths that human
reason would not in the ordinary course of
experience have discovered truths that come
to us by what we distinctively know as *a revelation*; but then these truths, when revealed, are
rationally given and rationally apprehended, and
to that extent they are not mere negative notions.

"If a representation," says Principal Caird, "is a true representation, it must belong to the same order with the thing represented. The relation between them is a thinkable relation and one which, though immature individual intelligence may not apprehend it, thought or intelligence in general is capable of apprehending. Nothing that is absolutely inscrutable to reason can be made known to faith. It is only because the content of a revelation is implicitly rational that it can possess any self-evidencing power, or exert any moral influence over the human spirit" (*An Introduction to the Philosophy of Religion*, p. 78).

Nor are we in any way helped by having recourse to Mansel's favourite distinction (as it was Kant's) between a speculative and a regulative truth—between a truth that satisfies the intellect and one that is simply sufficient for guiding conduct.[1] That distinction just means that, between the rational and the practical sides of man's nature, there is a chasm that cannot be bridged over. But in reality there is no such chasm; for, faith and reason, or practice and speculation, are not the extreme opposites that Mansel would make them out to be. It

---

[1] Mansel, however, is careful to point out that Kant turns the distinction in a direction entirely opposite to his own. While Mansel regards the finite manifestation of God to be the regulative truth, Kant regards the regulative truth to be the Absolute itself.

is quite true, what Butler says, that "probability is the very guide of life" — not, however, the *calculus* of probability (we must beware of the mathematicians here), but probability as a thing of likelihood and degrees, ranging from the merest presumption to a very high certainty; and this probability, as distinguished from absolute demonstration, you may, if you care, term faith. But then, it is a *rational* faith,—a faith resting on a very positive basis, on more or less of intelligible evidence, and not taking its tone from a mere mental impotence.

3. And this brings me to a third remark.

In Mansel's doctrine of faith and reason, there is an unmistakable arbitrariness, which leads to rather curious results. In Mansel himself, we have a wonderful combination of two striking qualities, but each of them in excess. On the one hand, he is extreme in his speculative *caution:* he will neither affirm nor deny in connexion with the objects of negative notions; he even rebukes Berkeley for his denial of the metaphysician's abstraction, "matter". "The fault of Berkeley," he says (*Prolegomena Logica,* p. 132), "did not consist in doubting the existence of matter, but in asserting its non-existence. It is characteristic of all negative notions, that we cannot possibly say whether their supposed objects exist or not." On the other hand, he is extreme in his *credulity*, having recourse to faith to an extent that certainly is not common among philosophers. But now mark the point where his credulity outruns his caution, and, in doing so, brings him into difficulties. Of spiritual beings, he has direct knowledge, he tells us, of himself, and of himself alone: his own ego is the sole object of his immediate consciousness; he does not know his fellow-men save indirectly—he simply *believes* in their existence. But he believes in their existence because of the evidence he has that they are egos like himself: in other words, his experience of his own ego is the ground of his belief in theirs. If so, why not believe in God on the same evidence? If our experience of ourselves authorizes us to believe in our fellow-men, what hinders this same experience from being the basis of our belief in God? If this basis be sound, then we may, indeed, make affirmations regarding God: but what then becomes of the negative notion and the impossibility of either asserting or denying the existence of its object? And if this basis be not sound, then must it not also fail us in the case of our fellow-men, and should not our only legitimate position be that of solipsism?

4. " But," it may be said, " Mansel does allow

us a certain kind of knowledge of God: he allows us the Infinite as a *negative* notion."

Yes, but what is a negative notion? It is the thinking away of limits from the limited, and trying to magnify indefinitely the circumscribed of our experience; as when, in endeavouring to realize infinite Space to ourselves, we start from the limited space of our experience, and then by degrees remove its boundaries farther and farther till we make ourselves believe that we have got a conception of the absolutely unbounded. But that is not Mansel's meaning. Mansel does not say that we conceive of God as a being endowed with all that in man is highest and best,—knowledge, wisdom, goodness, and the like,—only with the *limit* of man's attainment removed. He says that, as Infinite, God is wholly incognizable. " Religion," he says, " is not a function of thought: and the attempt to make it so, if consistently carried out, necessarily leads, firstly to Anthropomorphism, and ultimately to Atheism " (*Prolegomena Logica*, p. 257). He says, in other words, what Xenophanes had said before, and what pantheists, from Parmenides to Spinoza and from Spinoza to Hegel, have ever said.

In like manner, Matthew Arnold, in his *Literature and Dogma* (pp. 38, 39), has laid it down that the Hebrew conception of God is precisely that of a power that is not amenable to the categories of human thought, and has himself (p. 58) given his adherence to the Hebrew conception in the felicitous phrase —"the unexplored and the inexpressible". He says : "As he had developed his idea of God from personal experience, Israel knew what we, who have developed our idea from his words about it. so often are ignorant of : that his words were but *thrown out* at a vast object of consciousness, which he could not fully grasp, and which he apprehended clearly by one point only, that it made for the great concern of life, *conduct*. How little we know of it besides, how impenetrable is the course of its ways with us, how we are baffled in our attempts to name and describe it, how, when we personify it and call it ·the moral and intelligent Governor of the universe,' we presently find it not to be a person as man conceives of person. nor moral as man conceives of moral. nor intelligent as man conceives of intelligent. nor a governor as man conceives of governors,

all this, which scientific theology loses sight of, Israel, who had but poetry and eloquence, and no system. and who did not mind contradicting himself, knew."

So, ages before, but with deep piety, Marcus Minutius Felix, in his *Octavius*, had said of God : " Our intellect is too narrow to contain Him, and, therefore, we can never conceive so worthily of Him as when we conceive Him inconceivable. Whoever imagines that he knows the Divine Majesty, lessens it; and whoever does not lessen it, can never pretend to know it."

But clearly if, in the midst of all this negation, there be nothing positive, we are simply playing with words. If God be solely the antithesis of all that we ourselves are, Arnold's impersonal "it" is quite sufficient to describe Him. Not only do we not know Him, we cannot rightly be said to be ignorant of Him. For, according to Ferrier's luminous distinction, "There are *two* kinds of ignorance; but only *one* of these is *ignorance* properly so called. There is, *first*, an ignorance which is incident to some minds as compared with others, but not necessarily incident to *all* minds. Such ignorance is a defect, an imperfection. A Hottentot is ignorant of geometry: a Frenchman knows it. This kind of ignorance *is* ignorance. But, *secondly*, there is an ignorance or nescience which is of necessity incident to *all* intelligence *by its very nature*, and which is no defect, or imperfection, or limitation, but rather a perfection. For example, it is impossible for any mind to know that two straight lines enclose a space, or to know the *opposite* of any of the mathematical axioms: shall we say then that we are ignorant of these? That would be absurd. No man can be ignorant that two and two *make fire;* for this is a thing *not to be known* on any terms, or by any mind. This fixes the law of ignorance, which is, that " we can be ignorant only of what can (possibly) be known," or, in barbarous locution, "*the Knowable alone is the ignorable*" (*Remains,* i. pp. 482-3. See, also, *Institutes of Metaphysic,* 3rd ed., pp. 412, etc.).

The doctrine of the negative notion, then, lands us on the horns of a dilemma. If God be solely what we ourselves are *not,* then He is nothing to us ; while, if He is anything to us, He cannot be the bare negation contended for.

5. But, again, Mansel makes much of the doctrine of analogy. Although man's mental powers, he says, are neither identical with nor an exact copy of the Divine, they are *analogous* to the Divine.

Now what is meant by "analogous"? and how does the doctrine of analogy answer the purpose?

"Analogous" may mean one of three things. First, in Aristotle's terminology, Analogy means "*equality* of ratios or relations," as when we say, "The soul : the body : : the boatman : his boat"; where the two ratios on either side are exactly equal, and propositions true of the one are true of the other also. Next, with Archbishop Whately, analogy signifies "*resemblance* of ratios or relations,"—resemblance, not of the objects themselves, but of their *relations*. Thus, a man's parent is different from his master; but, inasmuch as both parent and master exercise a certain authority over him, there is an analogy in this relation of superiority. Thirdly, Analogy means "resemblance *of any kind* (whether of attributes or of relations) among objects, and such resemblance as is sufficient to form a basis of *probable* reasoning". This is Analogy as at present conceived by logicians.

Now, in which of these senses does Mansel use the term when he says that the human is analogous to the Divine? He himself tells us when he says, "that the relation between the communicable attributes of God and the corresponding attributes of man is one not of identity, but of analogy: that is to say, that the Divine attributes have the same relation to the Divine nature that the human attributes have to human nature" (*The Philosophy of the Conditioned*, p. 164). But surely, if this be so, the question at once suggests itself, How do you know this? Before you are able to declare that the two classes of attributes are not identical but only analogous, you must know the Divine as well as the human; and, if you do not know the Divine, it is illegitimate for you to talk of the Divine attributes at all.

Berkeley is far nearer the mark than Mansel here. "It is to be observed," he says, "that a twofold analogy is distinguished by the schoolmen —metaphorical and proper. Of the first kind there are frequent instances in Holy Scripture, attributing human parts and passions to God. When He is represented as having a finger, an eye, or an ear; when He is said to repent, to be angry, or grieved; every one sees that analogy is metaphorical. Because those parts and passions, taken in the proper signification, must, in every degree, necessarily and from the formal nature of the thing, include imperfection. When, therefore, it is said -the finger of God appears in this or that event, men of common-sense mean no more but that it is as truly ascribed to God as the works wrought by human fingers are to man; and so of the rest. But the case is different when wisdom and knowledge are attributed to God. Passions and senses, as such, imply defect; but in knowledge simply, or as such, there is no defect. Knowledge, therefore, in the proper formal meaning of the word, may be attributed to God proportionably, that is preserving a proportion to the infinite nature of God. We may say, therefore, that as God is infinitely above man, so is the knowledge of God infinitely above the knowledge of man, and this is what Cajetan calls

analogia proprie facta. And after this same analogy we must understand all those attributes to
belong to the Deity which in themselves simply,
and as such, denote perfection. We may, therefore,
consistently with what hath been premised, affirm
that all sorts of perfection which we can conceive in
a finite spirit are in God, but without any of that
allay which is found in the creatures. This doctrine, therefore, of analogical perfections in God,
or our knowing God by analogy, seems very much
misunderstood and misapplied by those who would
infer from thence that we cannot frame any direct
or proper notion, though never so inadequate, of
knowledge or wisdom, as they are in the Deity:
or understand any more of them than one born
blind can of light and colours" (*Alciphron; or. The
Minute Philosopher*, Dialogue, iv. § 21).

6. But now, apart from the speculative side
of our nature, what of God as given by other
parts of it? What of the emotional and ethical
sides of our being—what of our feeling of dependence on One Higher than ourselves and of the
demands of Conscience,—on which Mansel lays
especial stress? These, indeed, are important
elements in our philosophy of Theism: but they
are not the sole factors. When Mansel demands
that our "religious feelings and affections" shall

be regarded "as a distinct class of psychological facts, co-ordinate with, not subordinate to, the thinking faculty" (*Prolegomena Logica*, p. 256), he is on strong ground, and we heartily acquiesce. But when he further says "that religion is not a function of thought," we immediately dissent ; for, in thus saying, he is ignoring his own demand. To accept this last position is to break the co-ordination between intellect and our religious affections ; it is to make the latter superordinate and the former subordinate, if it be not, indeed, to sweep the former away altogether. If God is a datum of our nature, He is a datum of our *whole* nature, and not merely of a part of it.

III. Philosophico-Scientific Agnosticism.

6. *Mr. Herbert Spencer.*

No such illegitimate separation of the intellectual from the moral side of human nature as was made by Kant and by Mansel is made by Mr. Herbert Spencer ; and his agnosticism, accordingly, is more symmetrical. Discarding alike the Neo-platonic mysticism and Kant's practical reason as sufficient guarantees for theism, he bases his doctrine in the persistence of human belief. Yet, he is entirely on the side of Mansel and of Matthew Arnold in reaching, as his conclusion, a Deity that is unknown and unknowable. Indeed, he himself tells us, in the original Programme of his writings, distributed in 1860 and reprinted in the Preface to his *First Principles*, that his main object in the philosophy of the unknowable is "carrying a step further the doctrine put into shape by Hamilton and Mansel; pointing out the various directions in which Science leads to the same conclusions; and showing that in this united belief in an Absolute that transcends not only human knowledge but human conception, lies the only possible reconciliation of Science and Religion".

Put briefly, Mr. Spencer's position is as follows :

Knowledge is essentially relative—not human knowledge only, but *all* knowledge. Hence, knowledge of transcendent reality is impossible. Nevertheless, men have an ineradicable belief that transcendent reality exists. Such a belief has survived all hostile attacks, and is a fact of Evolution. Yet the transcendent Reality, the noümenon behind phenomena, is unknowable and incomprehensible, and we ought to "refrain from assigning to it any attributes whatever" (*First Principles*, 5th ed., p. 110). The ascribing of attributes to God, indeed, Mr. Spencer calls "the impiety of the pious"; and he likens the procedure of theologians who speak of God as knowable to that of a conscious watch,

which should "insist on regarding the watch-
maker's actions as determined like its own by
springs and escapements," and should also insist
on all other watches reverently doing the same,
or else submitting to being branded as atheistic.
Notwithstanding these brave words, however, he
himself cannot get along without predicating certain things of the Incognizable. *First*, positively :
he says that it is a *cause*,—"the Ultimate cause of
things" (*Id.*, p. 108); or, as he more frequently
expresses it, a *power*, "an Inscrutable Power
manifested to us through all phenomena." "A
Power of which no limit in Time or Space can be
conceived": or, from the side of Science. *force*,
"persistent Force ever changing its manifestations
but unchanged in quantity throughout all past
time and all future time" (*Id.*, p. 552); the "unknown Power" of which Matter and Motion are
the "conditioned manifestations," and of which,
too, "that Force as we are conscious of it when
by our own efforts we produce changes. is the
correlative" (*Id.*, p. 579): in other words, the "Universal Power which transcends consciousness,"
alike inscrutable in Mind as in Matter (*The Principles of Psychology*, vol. i. § 63). So, then. even
while maintaining it to be inscrutable, Mr. Spencer
distinctly ascribes to the Unknowable a dynamic
nature : he regards it as one and permanent. the

sole constant in the midst of change : eternal, too,
and practically omnipresent—"the Infinite and
Eternal Energy, from which all things proceed"
(*Ecclesiastical Institutions,* p. 863). *Second*, negatively : he says that it is not to be regarded as
personal—"duty requires us neither to affirm nor
deny personality," "Is it not just possible that
there is a mode of being as much transcending
Intelligence and Will, as these transcend mechanical motion ?" (*First Principles,* 5th ed., p. 109).

Now, what shall we say of this ?

Obviously, three questions here arise : —

1. On what evidence does Mr. Spencer regard
the Absolute or God as unknowable ?

2. On what grounds does he assert the existence
of this Unknowable ?

3. How does he characterize the Unknowable ?
For, after all, it is not absolutely characterless : Mr.
Spencer's attitude not being, as he himself main-
tains, one of "entire and contemptuous negation".

1. As to the first of these questions, the great
evidence is the philosophical one,—the Relativity
of Knowledge.

This doctrine Mr. Spencer accepts from Hamilton and Mansel ; but he gives it the widest possible
sweep, and alters it in one important particular.

While maintaining that knowledge is essentially relative, he is altogether opposed to the doctrine of the negative notion. So far, he says, is the absolute from being merely the negation of all the conditions of thought, that, on the contrary, we have a *positive*, though *vague* or indefinite, consciousness of it as the "actuality lying behind appearances". His argument is: "We are conscious of the Relative as existence under conditions and limits; it is impossible that these conditions and limits can be thought of apart from something to which they give the form; the abstraction of these conditions and limits, is, by the hypothesis, the abstraction of them *only*; consequently there must be a residuary consciousness of something which filled up their outlines; and this indefinite something constitutes our consciousness of the Non-relative or Absolute. Impossible though it is to give to this consciousness any qualitative or quantitative expression whatever, it is not the less certain that it remains with us as a positive and indestructible element of thought " (*Id.*, pp. 90, 91). And to the impossibility of getting rid of the consciousness of this non-qualitative, non-quantitative, Absolute, Mr. Spencer ascribes "our indestructible belief" in its actuality.

Now, with Mr. Spencer, in his rejection of the

doctrine of the negative notion, I am entirely at
one. On grounds already explained, and which
need not be repeated, I think that doctrine altogether untenable. But not less untenable and
not less self-destructive, does Mr. Spencer's substitute appear to me to be. That we have a
knowledge of the Absolute in the only true sense
of the Absolute when applied to God—a knowledge of Him in the qualities of His being, true
though limited, positive and real though not complete,—is the very point that I maintain. But a
"consciousness" of Him without any knowledge
of what it is, or whom it is, whereof we are conscious, leading to the indestructible "belief" in
His or its real existence, appears to me a thing
utterly fictitious, and the statement of it a contradiction in terms. We do not *believe* in that of
which we are conscious; we *know* it. We believe
only in what is not, in the strict sense of the term,
known,—in what is liable to more or less of doubt,
—what needs to be supported by evidence or by
reasoning, and the evidence may be defective and
the reasoning weak. Nor is it anything more
than putting words together in a meaningless
conjunction to say that we are conscious, even in
a vague or indefinite way, of the Unknowable. If
the object of consciousness be "inscrutable," if it
be not expressible either in quality or in quantity,

it is no object of consciousness ; and "the consciousness of something which is yet out of consciousness" (*The Principles of Psychology*, vol. ii.
§ 448) is more than "mysterious": it is self-contradictory.

And this Mr. Spencer himself by and by feels.
His unknown and unknowable, when he comes
to view it in the light of Science, is not that
colourless something to which no predicate can
be attached, but a very definite something whose
character is wonderfully well ascertained. It can
never be too often stated, as it cannot be too
firmly grasped, that the Absolute is the co-relative
of the Relative (the Infinite of the finite), not as
being its exclusive antithesis or contradictory, but
as being its complement or completion, and that, as
complement or completion, it stands to it in very
definite relations, which by us are distinctly, though
only partially, known.

2. So much, then, for the first question. What
now of the second? What of the grounds on
which Mr. Spencer asserts the existence of the
Unknowable?

The *logical* ground we have already seen and
examined : relative implies absolute. But the
really telling argument is, the fact of man's ineradicable belief.

Mr. Spencer is on very firm ground in his teaching about ineradicable beliefs.[1] Such beliefs, he says, " beliefs that are perennial and nearly or quite universal," have in them at any rate *partial* truth. Although he does not allow that a truth is proved merely by the fact that it is accepted by the majority of men, although he is very far from admitting that the voice of the people is necessarily the voice of God,-- he, nevertheless, maintains that " admitting, as we must, that life is impossible unless through a certain agreement between internal convictions and external circumstances ; admitting therefore that the probabilities are always in favour of the truth, or at least the partial truth. of a conviction ; we must admit that the convictions entertained by many minds in common are the most likely to have some foundation. The elimination of individual errors of thought. must give to the resulting judgment a certain additional value" (*First Principles*, 5th ed., p. 4). And in this position, I think he is impregnable. But he is not so secure in the method he adopts for discovering the element of truth " in things erroneous," or in ascertaining what is the thing

---

[1] This is in part the old argument *Consensus gentium*, of which Cicero makes so great a use. It has been brought prominently forward in recent times; *e.g.*, by Bishop Ellicott, in the Second Address of his *Six Addresses on the Being of God*.

that men universally believe, in the midst of their
diversity of modes of expressing it. His method
is : " To compare all opinions of the same genus ;
to set aside as more or less discrediting one another
those various special and concrete elements in
which such opinions disagree ; to observe what
remains after the discordant constituents have
been eliminated ; and to find for this remaining
constituent that abstract expression which holds
true throughout its divergent modifications " (*Id.,*
p. 11). In other words, it is the *comparative*
method, which can only leave you with a very bare
residuum, a pure simulacrum, an attenuated point,
as the object of general belief. And the residuum
is more meagre still when, on the same comparative
principle, we have to whittle it down so as to find
in it the common element of Science and Religion.
No wonder that Mr. Spencer's ultimate term
should assume a very ghost-like form. It is
simply this : " the Power which the Universe manifests to us is utterly inscrutable " (*Id.,* p. 46).

What then, under this head, falls to be said is,
That, granting the fact of men's ineradicable belief
in God as the noümenon underlying phenomena,
we do not grant that this belief centres in an unknown and unknowable God. On the contrary, it
amounts to a very firm conviction that God is par-

tially known—known in His manifestations,—and may be more and more fully known, as time goes on and experience deepens. So far is it from shutting out knowledge of God, that it refuses to set limits to the possibilities in this direction, and thus becomes a powerful motive to effort and a never-failing stimulus to religious progress. Unlike agnosticism, it forecloses nothing; and thus has nothing about it of the paralyzing influence that necessarily accompanies a creed which, in the name of Reason, claims to set bounds to reason, and, under guise of nescience, makes assertions that are competent only to omniscience. Mr. Spencer is right in demanding respect for the ineradicable belief; he is wrong in his analysis of that belief itself.

3. But now, thirdly, what of Mr. Spencer's own characterization of his Unknowable?

We have already seen that he makes it out to be Force; and, although he will not designate it a person, he ascribes to it permanence, unity, eternity, and practical omnipresence. But surely this goes far beyond the attitude of nescience; and yet, even at its best, it is altogether inadequate to express men's indestructible belief, on which he justly lays stress, and, in one vital point, is diametrically opposed to it. For, while men do have a perennial conviction

regarding the existence of the Absolute, and also
regarding His nature, they are not less definite in
regarding the Absolute as *personal*.   Personality
is the highest fact in the universe known to man :
and, if he is to interpret the universe at all, he
feels that this interpretation must be in terms of
the highest factor known to him, and not in terms
of anything lower.   Nor is there presumption,
much less "impiety," in thus ascribing Personality
to God, or in supposing Him to be endowed with
Intelligence and Will like our own.   There can in
this be no presumption, if we have a right to postulate the Deity at all.   On the contrary, there is
absolute necessity ; and light accrues from our procedure.   For, given a great Personal Being, who
underlies the universe and informs it, not a bare
Creator outside and simply working upon it, and you
can see how mind and matter, and the finite and
the Infinite, can meet.   There is a greeting of the
Spirit here, which means much.   But refuse this,
and your mere conception of Force does not help
you.   Hence, the weakness of simply dealing
" with Evolution at large Inorganic, Organic, and
Super-organic– in terms of Matter and Motion ".
Matter and Motion can do great things, but they
cannot explain spiritual phenomena ; even Anaxagoras saw that they pre-supposed *Mind*.   Personality is not found there ; and Mr. Spencer himself

has to take Spirit as utterly distinct from Matter,
consciousness as distinct from nerve force, and to
leave the union of the two an entire mystery.

But more than this, Mr. Spencer's Force, as
not being personal, is a pure abstraction. It is
impossible, therefore, to accept it as the true object
of Religion. He himself feels this when he says :
" Indeed it seems somewhat strange that men
should suppose the highest worship to lie in assimilating the object of their worship to themselves.
Not in asserting a transcendent difference, but in
asserting a certain likeness, consists the element of
their creed which they think essential " (*Id.*, p. 109).
But there is no strangeness about this, if the Object
of Religion must be one that shall meet men's various
needs. It is strictly necessitated on psychological
grounds. There are certain things, indeed, on the
side of emotion, that Force might conceivably be
competent to effect. It might impress us with awe,
or it might affect us with fear ; it might even, in
another aspect, please us as the beautiful or soothe
us as the mild ; it might also place us in the attitude
of wonder and of meditation, and give exercise to our
intellectual curiosity. But it could not draw forth
our prayers, in expectation of light and help and
guidance from it ; nor could it elicit that piety and
devotion, that moral reverence and deep veneration,
that tender submission and feeling of trust and

love, that are characteristic of Religion.   We might
yield to it as coercing us, or resign ourselves to it
as to the inevitable ; but we never could cheerfully
submit to it as acquiescing in it.   Nothing but
Personality can constrain us ; and to none but a
living Person, supreme in wisdom and in love, can
we yield a full and willing homage.

Once more, what of morality and conscience ?
The cosmic order and the moral order, regarded
simply as force, are not homogeneous ; and a bridge
has to be erected between physical order, or fixed
natural law, and the harmony of the soul.

Briefly then : Mr. Spencer's Unknowable, in so
far as it is characterized, ceases to be the unknowable ; but, even when characterized, it is not sufficient for man's religious needs.   Its power,
though bought at the expense of inconsistency,
turns out to be impotence.

7. *Professor Huxley.*

There is a type of agnosticism yet to be considered,—that which is identified with Professor
Huxley, and which is associated with the first
introduction of the name "agnostic".

Professor Huxley himself has laid down his
position for us, and we cannot do better than
listen to his own words.

In his famous article in the *Nineteenth Century*

for February 1889, reprinted with minor alterations, in the *Essays upon Some Controverted
Questions* (1892),—after recording that in his youth
he "was brought up in the strictest school of
Evangelical orthodoxy," and after emphasizing the
fact that, of the books and essays that he early
read, two left on him an indelible impression, one
Guizot's *History of Civilization*, the other Sir
William Hamilton's Essay "On the Philosophy
of the Unconditioned," in the *Edinburgh Review*,
—he goes on to say[1]:-

"When I reached intellectual maturity and
began to ask myself whether I was an atheist, a
theist, or a pantheist: a materialist or an idealist;
a Christian or a freethinker: I found that the
more I learned and reflected, the less ready was
the answer: until at last, I came to the conclusion
that I had neither art nor part with any of these
denominations, except the last. The one thing
in which most of these good people were agreed
was the one thing in which I differed from
them. They were quite sure they had attained a
certain 'gnosis,' had, more or less successfully,
solved the problem of existence: while I was quite
sure I had not, and had a pretty strong conviction
that the problem was insoluble. And, with Kant

---

[1] My quotations are throughout from the *Essays*, not from the *Nineteenth Century*.

and Hume on my side I could not think myself
presumptuous in holding fast by that opinion. . . .
This was my situation when I had the good fortune
to find a place among the members of that remark-
able confraternity of antagonists, long since de-
ceased, but of green and pious memory, the
Metaphysical Society.   Every variety of philosophical and theological opinion was represented
there, and expressed itself with entire openness ;
most of my colleagues were-*ists* of one sort or
another ; and, however kind and friendly they
might be, I, the man without a rag of a label to
cover himself with, could not fail to have some of
the uneasy feelings which must have beset the
historical fox when, after leaving the trap in
which his tail remained, he presented himself to
his normally elongated companions.   So I took
thought, and invented what I conceived to be the
appropriate title of 'agnostic'.   It came into my
head as suggestively antithetic to the 'gnostic' of
Church History, who professed to know so much
about the very things of which I was ignorant ;
and I took the earliest opportunity of parading
it to our Society, to show that I, too, had a tail,
like the other foxes.   To my great satisfaction, the
term took."   Very well : what more ?   "Agnosticism in fact," continues the Professor, "is not
a creed, but a method, the essence of which lies in

the rigorous application of a single principle.
That principle is of great antiquity; it is as old as
Socrates; as old as the writer who said, 'Try all
things, hold fast by that which is good': it is the
foundation of the Reformation, which simply illustrated the axiom that every man should be able to
give a reason for the faith that is in him: it is the
great principle of Descartes: it is the fundamental
axiom of modern science. Positively the principle
may be expressed: In matters of the intellect
follow your reason as far as it will take you
without regard to any other consideration. And
negatively: In matters of the intellect do not
pretend that conclusions are certain which are
not demonstrated or demonstrable. That I take
to be the agnostic faith, which if a man keep whole
and undefiled, he shall not be ashamed to look the
universe in the face, whatever the future may have
in store for him. . . The only negative fixed
points will be those negations which flow from
the demonstrable limitation of our faculties. And
the only obligation accepted is to have the mind
always open to conviction. Agnostics who never
fail in carrying out their principles, are, I am
afraid, as rare as other people of whom the same
consistency can be truthfully predicated. But, if
you were to meet with such a phœnix and to tell
him that you had discovered that two and two

make five, he would patiently ask you to state
your reasons for that conviction, and express his
readiness to agree with you if he found them
satisfactory. The apostolic injunction to 'suffer
fools gladly' should be the rule of life of a true
agnostic. I am deeply conscious how far I myself
fall short of this ideal, but it is my personal conception of what agnostics ought to be."

Now, with regard to this, the first thing to be
observed is, the great similarity between Professor
Huxley's experience and that of Simonides, pre-
viously referred to. Said Simonides to Hiero,
concerning the definition of God, "the longer I
meditate upon it, the more obscure does it seem to
me to be". Says Professor Huxley, " I found
that the more I learned and reflected, the less
ready was the answer".

Observe, next, that Professor Huxley regards
agnosticism as "a method," not as "a creed";
nevertheless, there are sure enough indications
that he is not without his firm convictions. Regarding the problem of existence, he says,—" I
had a pretty strong conviction that the problem
was insoluble". And, earlier in the article, he
says. " Near my journey's end, I find myself in a
condition of something more than mere doubt
about these matters"; while, later on, he writes,

"I had, and have, the firmest conviction that I never left the '*rerace ria*'—the straight road; and that this road led nowhere else but into the dark depths of a wild and tangled forest". Add to this that, in succeeding articles in the *Essays*, he is positive and dogmatic enough in his attack on the Christian Gnosis, and on the conception of Jesus given to us in the four Gospels.

But, lastly, observe that his agnosticism, *as a method*, is, as *he* enunciates it, a very innocent and a very unhelpful process. Nobody will be found who does not acquiesce in his leading principle, both in its positive and in its negative aspect. Ever since the days of Justin Martyr, controversialists of all schools have begun with the claim, "Reason directs those who are truly pious and philosophical to honour and love only what is true," and have ended with the appeal, "If these things seem to you to be reasonable and true, honour them: but if they seem nonsensical, despise them as nonsense" (Justin's *First Apology*, chapters ii. and lxviii.). But if there is no dissentient, that looks somewhat suspicious: for, just because of this universal acquiescence, coupled with the fact that there is untold diversity in the opinions of those that acquiesce in it, it cannot of itself be effective for very much in helping to form opinion or to solve difficulties. It is unquestionably right, in matters of the intellect, to "follow your reason as far as it will take you without regard to any other consideration": it is undoubtedly your bounden duty "not to pretend that conclusions are certain which are not demonstrated or demonstrable". But the very matter in question is, "How far can your reason take you? What constitute the limits of the demonstrable?" And, until you satisfy us with a *critique* of reason, your principle is simply the verbal enunciation of a truism, which every man will accept, and will forthwith apply in an individualistic fashion, interpreting it in the way that suits himself.

Nothing, then, need be feared from the agnostic principle as here laid down: taken in itself, it is very just and very harmless. But the shafts of Professor Huxley's agnostic wit are not dependent solely on his principle: they are barbed from another source,—namely, from Science: and they are not aimed direct at Theism, but are shot into the heart of the Bible Revelation, more particularly of the Christian part of it. It is the old story of the incredibility of miracles, especially of Christian miracles as recorded in the Gospels. These, it is maintained,—witness, for instance, the destruction of the Gadarene swine,—are wholly unbelievable: they contradict what Nature reveals to us as most certain, and what experience testifies to, and they fail to satisfy the demands of scientific proof.

Now, into the discussion about Christ's miracles, it is not our business here to enter. These must stand or fall according to the evidence adduced. But, as to the matter of the *possibility* of miracles itself, I may be permitted to say that, if Theism be true, such possibility is axiomatic. If God is, He is greater than Nature and controls it. For, a miracle is not, as Hume defined it, a "violation" or "transgression" of the laws of nature, it is not even a "suspension" of these laws: *it is a higher manipulation of Nature's forces than we are accustomed to, owing to a special Divine volition for a special purpose.* The old Roman soldier might have taught Hume here. When the Centurion of Capernaum sent to Jesus requesting Him to cure his servant boy, who lay sick and at the point of death, he gave as his reason, "For I also am a man set under authority, having under me soldiers, and I say unto one, Go, and he goeth; and to another, Come, and he cometh: and to my servant, Do this, and he doeth it". *That* is the true conception: the forces of Nature all marshalled, like so many soldiers, ready to obey the Captain's will "doing His commandments, hearkening unto the voice of His word": and the

Captain Himself possessed of full knowledge of these forces and full power over them. Discipline and obedience everywhere, just as in an army; yet all under the direction of a central authority. And even the soldier who leaves the ranks, while his comrades are at drill, to execute the superior officer's special behests, is as much subject to discipline as they. His *extra*ordinary action is no breach of the prevailing order, but a further exemplification of it. So, a miracle is no " violation " of nature, or " transgression " of it; but rather, when rightly interpreted, a manifestation, through the very instrumentality of Nature's laws, of the Supreme Power that gives to Nature its being and that constitutes its inner meaning. " One force may override another, and two laws may each be obeyed and may each disguise the action of the other. In the intimate constitution of matter there may be hidden springs of force which, while acting in accordance with their own fixed laws, may lead to sudden and unexpected changes. . . . To the ancients it seemed incredible that one lifeless stone could make another leap towards it. A piece of iron while it obeys the magnetic forces of the loadstone does not the less obey the law of gravity." There is such a thing as what Jevons calls a " Hierarchy of Natural Laws," and " there is absolutely nothing in science or in scientific method to warrant us in assigning any limit to this hierarchy of laws" (*The Principles of Science,* book vi.).

Physical science, therefore, has nothing to say against the possibility of miracles. Nor does the question fall within its sphere, but needs for its determination principles that go beyond Nature. Whether, on the other hand, at a particular date and in a particular spot, a miracle, as alleged, did actually take place, is a point to be settled by a consideration of the whole evidence. There can be no question that, as Professor Huxley says, "when a man testifies to a miracle, he not only states a fact, but he adds an interpretation of the fact. We may admit his evidence as to the former, and yet think his opinion as to the latter worthless." But it must be borne in mind, also, that the miracles of our Lord are *parables* as well; they are not only proofs of His mission, they are revelations of His character. And so, in determining the value of the early witnesses' interpretation of them, we have to consider, among other things, these three questions :—
(1) The *kind* or *nature* of the miracles —whether they are works of mercy or works of malevolence or of deceit ; (2) the *motive* of the miracle-worker —whether self-interest or sympathy with mankind,

whether personal selfishness or universal welfare ;
(3) the *end* or *object* of them— whether they be
"signs" as well as wonders, the evidence or token
of a Divine mission (in which case, the substance
of the mission itself must be taken into account),
or merely the display of the worker's own superior
power, no heavenly message being concealed under
them.

But, although Professor Huxley's vehement
onslaught on the Christian miracles is not a phase
of his agnosticism that specially concerns us here,
there is another phase of it that has distinct
relevance to our subject. This is his attempt, in
imitation of Hume, to determine the historical
origin of Religion, and his emphatic assertion in
Comtian fashion, of the decadence or decline of
Religion, under the dissemination of scientific
notions, at the present day.

As to the first of these the rise of supernaturalism among men,—here is what he says in
the "Prologue" to his *Essays upon Some Controverted Questions* (pp. 3, 4) : —

"Experience speedily taught them that the
shifting scenes of the world's stage have a permanent background ; that there is order amidst
the seeming confusion, and that many events take

place according to unchanging rules. To this region of familiar steadiness and customary regularity they gave the name of Nature. But, at the same time, their infantile and untutored reason, little more, as yet, than the playfellow of the imagination, led them to believe that this tangible, commonplace, orderly world of Nature was surrounded and interpenetrated by another tangible and mysterious world, no more bound by fixed rules than, as they fancied, were the thoughts and passions which coursed through their minds and seemed to exercise an intermittent and capricious rule over their bodies. They attributed to the entities, with which they peopled this dim and dreadful region, an unlimited amount of that power of modifying the course of events of which they themselves possessed a small share, and thus came to regard them as not merely beyond, but above Nature. Hence arose the conception of a 'Supernature' antithetic to 'Nature'— the primitive dualism of a natural world 'fixed in fate,' and a supernatural, left to the free play of volition which has pervaded all later speculation and, for thousands of years, has exercised a profound influence on practice."

Now, upon this doctrine, we may remark :-

(1) First, that the account here given of the

origin of supernaturalism, however like history it may appear to be, is not really history. It is simply a conjecture, simply a surmise, and must not be taken as indisputable fact. But (2). next, there is no such naïve distinction as is here drawn between experience teaching (primitive) man aright in his relations with external nature. and "infantile and untutored reason" leading him astray, or, at least. not guiding him unerringly, in the matter of the supernatural. The opposition between Experience (as the non-rational) and Reason is utterly unwarranted. There is even no just ground for disparaging "Imagination". If Imagination has a place in Religion. has it not also a place in Science? We know Professor Tyndall's answer; we know the answer given by Sir Archibald Geikie in his Presidential Address this year (1892) to the British Association; and Professor Huxley, with his own brilliant biological speculations, cannot answer differently. Even Experience, to which Professor Huxley ascribes man's early knowledge of the regularity of Nature. is impossible without imagination. For, Experience implies *memory*, or recollection of the past. and *expectation*, or anticipation of the future: and if Professor Huxley can explain Memory and Expectation without a reference to imagination he will accomplish a feat that will put psychologists to the blush. But (3), lastly, even supposing that the origin of supernaturalism was precisely in fact as it is here represented to have been, that would in no way invalidate the truth of Theism; it would simply show that Theism has, like every other rational conception, gone through a process of development, that it is subject to the law of evolution.

The stress of the objection, then, must be shifted from the region of origin to that of the present-day prospects of Religion. These, it is urged, are very far from bright. Not only are we met by the fact that the study of nature has amply rewarded mankind, "developing the Arts which have furnished the conditions of civilized existence; and the Sciences, which have been a progressive revelation of reality and have afforded the best discipline of the mind in the methods of discovering truth," while the study of Supernature has only led to diversity of opinion and mutually exclusive Religions, the adherents of which "delight in charging each other, not merely with error, but with criminality, deserving and ensuing (*sic*) punishment of infinite severity": not only this, but natural knowledge and supernatural knowledge are to-day directly contrasted in the hold that they have over cultured mankind. Says

Professor Huxley:—"In singular contrast with natural knowledge, again, the acquaintance of mankind with the supernatural appears the more extensive and the more exact, and the influence of supernatural doctrines upon the conduct the greater, the further back we go in time and the lower the stage of civilization submitted to investigation. Historically, indeed, there would seem to be an inverse relation between supernatural and natural knowledge. As the latter has widened, gained in precision and in trustworthiness, so has the former shrunk, grown vague and questionable; as the one has more and more filled the sphere of action, so has the other retreated into the region of meditation, or vanished behind the screen of mere verbal recognition. . . . Men are growing to be seriously alive to the fact that the historical evolution of humanity, which is generally, and I venture to think not unreasonably, regarded as progress, has been, and is being accompanied by a co-ordinate elimination of the supernatural from its originally large occupation of men's thoughts " (*Essays*, pp. 6, 7).

Now, I do not think that any calm and dispassionate man will deny that there is some truth here; but neither do I think that he will hesitate to say that there is exaggeration. That supernaturalism has gone through many phases and is ever undergoing a purifying and refining process as time passes, is very true; but the same thing is also true of naturalism. Neither natural nor supernatural science sprang full-armed from the brain of Zeus. Again, it is not proved that supernaturalism is losing its hold on men's convictions, or is ceasing to influence their conduct. On the contrary, what seems to be true is, that, while thinking men are now taking a less mechanical view of God's relation to outward nature than was taken formerly, they are working towards an ever-deepening consciousness of His permeating presence in Nature, and of the necessity of presupposing Him in all things. The forms of their conception change, and their *outward modes* of recognizing the supernatural change; but their convictions remain secure.

Neither the argument from origin, then, nor that from religion's decline is very formidable. Even if the facts on which the first is founded were literally correct, they are irrelevant: and the measure of truth that is contained in the second is far from decisive.

III.

We are now ready to advance from agnosticism. But, before finally dismissing it, we may as well, in a sentence or two, gather up our arguments and state the conclusion.

As the result of our discussion, we have seen that there is nothing against Theism arising from the leading agnostic theory as to its *origin*, nor is there anything against it arising from the present reception and the immediate future prospects of Religion in the world. But we have seen, further, that there is nothing in the principles of agnosticism, as philosophically presented, that necessarily shuts us out from knowledge of the Deity. We must, indeed, for purposes of clear thought and the conveniences of exposition, consider the finite and the Infinite apart; but this separation in the consideration of the two must not be allowed to blind us to the fact that it is only a logical device necessary for the understanding, but not representing the truth in its entirety. If we turn the two terms into bare abstractions, then, indeed, we may find them unmanageable; but this is not their real nature, and we have fallen into error. Knowledge also is relative, if by that you mean that it implies a knower as well as something known; but how this should debar us from the possibility of knowledge, is far from self-evident. That things are as they are found to be is not an unmeaning paradox; although it is quite true that things are often different from what they *seem* to be. That consciousness, too, is not a kind of envelope, a circumambient aether, going round and clasping phenomena so as always to keep them separate from noümena, is constantly to be borne in mind. "Enveloping," "circumscribing," "clasping," are words embodying a too materialistic conception to be strictly applicable to consciousness: they are not so much inadequate as irrelevant. Neither does it follow that, because man's faculties are *limited*, they are not valid to *any* extent. It only follows that there are heights and depths in the Divine nature that we cannot fully penetrate. This is what I take to be the real truth implied in calling God "the unexplored and the inexpressible". I like that phrase; and I like the other phrase of Matthew Arnold's, "words *thrown out* at a vast object of consciousness". But I like equally, in this connexion, the devotional language of Ben-Sira: "When ye glorify the Lord, exalt Him as much as ye can; for even yet will He far exceed: and when ye exalt Him, put forth all your strength, and be not weary: for ye can never go far enough" (*Ecclesiasticus*, xliii. 30). Nor, lastly, can you argue that, because God is the *perfection* of all that we regard as highest and best - wisdom, goodness, justice, truth, therefore, He is practically unknown by us, inasmuch as we ourselves have never attained perfection, and, until we have done so, we cannot really know the All-perfect.

For, surely, the *perfection* of a quality has reference to *degree*, and makes no difference in regard to the nature or essence of the quality itself; while the fact that we ourselves are *potentially* what we *ideally* conceive, is the all-important thing : if the Infinite be *implicit* in us, it also really *is*.

Put in a sentence, the pith of the agnostic objection, from the side of philosophy, is : That the human mind cannot transcend experience. And, put in another sentence, the pith of the answer to this objection may be very suitably given in the words of Professor Otto Pfleiderer (*The Philosophy of Religion*, Eng. transl., vol. iii. p. 254) : " Every act of thought is a transcending of immediate experience, which only affords the raw material of separate sensations ; and every general notion, most particularly that of 'law'—the fundamental notion of all scientific thought—is an unconditioned which sets itself above conditioned phenomena ; and any act of thought that is conscious of the finiteness of the individual objects it deals with, has therewith at once transcended the limits of the finite, and has along with the notion of finiteness embraced also its correlative, infinity ".

LECTURE V.

GOD A NECESSITY OF HUMAN NATURE.

PHILOSOPHY, in order to be valid, must rest upon and begin with Experience. We do not first have philosophy and then experience: we start from experience, and next pass on to philosophy.

This is the order of fact, and, therefore, the order to be strictly observed in proceeding to theory. As fact, man did not commence philosophizing before he had anything to philosophize upon: he had first the data of experience, and then he tried to interpret and understand them. In theory, if we begin philosophizing without paying due regard to our material, we shall do less than weave the spider's web—we shall rear a phantom structure, suitable for phantoms only.

This, which applies to experience in general, is distinctly applicable to theistic experience in special. It is not a philosophy unrelated to fact that we here desiderate, but one founded on facts and explanatory of them.

What, then, is the experiential basis of theistic

religion? What, in other words, is the psychological foundation of Theism both (*a*) in its spring, and (*b*) in the nature of that Divine object whom the religious consciousness affirms, and to whom the religious sentiment goes forth?

I.

In answer to the first of these questions,—What is the spring of theism? the testimony of Experience is :—

Man, by a necessity of his nature has been driven to the conception of and belief in God as objectively existing. And this conception and belief, whose stability is amply confirmed by evolution, has had the twofold characteristic, (1) of being emphatically on the line of what is highest and purest in existence, and (2) of stimulating men to the practice of righteousness and of helping them to reach higher and still higher achievements : in other words, it has been both a condition and a means of human progress—it has aided in initiating and it has furthered the higher civilization. But, this being so, it is impossible to believe that what is thus a necessity of our nature, and has conditioned human progress, what has powerfully operated in the direction of culture and improvement, of intellectual light and moral character, and has been a chief source of happiness to mankind.

should itself be an utter and entire delusion. For, if we cannot trust our higher nature, there is nothing else that we can trust ; and, however much we may puzzle ourselves with the question as to how it is possible to pass from subjective to objective existence, the validity of the fact that this passage has been made ought to be sufficiently established when it is shown that human nature has been necessitated to make it.

That is the testimony of, and argument from, Experience ; but we must elucidate it somewhat in detail.

First of all, however, let it be observed that, in saying that God is a necessity of human nature, we are not asserting that every man is, and all men have been, definitely *conscious* of this necessity. Human nature may be bound up with the Divine without every individual man being explicitly aware of it : for, a need may be simply implicit, and, if implicit, particular individuals or particular peoples may not fully awake to it till a particular stage of development has been reached.[1] A man, or even a nation, may be in religion, as in other things—

---

[1] Want *unfelt* is what Prof. J. Grote calls *egence.* Want *felt,* or craving and yearning, is what he calls *desiderium.* " Want or egence, and *want-feel* or craving, are not exactly the same thing : there may be real want unfelt, and there may be mistaken want-feel" (*A Treatise on the Moral Ideals,* p. 27).

> An infant crying in the night :
> An infant crying for the light :
> And with no language but a cry ;

and yet this " cry," to him that understands it, may be full of meaning. It may mean nothing less than that man is himself akin to the Deity—that, in Bible language, he is " made in the image of God". The story of Prometheus stealing fire and wisdom from the gods and imparting them to man, has a deeper meaning in it than appears upon the surface. If, as Aristotle long ago saw, man's normal condition be civilization, not barbarism, we can hardly expect to get the true conception of his nature if we take the lower or barbaric state for our ideal standard ; and Evolution has taught us the great truth that man's theistic notions are "necessary products of progressing intelligence" (Mr. Spencer's *First Principles*, 5th edition, p. 13).

God, then, is a necessity of human nature. How so ?

(I.) First, because, as man is what he is, the idea of God, as we see from history and from present fact, inevitably arises in him. But, if it inevitably arises in him, it ministers to a human want, and is thereby a necessity.

The doctrine of human Wants, as distinguished

from mere desires or wishes, calls for consideration.

These three things—desire, wish, want—need
to be carefully discriminated. *Desire* contains
three factors: first, the conception of an object
regarded as in itself desirable; secondly, a felt
craving for that object by me; thirdly, action or
effort towards the attainment or realization of this
desired and desirable object. In *wish*, there is not
necessarily implied more than the mere fact of *my*
craving (more or less intelligently) for an object:
there is no implication, one way or another, as to
whether the object is or is not in itself really a
desirable one, though there is an implication of my
regarding it as pleasure-giving or pain-removing.
Want implies all the three factors of Desire, with
the further implication that desire has here become
an index of reality, a guide to truth. In other
words, Want is that kind of desire to which the
human system (animal or spiritual) is organic: it
is not only a need or craving which finds satisfaction in particular objects, it is also a need or
craving whose very existence presupposes the
existence of those objects.

Now, among Natural Wants (which I divide in
a twofold way, into those that are the condition
of bare animal existence and those that are the
condition of spiritual life and growth), there are

certain points of agreement and certain well-marked differences.

(1) The first great distinction to be drawn is, that some natural wants are temporary, recurrent, or periodical; while others are permanent or enduring. To the former class belong all bodily wants, such as thirst and hunger; to the latter class belong knowledge, friendship, and other spiritual needs.

(2) Next, temporary or recurrent wants are soon satisfied, and, if over-satisfied, breed satiety: they are also regarded as in a manner external to us, we do not identify them with our inner self. Permanent or enduring wants, on the other hand, have an *insatiableness* about them that is very striking, and they never breed satiety; in a very special sense, also, we identify ourselves with them.

Now, note this distinction, for it gives us the principle of limitation. Purely recurrent wants, such as hunger and thirst, do not increase in magnitude the more you satisfy them; on the contrary, they have a quite definite range, and satiety is soon reached. But wants of the enduring kind—intellectual and moral—do increase the craving, aspiration, or longing, the more they are satisfied: they do not allow you to rest in any particular attainment, but always urge you on to something further; the capacity increases with exercise. This is only saying, in a different way, that these enduring wants are those alone that have reference to *an ideal*; they point us onward to something presumably realizable, but never fully realized. Hence, the recurrent wants are rightly regarded as the lower, and the permanent as the higher. Hence, too, in Ethics, special value is attached to these last as motives influencing the will or determining conduct.

(3) Thirdly, the objects of the lower wants are material, those of the higher wants are spiritual. The object of thirst is drink, and of hunger, food; while the objects of (say) knowledge and friendship are not of this kind.

(4) Fourthly, there is a distinction between the members of the higher class themselves. While some are egoistic, others are disinterested: *i.e.*, while in some the individual would appropriate the whole of the object, in others the object is such as may be shared in by any number of individuals, without any one feeling that he is robbed by his neighbour. Ambition and Esteem are of the grasping kind; true Friendship and Knowledge go beyond self-love.

(5) Lastly, the objects of some of the members of the higher class are persons; of others, not. Friendship, for instance, can exist only between

persons; the personal implication is not a necessity
in Knowledge.

These, then, being the distinctions, the question
arises, whether the existence of a natural want
always implies, directly or indirectly, the existence
– the real, not simply ideal, existence—of its
object.

The answer is clearly affirmative, so far as
recurrent wants are concerned. Hunger could
never be, had there not also been such a thing as
food to satisfy it. The craving of thirst presupposes the reality of water to allay it. Both
thirst and hunger are states of a living organism:
and they speak to the fact that, ere such an
organism could be, the food and nourishment
necessary to its existence must be too. So, we
may readily grant that some at least of the permanent or higher wants imply the actual existence
of their object. Friendship would be inexplicable,
except upon the supposition of the existence of
living persons between whom the emotion could
exist.

But is this equally the case with Knowledge?
The immediate objects of knowledge (you say) are
relations, and relations are of the mind. Yes,
but then relations imply the existence of things
related. Relations as existences *per se* would be

absurd. While, therefore, Truth, which is the immediate object of knowledge, being of relations, may correctly enough be designated ideal; nevertheless, that to which truth ultimately refers, and which makes it possible, is equally reality with food and drink and friends and the other objective things wherewith natural wants are concerned.

What, then, of our Theistic craving? As this is a natural want, it must have an object: but need the object have a distinct personal existence (like our friends), or is it simply an idea of the mind —a fictitious entity, a pious imagination? It may be plausibly argued that a subjective or ideal existence is all that is legitimate; for, God is an object invisible and intangible. But, in that case, we ought to find in man some traces of a consciousness that this Being believed in is a mere imaginary entity; just as we find in healthy natures a quite distinct consciousness of the difference between what is actually real and what the mind simply *feigns* to be such. But, so far is this from being the case, that in monotheistic, polytheistic, and pantheistic religions alike, we find that the Deity believed in is always regarded as truly existent; and, in philosophical pantheism, He is conceived as the sole existence. Moreover, men, by a kind of natural instinct, invariably represent the cravings of their religious being as a hunger and a thirst; thereby unconsciously assimilating them to wants whose objects are unquestionably existent. They further feel their own finiteness, and are dissatisfied with the finite: and this is testimony to something in them higher than the finite, and thereby God is secured to them.

God is a datum, then, of man's nature, inasmuch as He is the object of a natural want. To this want, man's spiritual system is organic—which means not only that human nature is dependent for its *satisfaction* on Him, but also that the want itself could not have *arisen* apart from Him.

Nor is it any argument against this to say that we cannot see how the human and the Divine can meet. This inability to see how is only part of a much wider inability. Can we see how mind and matter can meet, or spirit and nature? Yet there we have their union in external perception: and spirit can go forth to, understand, and assimilate nature. Or, can we see how one man can communicate his thoughts to, or exercise a guiding influence over, another? Yet, the power of friendship and the inseparable union of hearts here is a fact, as it is equally a fact that sociality is the atmosphere in which the human spirit thrives. Altruism, again, especially in the form of self-sacrifice: can you fully understand its rationale?

Yet, self-sacrifice is an indubitable fact of experience. If we can show that theism is a want of human nature, it is enough. The implication therein is, that God exists and that man himself is allied to Him.

In this way, the being of God becomes more than an *hypothesis*. Even as an hypothesis, it would be needed in order to the full explanation of the facts, just as the assumption of æther is necessary for Science in order to account for the phenomena of Optics. Hypotheses have undoubted value; and scientific speculation knows how to use them. But, once base theism in human nature, and God's existence becomes a rational certainty: it is the necessary presupposition of the case.

But, although this be so, there is no need, further, that theism, being natural to man, should also be identical in all men. The form of theistic expression will vary according to the endowments of particular peoples, and according to the environment. Man is everywhere a rational being, and yet the degree of rationality is very different in different persons, and different nations have embodied it in different forms. So, religion may be the common property of mankind, and yet endless diversity may be discoverable in the forms of it, and in the degrees of it, among men. Yea, such diversity *must* be discoverable, if man is a progressive being, and if progress be conditioned by natural situation and life's circumstances. If the races and peoples of the earth have to work out their own laws, and form their own language, and create their own institutions, they have also to work out their own religions. Man's nature (rational, social, and religious) is, in its groundwork, everywhere the same : but, in its quality and actual endowments, it admits of unlimited variety, and the development of its capacities is dependent on the opportunities afforded.

Objections.

But, that we may the better understand the nature of the argument, let us examine a few of the leading objections to it.

1. First of all, it is said : Theism cannot be based in human nature, otherwise it would be *universal;* but we know that the idea of God is not found among some existing savages, and existing savages represent primitive man.

To this one may reply :—

(1) First, that we must not be too positive in identifying savages of the present day with primitive man. For, both Comparative Philology and much of Ethnology refuse to countenance such an assumption ; and, so long as that is the case, neither

science nor logic warrants the inference that what is true of modern savages is, therefore, true of early man.[1]

(2) But, secondly, even granting that some savages may be without the idea of God, and granting further (for the sake of argument) that they could be proved never to have had it, this is no argument against the validity of that idea. For, *lateness* of evolution is characteristic of our highest truths and notions—those of geometry, for instance,—and such truths and notions have arisen in limited areas of the earth and have taken time to travel; and, still, these are natural to man. "Natural to man" means implicit in his nature (no matter at what point of time, or in what nation, the implicit may first become explicit); and "universal" does not mean "consciously acknowledged by all," but what is seen to be necessary as an element in human nature when man is viewed *as* man, or when we take his nature in its highest or ideal form.

2. But, secondly, it may be said: It can be

---

[1] "To take for granted that what the savages now are, perhaps after millenniums of degradation, all other people must have been, and that modes of thought through which they are now passing have been passed through by others, is a most unscientific assumption, and you will seldom meet with it in any essay or book without also finding proof that the writer did not know how to deal with historical evidence" (P. Le Page Renouf, *Hibbert Lectures*, p. 125).

shown that man formed his idea of God out of very lowly material (the oldest religious documents we possess—the Vedic hymns, for example—show us that):[1] and this fact of lowly origin affects the product when attained.

To this I answer:—

(1) First, why should it? Saccharine - the purest, the whitest, the sweetest of substances -is produced from coal tar; yet, its virtue is not thereby affected. High and low, base and noble, are really terms inapplicable to the raw material of spiritual evolution. *All* elements are alike noble, when you view them from the higher and proper standpoint. We can even suppose, without detriment to the theistic product, that religion was primarily associated with *fear*,—fear in the presence of the overpowering and destructive forces of nature -storms, tempests, earthquakes, and the like. Fear,[2] indeed, I readily believe (and physiolatry seems to confirm it), had a part to play in the development of (though it was not competent to originate) the religious sentiment: and thus far Hobbes and Hume are right. And yet, that only means that the circumstances of human life have been such as

[1] Probably the oldest piece of poetry in the literature of the world belongs to Egypt; and this is the fifteenth chapter of the *Book of the Dead*, "which is a hymn to the rising and to the setting Sun".

[2] The distinction between Awe and Fear will be dwelt upon in Lecture VII.

to impress man with a feeling of his own impotence and dependence, and thereby to arouse in him the consciousness of a God. But, while Fear had thus its function, surely Gratitude and Love must have been operative too. For, Nature has beneficent as well as destructive forces; and the divinizing of sun and moon and earth by nature-worshippers testifies to the fount of affection welling up towards the Originator of our being, as much as the divinizing of its destructive forces testifies to our sense of helplessness or dependence. Nor must we forget the significant fact of beneficent theophanies. Castor and Pollux came to give *help* at Lake Regillus: and the story of Baucis and Philemon presents the winning and humane side of the Divine conception.

(2) But, secondly, while admitting that some old documents show us man forming gods out of lowly materials, we must be careful not to exaggerate this fact. Other ancient documents, some of them among the oldest we possess, or, at any rate, embodying a very early tradition, show us man beginning at the higher plane. However critics may ultimately apportion the parts of the Old Testament Scripture, it is generally admitted that the teaching regarding the Mosaic Cosmogony is exceptionally old. Well, this teaching, as given in the opening chapters of our Bible, represents God

as "creating man after His own image," "in His own likeness"; and represents man as standing, at the first, in a felt relation to Him—though, no doubt, with his conceptions still needing to be deepened and developed. It is not part of my duty here to examine the place and scientific value of the Bible teaching; but it *is* part of my duty to emphasize the fact that here, in extremely ancient documents, recording a confessedly ancient belief, views about God and about man's relation to Him are laid down from the higher platform, and occupy a unique position.

(3) Lastly, no document of any people in existence shows us man forming God at the very beginning. For, the very oldest extant documents of any people (the Vedic hymns, for instance) refer to a time when the people in question had far advanced in their history, and when their religion had, through sacerdotal and other influences, assumed a shape—we know not how—different from what characterized it originally.

3. But, next, it is objected: Men have now outgrown religion (at least, they have done so in highly civilized lands); and this proves that theism is not a necessity of human nature, but, at best, was only necessary as a stage in human progress.

This objection (repeated by Professor Huxley,

and enforced with all the charms of literary style by Renan) is put most strikingly by Comte: and we shall take it as presented by him.

It was one of the most characteristic of Comte's positions that historical evolution has followed the law of three successive stages. Both the individual and the race (he held) have begun, in their interpretation of external things (facts, incidents, and events), by ascribing them to beings endowed with power and personality, yet supernatural: in other words, by regarding them as produced by deities. The lowest form of such divinizing of the causes of external events is Fetishism,—which consists in ascribing life and personality to whatever in outward nature arrests the attention or engages self-interest;[1] and a well-known higher form is

[1] A dispute has arisen between Comtists and naturists as to the proper conception and definition of Fetishism. Is a fetish simply a concrete material object (a stone, a piece of wood, etc.) *personalized*: or is it a concrete material object regarded as the embodiment of a spirit introduced into it from without? The truth seems to lie with Count Goblet d'Alviella (*Hibbert Lectures*, p. 109 n.), who distinguishes between "*primary* fetishism, in which man, personifying natural objects, chooses one as an auxiliary or protector; and *secondary*, or derived fetishism, which implies the incorporation of an independent spirit in a material object". This does not, however, prevent him from wishing to restrict the term to the second of these meanings; in which case, an obvious distinction is obtained between a fetish and an idol—this latter being simply "an elaborated fetish," one on which human workmanship, in the shape of painting or of sculpture, has been more or less expended. "The fetish is an object

seen in the worshipping of sun and moon and
stars, and in the sacred veneration that has been
paid from very early times to mother Earth.   This
is the first stage in the threefold development
(itself also consisting of three steps—fetishism,
polytheism, monotheism[1]); and Comte has called
it the *theological.*   Next comes the stage when
people begin to form abstract ideas, and to explain things and events in accordance therewith.
Everything that happens is now conceived as
having an efficient cause, but the cause is no
longer external: it is the thing's own peculiar
energy or force, its inherent essence—such as
attraction, repulsion, etc.   These inherent forces
are all considered as possessing a distinct existence of their own, they are hypostatized abstractions: and merely to give them a name is to
explain them.   Phenomena are still regarded as
caused, but not by supernatural wills, only by
abstract entities.   This is the *metaphysical* stage.
Last of all comes the stage when people begin to
see that neither theological nor metaphysical inter-

---

supposed to be inhabited by a spirit to which superhuman power is
attributed, and the idol is the fetish so fashioned or retouched as to
reproduce the appearance of the spirit supposed to reside in it."

[1] This threefold gradation dates from De Brosses (say, 1760), to
whom is ascribed the introduction both of the name and of the
theory of Fetishism.   See Professor Max Müller's *Hibbert Lectures*.
pp. 58, 59.

pretation is worth anything, that the "search for causes" is wholly illusory and must be abandoned, but that the whole of existence is explainable on *natural* principles : we need nothing supernatural, we need nothing metaphysical ; Science—systematized knowledge of phenomena, commanding the assent of experts, and verified by its power of successful prevision—is all-sufficient. This is the last or scientific stage : Comte calls it *positive*.

And these three stages Comte regards as valid, not only for the individual, but for the race : and he claims to have established, by a wide induction of particulars and by legitimate inference, that men have actually gone through them —that, in other words, the stages represent the actual course of history. Just as there have been times when the world was swayed by the theological idea, so have there been times when the metaphysical conception was supreme ; and now, at the present day, we have reached the last and highest stage, the positive. It is the characteristic of the nineteenth century that it has done with theology and done with metaphysics, and has pinned its faith to science.

Now, with regard to this bold and sweeping theory, it may be remarked :—

1. First, that, if the law of the three stages

were established, it would certainly simplify the interpretation of life and of the universe; but it would simplify it by rendering interpretation altogether impossible. For, if what men have regarded as highest and best turn out to have been a groundless fancy, what security have they that anything else in which they trust may not be equally fictitious? If religion be a fiction, and metaphysics a delusion, there is an uncomfortable feeling that science itself may not have the stable existence that we suppose it to have, and that even the positive stage may not be able to resist disintegration, standing alone.

2. But, secondly, has Comte succeeded in establishing his law of the three stages? Is his theory sufficiently borne out by history? It is impossible, without actually producing his works themselves, to give an adequate idea of the mass of material that he marshals for the purpose of proving the affirmative; and it is equally impossible to give any adequate impression, without copious extracts, of his own intellectual acumen in working up this material, and generalizing upon it. But while wishing to give all weight to the facts adduced, and to do reverence to the genius of the great generalizer himself, I cannot say, in the face of history, and of the facts patent to every one of us in our daily experience, that he has succeeded in making

good his contention : rather, he seems to me to have fallen into the error of over-generalization.[1] For, in the first place, tested by any period of history that any of us may happen to know, his so-called stages may easily be seen not to have been successive, but *contemporaneous in the past*; and, in the next place, we know that they are *contemporaneous in the present.* It is not the case that, though we live in an age pre-eminently scientific, we have parted with metaphysics and theology. It is not the case that, in the past, theology has been succeeded by metaphysics, and that the latter has dissolved the former. On the contrary, " it was by the most sublime metaphysics," as Fenelon argued in one of his letters to the Cardinal de Noailles, when urging the necessity of great theologians being metaphysicians, " that St. Augustine developed the first principles of the truths of religion against pagans and heretics. It is by the sublimity of this science, that St. Gregory Nazianzen deserves, by way of pre-eminence, the title of theologian. It was by metaphysics that St. Anselm

---

[1] For admirable critiques of Comte's doctrine, see Professor Flint's *The Philosophy of History* (bk. i. ch. xii.) and Dr. Martineau's *Types of Ethical Theory* (part i. bk. ii.). In the text, I pass by all detailed criticism as not being necessary for my purpose,— as, for example, the point so vigorously urged by Professor Max Müller, Professor Otto Pfleiderer, and others, that neither history nor psychology supports Comte's assumption that religion had its origin in fetishism.

and St. Thomas became, in the later centuries, the great luminaries of their time." Again, in the very highest civilizations, thinking men have always been metaphysical; and it may almost be said that, the higher the civilization, the more metaphysical they have been. In ancient Greek days, with Plato and Aristotle in the ascendant, Metaphysics held a prominent place in human interest. It was in nowise different in ancient India, Egypt, Assyria, Persia, Arabia. Metaphysics and civilization went hand in hand then: and they go hand in hand still. "Metaphysics is an indestructible fact in Human Nature, shown more powerfully, instead of less, as Comte supposes, with a nation's growth;" which "is also proved by what Bacon calls 'Prerogative instances,' as the written Metaphysics which the world has preserved, was produced only by the highest intellects of the nations foremost in each period of history," and the same is proved by modern philosophy, "which is a product of the three foremost nations of Europe—England, France, and Germany" (Mr. W. Graham's *Idealism*, p. xxvi.).

Nor do I think that Science itself is able to avoid being largely metaphysical. Such is the character of its leading conception, "Force"; and, so long as speculation on "Atoms" and similar scientific entities goes on (and that, presumably, will be till the close of science itself), so long will metaphysics be secured, even when nominally denied, to mankind.

But what is true of Metaphysics is equally true of Theology. Even Comte himself could not rest in mere nature, with its co-existences and its successions, but was driven on to the origination and advocacy of the worship of Humanity. He who despised metaphysics and abstract thinking, ultimately set up an abstraction as the object of his devotion. And all the present-day talk of "pancosmism," "cosmic unity," "cosmic emotion," and the like: what is it but just the positivist's confession that religion and metaphysics are natural to man, and that, if you shut them out in one form, they will inevitably make their appearance in another?

The truth seems to be almost exactly the reverse of what is maintained by Comte. The three states —the theological, the metaphysical, and the positive —are in themselves very real: they simply represent the three great questions that the human mind is ever putting regarding things, –*viz.*, (1) Whence do they arise; or what is the source of their production? (2) What is their own inmost nature; what all is implied in the fact that they *are?* (3) How are they related to each other: or what are the laws that distinguish them as ordered phenomena ? But these three *states* are not three *stages*, nor does the one supersede the other. On the contrary, it is established by history—unless you take history as meaning arbitrarily selected periods, strung together according to one's own fancy—that they are, and all along have been, contemporaneous ; and that, as Channing powerfully expresses it, "the human race, as it advances, does not leave religion behind it, as it leaves the shelter of caves and forests ; does not outgrow faith, does not see it fading like the mist before its rising intelligence. On the contrary, religion opens before the improved mind in new grandeur. God, whom uncivilized man had narrowed into a local and tutelar Deity, rises with every advance of knowledge to a loftier throne, and is seen to sway a mightier sceptre. The soul, in proportion as it enlarges its faculties and refines its affections, possesses and discerns within itself a more and more glorious type of the Divinity, learns his spirituality in its own spiritual powers, and offers him a profounder and more inward worship" (*Discourse on Christian Worship*, Works, vol. ii. p. 191).

In brief, then : the truth embodied in Comte's three stages is the truth that there are three states, not mutually exclusive and incompatible, but mutually supporting and co-existent ; and the development that is indisputable is, not the development of throwing off one and putting on another, but the progress in elevation and refinement *in each* that comes with wider and deeper experience and the onward march of time. We do now, indeed, live in a distinctively scientific age ; but Religion, with its implicated metaphysics and theology, is not less real or less intense to us than it was to our ancestors, nor is it less widely diffused to-day than it once was. On the contrary, that great religious ferment which we see going on all over the civilized world, and that power which religious controversy has of drawing men of all classes and professions into it, testify to its *perennial* interest for men ; and the fermenting process itself—what does it betoken but the further purification and refining of the religious idea, which, like other great and living conceptions, can grow and gain strength in us only through conflict and through strife ?

Consequently, I do not think that it is proved, or can be proved, that men have outgrown religion : nor is the presumption warranted that they will one day finally dispense with it. What the evidence goes to prove is, that in religion there is progress, as in everything else ; and that man's religious conceptions keep steady pace with his intellectual and moral advance.

4. There is just one other argument against Religion's being a necessity of human nature that needs to be mentioned; but a bare mention of it will be quite enough.

It has been said: Religion is invalid because it is a pure device of the priests, and a device for their own aggrandisement.

This argument is not now often heard; but it was the common Deistic argument of last century: and it was frequent, in a modified form, in the seventeenth century, from Herbert of Cherbury downwards.

But, however relevant it may sometimes have been to certain forms in which Religion has clothed itself among men, it is obviously quite irrelevant to Religion itself. The argument is a clear *hysteron proteron*. For, apart altogether from the circumstance that it lacks historical support, and apart from the further circumstance that it is entirely opposed by the universality of religious belief,— *in the very fact of a priest* you presuppose the existence of religion; and, surely, there must have been something in man's nature to appeal to before the priest could have got his device accepted. Priest-craft is one thing, Religion is another; and, save that the former puts on the guise of the latter, there is no other necessary connexion between the two.[1]

[1] Moreover, the accusation is not borne out by historical fact. Religious belief is too universal, is too variously expressed, and has

(II.) We pass, then, to the second point included in the primary argument,—*viz.*, the *utility* of Religion. It is maintained, on the testimony of history and of experience, that the idea of God and belief in Him has been and is potent on the side of righteousness and enlightenment—in other words, that it both *furthers* and *conditions* spiritual growth and human progress.

In this way, its place as a natural want is specially justified. For, in applying utility as the ground of distinction between what is "natural" and what is "unnatural" in the spiritual part of human nature, we are only extending the ruling test, so amply appealed to by biologists, of the natural and the unnatural in physical organism. *That* is a natural want of the physical organism which conduces to the health and development of the organism, while that is unnatural which obstructs the development and promotes dishealth or degeneration.

Now, in order to appreciate the full force of our contention, it would be necessary to traverse

---

arisen under too great a variety of circumstances, to be compatible with the supposition of a priestly origin. The evidence is all the other way; and "even as a mere question of probabilities, it cannot rationally be concluded that in every society, past and present, savage and civilized, certain members of the community have combined to delude the rest, in ways so analogous" (Mr. H. Spencer, *First Principles*, 5th edition, p. 14).

the whole of human history, and to appraise the various movements in ancient and in modern times that have forwarded the happiness and good of the race. This, of course, cannot be attempted here. I must take for granted that, from what each knows of religion and its history, you will allow that Religion has done good in the world, and has been a means of human felicity. It has taught men subordination and mutual respect, and has been a bond of union among them, uniting families, communities, nations, in the sense of a common faith. It has encouraged self-sacrifice and self-denial, not only in the form of surrendering a present good in view of one that is more distant, but also in drawing forth the disinterested affections of man's heart and in presenting to him an Object *for* whom, as well as *in* whom, he might live. It has trained heroes, therefore. But heroism and intelligence go hand in hand--as the ancient Greeks very well saw when, by a proper instinct, they made the goddess of war the goddess of wisdom too. And so it is essentially a refining, - as well as a purifying, conception; and mankind has ever been the gainer by attachment to it.

All this, and much more of the same kind, I must take for granted as admitted; and I will confine myself to rebutting the reasonings of those who attack Religion on the side of the harm it is alleged to be doing, or to have done—on the misery it has caused, and the obstruction it has offered to intellectual and scientific advance.

But, first, note the limitation of our original statement. It is not maintained that nothing but religion has done good in the world; it is only said that religion has been a factor, a leading and conspicuous factor, in man's improvement. It would be absurd to forget what we owe to the Art, the Philosophy, and the Letters of Greece; to the Legal and practical wisdom of Rome; to the mighty civilizing influences of the ancient empires of Egypt, Assyria, Persia, and so forth. We have no need to exalt Religion at the expense of the non-religious elements in man's advancement: it is enough if Religion be seen to have been a great power in the onward march of civilization and refinement. Grant that Religion has been a great purifier of Morals, the inspirer of noble and heroic deeds, the elevator of character and of manners, the minister of union and order, the suppressor of vice and incentive to virtue,— and I ask no more. If, notwithstanding these noble consequences, you still persist in calling it a dream, then I can only answer in the words of Joseph Truman,—"Dreams are not idle; dreams have saved the world".

What, then, says the objector? He says:—

1. First, that Religion is, and always has been, *superstition;* and that superstition is the greatest curse the world has ever seen,—cramping, numbing, paralyzing, and contracting men's natures, beating all independence out of them, and producing a cringing, spiritless, and unmanly disposition.

That is a strong indictment, and needs to be definitely met.

What, then, let us first ask, is Superstition?

Superstition, as I define it, is *looking upon the unknown as something hostile to us, with irrational dread of its consequences, together with irrational effort to frustrate or to avert its baneful action.* Its cramping power lies partly in its being fear, but partly also in its being irrational; and the objectionable thing about its efforts to get rid of this fear is that these efforts also are irrational.

Now note, first, that Superstition is not confined to Religion; and, secondly, that it is not of the essence of religion.

Superstition is not confined to religion: for, first of all, it is fear of impending danger, but irrational fear begotten of ignorance,—and ignorance with its attendant fear is very far-reaching in its operation. We see it in the timidity of a novice in handling an unknown, suspicious-looking article, lest it should turn out to be dynamite; and we see it in that most general of all fears—the fear of Death. So long as human knowledge is incomplete, so long this kind of fear will remain; but increase of knowledge means decrease of fear. We know what familiarity with the various drugs in a druggist's shop can do. At first, most of them are dreaded as poison, and are delicately handled; but, by and by, poison itself loses its terrors, and the young apprentice can move about unconcerned amid so much that is powerful for destruction.

But, next, Superstition rests on the fact that future events in the world are to man contingent— they may or they may not happen; and on the two further facts of man's self-interest and his desire to have all go well with him. But there is nothing in all this specifically religious.

Lastly, superstition is traceable, in part, to certain fallacious tendencies of the human mind which have a much wider sweep than religion. These tendencies are two in number:—

(*a*) First, the tendency to hasty generalization: particularly, to what logicians know as *post hoc ergo propter hoc*,—that is, to inferring from the fact that one thing follows another that, therefore, it is caused by that other. This is the basis of the doctrine of prodigies, omens, dreams. Thus: from observing frequent instances of ill-luck happening to persons who put on the right foot shoe before the left in dressing, people came to the conclusion that the ill-luck was the consequence of beginning with the right foot, and so dreaded ill-luck whenever they inadvertently fell into that mistake, and, perhaps, like an ancient pagan, refused to quit the house till such time as the evil omen was averted. That was superstition, though not of a religious kind.

(*b*) Next, it is a law of the human mind that, whenever we do a thing often, or get into a habit of doing it, we feel uncomfortable any time we neglect it, and are prompted to remove this discomfort by any means however ridiculous. It is recorded of Dr. Johnson, according to Macaulay, that, being in the habit of touching every post in the streets through which he walked, he was so uneasy if accidentally he omitted any one of them that he turned back and touched it. And Boswell tells us: "He had another particularity, of which none of his friends ever ventured to ask an explanation. It appeared to me some superstitious habit, which he had contracted early, and from which he had never called upon his reason to disentangle him. This was his anxious care to go out or in at a door or passage, by a certain number of steps from a certain point, or at least so that either his right or his left foot (I am not certain which) should constantly make the first actual movement when he came close to the door or passage. Thus I conjecture; for I have, upon innumerable occasions, observed him suddenly stop, and then seem to count his steps with a deep earnestness; and when he had neglected or gone wrong in this sort of magical movement, I have seen him go back again, put himself in a proper posture to begin the ceremony, and having gone through it, break from his abstraction, walk briskly on, and join his companion." That, again, was superstition, but not of the religious stamp: it arose from the discomfort of disrupted habit.

What, then, is distinctive of *religious* super-stition? Simply this,—that superstition, when allied with religion, assumes a particularly virulent form: it cramps and paralyzes the natures of those that are ruled by it, and prompts to exceptionally irrational and debasing rites and ceremonies.[1] This, indeed, is true. But it is no argument against Religion itself, but only an argument against the use that the superstitions make of it;

---

[1] Examples of the irrationalities of superstition, as shown in old Greek days, are given in Theophrastus's character-sketch of the Superstitious man (No. xxviii. in Professor Jebb's edition of *The Characters of Theophrastus*).

it is only another, and a most striking, instance of what is more generally observable,—*viz.*, that the corruption of what is best is worst.

But, awful and disastrous though the consequences of superstition are, I doubt whether, under all circumstances (Bacon notwithstanding [1]), superstition is an unmitigated or unmixed evil. It has this good effect, at any rate, of still keeping alive some consciousness of the supernatural and not allowing people altogether to lose their sense of guilt and of responsibility to a higher Power. Indeed, I can conceive a state of things where it would exercise a decidedly beneficial and beneficent function. Better far be superstitious than wantonly irreverent. Better superstition, too, than dogged indifference to religion, and supercilious contempt. Better rear an altar to an "unknown God" than not rear an altar at all.

And this is in full analogy with the uses of Fear in general. So long as there are causes of danger to man, so long will there be need for fear. It is the function of fear, in our mental economy, to teach us caution, and so prevent foolhardiness and irrational bravado. It educates us to prudence, and is thus a means of saving life. It says to us, "Be not over-rash". Furthermore, it is indispensable to the magistrate and the educator,

[1] See his *Essay* "Of Superstition".

in enforcing wholesome obedience; and its place in Morals and in Religion is as a preventive of wrong-doing and a guard to self-respect.

I do not, then, consider the argument from religious superstition, or rather from superstition when allied with religion, to be of very great force; and I do not think it would be regarded by others as at all weighty if it were clearly perceived and kept in mind that superstition is *not the effect* of religion, but only something that finds in religion one of the most suitable fields for its development and operation.[1]

2. Is it otherwise with the second objection to the utility of Religion? It is said : " Religion has frequently been the cause of the bitterest persecution among men ". What then? Does it thereby stand condemned as wholly detrimental to mankind ?

Note, first, that Persecution, like superstition, is not confined to religion. We meet with it in every sphere of opinion and of action where men's interests or their pretensions conflict—in politics, literature, society, commerce, as well as in religion.

---

[1] The superstitions of Voltaire, Robespierre, Napoleon, and other distinguished freethinkers of a century ago, are well known.

But note, next, that it may arise from one or more of various causes. First, it may be simply a form of that cruelty or malevolence that seems native to man—that delight in inflicting pain or suffering on a brother, purely for the delight's sake. Secondly, it may arise from wounded pride or thwarted domination—when a man feels himself hurt and his dignity humbled by his being unable to get others to think as he does or to act as he dictates: in other words, it may be impatience or intolerance of any opinion different from or opposed to one's own; with the consequent effort to *compel* others to accept our views in cases where we are unable to *persuade* them by reasoning. Thirdly, it may originate in earnestness or zeal—in a man's deep conviction of the truth of the cause that he has espoused, and of its vast importance for the good and welfare of his fellow-men. Fourthly, it may be begotten of class interest or personal selfishness—when a man suspects that opposition to, or dissent from, the cause that he upholds means the extinction of his own trade or profession, or the annihilation of his own immunities.

Clearly, the first two of these causes have no application to religion: they are anti-religious, and cannot claim any high place among human motives. The fourth, also, is non-religious, and might be passed by as such, were it not that, unfortunately, it is very apt to attach itself to religion and to play great havoc there. Caste, particularly in the pretensions of the priests, has ever been prone to plead religious sanction; and the priestly class have always been the greatest persecutors— often on the ground of caste-distinctions. But this is really outside religion. Even if Religion implied —which it does not—sacerdotal pretensions, it certainly does not empower the priests to persecute recalcitrant brothers so as thereby to enforce their own claims.

The only cause of persecution that may with considerable plausibility be maintained to be religious is the third,—*viz.*, when a man takes to persecution out of religious zeal, and is prompted to his action by unselfish conviction. This is the persecution of fanaticism. In its eagerness to accomplish its end, it is impatient of delay, and so will remove by force all resistance.

But here let us distinguish. *Zeal* is one thing, *discretion* is another; and, while earnestness and enthusiasm are noble and commendable, they need ever to be guided by judgment. It is certainly in favour of religion that it has the power of captivating the heart and securing a fervent devotion; but it is unreasonable to demand of it that it shall also impart sound judgment, so that its adherents shall

differ from all other men in never allowing their
zeal to outrun their discretion. Enough if it do
not sanction, much less require, persecution, and if
the enlightenment which it promotes is condemnatory of all attempts to further its interests in this
way.

You see, then, the argument. Misguided views
of religion cannot justly be laid at the door
of religion itself; and we are not to tax religion
with consequences which are rightly chargeable to
the abuse of it.[1]

---

[1] Abraham Tucker has some wise words on "Religion," under
that title, in his *Light of Nature Pursued.*

LECTURE VI.

THE IDEA OF GOD,
AS PSYCHOLOGICALLY DETERMINED.

II.

We pass, now, from the first question in connexion with the psychological foundation of Theism, from that which has reference to the spring or source of theism, to the second,—*viz.*, to that which is concerned with the nature of the Divine Object to whom the religious sentiment goes forth.

And, first of all, let me repeat that, as the essence of mind or spirit is activity, the law of human experience is necessarily that of mental or spiritual *progress:* it is not simply change, but advance.

By progress or advance is meant development, and not mere growth. A thing may grow without developing. In that case, its successive increments add only to its bulk, and are likely enough to be undesirable accretions. Development is from within, and *that* is true evolution. It is movement towards an ideal ; and every step not simply passes beyond and leaves behind that which preceded it, but is rendered possible only by having due regard to all that went before. In development, the material of the past is taken up into that of the present and is transmuted. Nothing that is on the line of evolution is ever really lost : it is assimilated and carried forward, and appears in the final product *transformed*.

Hence, knowledge is never rounded or completed at any one particular point of time, but, on the contrary, deepens, enlarges, and advances by a never-ceasing movement. And, as our mental horizon expands and one intellectual achievement is ever seen to lead onwards to another, we soon come to find that the range of advance is practically limitless, and that our happiness is placed in a continually-unfolding Truth. This applies both to thought and to action : indeed, it is the general condition of spiritual health. Here, at any rate, there is no life in stagnation, except such as corruption breeds.

From this, therefore, it obviously follows that God is not fully definable by us, because He is never fully known by us : our knowledge of Him develops with our increasing experience. Of necessity, the God given in experience is that of a Being not fully, yet partially, known ; but, if partially known, then not unknowable. "Not the definitely known God," as Professor Veitch puts it, "not the unknown God is our last word, far less the Unknowable God, but the ever-to-be-known God" (*Knowing and Being*, pp. 322-3). God is always greater than our conception of Him; yet we can say that, whatever else He may be, He is the perfection of all that in ourselves is highest and best, of all that is eternally valuable, that has spiritual nobility and worth.

In this truth, certain well-known spiritual facts find their explanation. If the soul can live only by expansion, then immediately we see,—(1) First, how new phases of the Divine Being should be ever and anon presenting themselves to mankind, and how clearer views of old phases should be obtained, as the ages roll. (2) Secondly (as a corollary from the first), how some phases of Divine Truth should be late in being discovered by men, and yet the latest discovered should be the highest. With deepened and lengthened experience, the hidden things of God come to light and are revealed to prepared souls. (3) Thirdly, how the test of the worth of a newly discovered or specially emphasized aspect of Divine Truth should be the readiness with which men respond to it when declared—in other words, should be the power it has of drawing men towards it and of keeping them attached. It is both "light-giving" and "fruit-bearing". (4) Fourthly, how different ages or different nations should, through social or other causes, be led to put special stress on one particular aspect of the Divine Being,—as when people, in strict monarchical days, emphasized God's Sovereignty, or when, as at the present moment, the emphasis falls upon His Fatherhood. The meaning of this just is that new life, and, therefore, new significance, may be thrown into an old truth owing to the peculiar circumstances of the leading non-religious conceptions of the time. Everybody knows the modifying effect produced upon our idea of the Creatorship of God which is being wrought before our eyes by the present dominant conception of Evolution.

From all this, it follows that Religion is wider than any one of the great historical religions of the world—much more, is wider than any outward ecclesiastical embodiment of religion now existing or ever known to have existed. Hence, too, it follows that each of the great historical religions of the world has embodied and carried forward some portion or portions of Divine Truth. But hence, further, it follows that Natural Religion may be deeply indebted to Revealed Religion, even when not identifying itself with it. In so far, at any rate, as the truths of Revealed Religion are but purified and ennobled forms of the truths of Natural Religion, they commend themselves to the enlightened searcher (altogether apart from consideration of the authoritative source whence they issued), and must be taken as a spiritual advance. I do not lay the foundation of Theism in what is usually known as Revelation; but the teaching of Revelation beneficially reacts on that of Natural Theism: and, to that extent at least, it here claims our allegiance.

This being understood, let us now take up the question definitely before us. What is the Idea of God, as psychologically determined?

(I.) The first thing that here demands our consideration is the PERSONALITY of God.[1]

But what is meant by Personality?

Personality is nothing apart from Mind. Now Mind, according to the general testimony of modern psychology, is a compound of three things, —Intellect or Cognition, Feeling, and Will: and these three things are conditioned by Consciousness.

---

[1] For, in regarding God as a Being, we necessarily regard Him as "not only All, but Lord over all; not a Something, but a Person; no It, but a *Thou*" (Van Oosterzee, *Christian Dogmatics*, Eng. transl., p. 244).

Personality, then, may be defined as intelligence, feeling, and will gathered up into a centre of conscious being. It is not intelligence, feeling, or will taken in separation, nor is it these regarded simply as a *logical* unity ; it is these regarded as an *organic* unity—held together by a living subject, which gives continuity to the various groups of states and unity to the whole.

Let me explain.

Intellect, feeling, and will we all know ; but we know nothing of them, in the first instance, except as experienced in ourselves. Now, as so experienced, they are given us, not as three isolated and independent facts, but as three mental factors combined in a conscious self or subject. This self or subject, which admits of no further definition, is what is understood by Person. It admits of no further definition, for it is itself the most ultimate of facts ; only, we may set over against it its partial and its complete contrasts—and this is, in a manner, to define it. The complete contrast is Thing or lifeless object ; which, although (as the very etymology shows) it is nothing if it is not a *subject of thought*, is, nevertheless, not itself Thought. And the partial contrasts are living objects to which we ascribe organism, but not self-consciousness,— namely, plants and animals. A thing is not a person : a plant is not a person ; we do not even, strictly, regard a brute beast, however high in the zoological scale, as a person. Personality, in so far as terrestrial beings are concerned, is confined to Man; and in this we have his leading characteristic.[1]

Unfortunately, however, Personality in the English language is an ambiguous term : it has both a specific and a generic application. Consequently, what is distinctive in an individual—it may be, pronounced self-will or excessive self-conceit ; it may be, commanding power of intellect or the fascination of character or the constraining authority of a born leader of men ; it may be, the consummate generalship of Wellington or the consuming ambition and indomitable courage of Napoleon,—but, whatever it is, this distinctive feature is usually denominated personality. But this is an abuse of words, and is greatly misleading. The personality here indicated is merely an exaggeration of some one trait of human nature ; it is what is *peculiar* to an individual, thereby marking him off from other individuals ; and it may as readily be a weakness as a strength, a defect as a virtue, an imperfection as a perfection. Call it

[1] An interesting account of the history of the term " Persona," though not with much relevance to our present purpose, is given by Professor Max Müller in his *Biographies of Words and the Home of the Aryas*, pp. 32-47.

individuality, if you care, or peculiarity, or idiosyncrasy; but not personality. Personality is a unity of all the three elements of selfhood, and not a mere excess of one; and the ideal personality, such as we attribute to God, is not the perfection of intellect or of feeling or of will, but the perfection of all these three, held together in entire harmony.

But even personality in its generic meaning may be misunderstood. Green defines it as Self-consciousness,—*i.e.*, as the quality in a subject to become an object to itself. In the *Prolegomena to Ethics* (p. 191), he says: "Personality is a term that has often been fought over without any very precise meaning being attached to it. If we mean anything else by it than the quality in a subject of being consciously an object to itself [*i.e.*, Self-consciousness], we are not justified in saying that it necessarily belongs to God and to any being in whom God in any measure reproduces or realizes Himself." Again, he says: "Self-objectification is at least the essential thing in personality". And, no doubt, Self-consciousness, as thus defined, is part of Personality; but it is not the whole. If self-consciousness were all, it does not appear how, out of this, can be got Character or any of the qualities that are distinctively ethical; nor does it appear how Emotional qualities can emerge. The Ego is more than self-reflection —it is the conscious active meeting-point of cognition, will, and feeling; and no definition of Personality can be satisfactory that does not recognize this—in other words, that does not repose on an adequate analysis of Mind. Least of all can such a definition be satisfactory as applied to the Personality of God; for, it simply suggests that "thinking upon thought" which, however real in itself, could, if standing alone, only characterize a Deity like Aristotle's—a solitary individual, living apart from the world, and occupied solely in contemplation. "God," said Aristotle (*Metaphysics*, xi.), "must think upon Himself; the thought of God is the thinking upon thought." If that be the synonym for Self-consciousness, it is, obviously, not a full rendering of Personality. Will, morality, and providence are wanting, and that supreme characteristic of Deity which Christianity denominates Love.

Personality, then, in the philosophical sense, means Selfhood; and this means the conscious activity of a living subject, manifested in feelings, thoughts, and actions, or what is emphatically now-a-days called Attention. It is not possible to explain the mind and mental experiences simply by taking the mind as a passivity. If it is passive so far as the receiving of sensations or impressions is concerned, it is essentially active in the working up of these sensations into knowledge, and in the elaborating of purposes and the effecting of resolves: in other words, it has both an intellectual and a moral aspect. And this essential activity of the mind gives us its distinctive feature, and affords us the starting-point for rationality and the reasoned interpretation of existence.

It is on this account that I have frequently referred to Personality as the highest fact in our experience, and, therefore, the category through which experience is to be understood. And it may be worth while to devote a moment's consideration to what is here meant by "highest fact in our experience"; for, although it would be generally admitted that the universe, if interpretable at all, is to be interpreted in terms of the highest fact known to us, and not in terms of anything lower, it may yet be questioned whether personality *is* this highest fact. The test of higher and lower, it may be maintained, is generality: in other words, higher and lower have no meaning except as signifying that the more general is higher than the less general; and, if so, the impersonal is in this sense higher than the personal, for it includes all lifeless things and all plants and animals lower in the scale of existence than man,—and, consequently, impersonality is the interpreting category, not personality.

But "generality" is not the true criterion of higher and lower here. The true criterion is, not the logical *extension* of the notion, or the number of individuals included under it, but the logical *intension* of the notion, its depth or comprehension, the amount of meaning it conveys. Wherefore, personality is higher, as being *more illuminative*, than impersonality : and, as the impersonal has itself no signification unless on the presupposition of the personal, the inanimate is seen ultimately to repose on life, and the non-conscious is explainable only on the postulate of underlying consciousness.

In this way, Personality, if the grounds of theism be psychological, is seen to attach to the Deity ; for, it is only when gathered up in a person and manifested in personal act that the very highest excellences—such as wisdom, love, mercy, righteousness—are intelligible to us, and it is only thus that they can affect us as really noble, or stimulate us to the imitation of these prime virtues in ourselves.

Hence, such a conception of God as that of Matthew Arnold, " the stream of tendency," " the Eternal not ourselves that makes for righteousness," is both inadequate and ineffective. It is inadequate, because an Eternal that is simply a "stream of tendency" does not, being impersonal, include the chief characteristic that human nature demands. It is ineffective, because it affords us no sufficient motive or stimulus to bring ourselves into harmony with it. All experience goes to show that it is a person that can most effectually move a person: indeed, that it is only a person, according to the doctrine (which holds as much in the spiritual as in the biological world) that life can only come from what is living. And, although by impersonal agencies we may be compelled into conformity with a particular drift or current, although by these we may be coerced into an outward harmony with what is given as righteousness,—nevertheless, this is something entirely different from a cheerful and willing obedience to a Righteous Being, in whom all righteousness is contained and by whom the perfect righteousness is exhibited.[1]

Objections.

The objections to ascribing Personality to God are apparently many, and they come from monotheists, pantheists, non-theists alike. But they all circle round one and the same idea,—namely

[1] See, also, Lecture X.

this, that personality means *limitation*, whereas God must be the unlimited.

But how, let us ask, is personality limitation; and in what sense is God conceived as the unlimited?

By " limitation " is meant several things, and these must be clearly distinguished.

1. In the first place, it means definite or restricted in *quantity ;* as, for example, limited in knowledge or in will or in power.

Now, limit in this sense is not applicable to God : it is a characteristic of finite personality alone. But, then, being restricted to finite personality, it is not essential to personality. It is imperfection or incompleteness adhering to a certain class of persons. But remove the imperfection or the incompleteness, and personality is not thereby negatived. On the contrary, it only then comes forth in all its true essential character. Difference in magnitude is not difference in kind ; and, though you alter the quantity, the quality remains the same.

2. Next, limitation may mean *defect.*

In this sense, too, it is restricted to finite personality. Men are both erring and sinful ; but neither sin nor error can be ascribed to God. But, then, neither sin nor error is of the essence

16

of personality : they are simply accidents incidental to man.

3. Thirdly, limitation may be applied to a thing to designate the fact that it is a certain individual thing and not another,—as when I say, " This is a thought and not a feeling, or a feeling and not a volition ".

But, surely, there is no appropriateness in this application of the term. There is sense in saying that a thing is limited when it does not realize the ideal of the type to which it belongs ; but none in saying it is limited because it is itself and not something else, or everything else, at the same time. There is no limit to God's knowledge, or to His love, or to His will : each of these, we must believe, is perfect—has attained the ideal of its own kind. But it is nothing less than the height of unreason to say that each of these is limited because, while being itself, it is not also the others. To demand that there shall not be the limit of distinctions in God is to demand that the Deity shall be some vast dead uniformity, which, if actually existent, would be utterly inoperative.

4. Hence, fourthly, it is no limitation, in any just sense, when we apply Reason and Reason's laws to God. This we saw already when examining Mansel's agnosticism (Lecture IV.). It is simply unmeaning verbiage to say, that God can make a

thing both be and not be at the same time, or that He can undo an act that is done.

5. But the great bugbear of limitation arises, I presume, under a fifth signification of the term. Limit, it is said, means the duality of self-consciousness—the need in every conscious being of an object of consciousness as well as a subject of consciousness, of a non-ego as well as an ego, of something thought about no less than of a thinker; and this necessity of an object to a subject limits the subject, makes it relative and dependent, and so cannot be transferred to God. " Personality," says Mansel, "as we conceive it, is essentially a limitation and a relation. Our own personality is presented to us as relative and limited; and it is from that presentation that all our representative notions of personality are derived. Personality is presented to us as a relation between the conscious self and the various modes of his consciousness. There is no personality in abstract thought without a thinker: there is no thinker, unless he exercise some mode of thought. Personality is also a limitation; for the thought and the thinker are distinguished from and limit each other; and the several modes of thought are distinguished each from each by limitation likewise" (*Limits of Religious Thought*, p. 56).

Now, the nature of Thought is, indeed, a

duality; a subject needs an object, thinker implies something thought. But what propriety is there in calling this a limitation, or in affirming that it would be derogatory to God? It would only be derogatory to God, would only be a "limitation" in any valid sense, if the object of thought were itself something apart from God (the Thinker) and co-ordinate with Him. The object of thought need not even be material: it may be simply a subject-object, an "eject" (giving a new meaning to Clifford's term),[1]—it may be simply thought itself. But, even in the case of the *material* world regarded as object of thought: this is not a self-existent independent reality (only a crude philosophy could represent it so), and, therefore, cannot be a limitation.

Even *potential* existence is no true limitation. The potential to God, indeed, could not be, if God be conceived simply as a Deity dwelling apart, having no relation to Time—transcendent, but not immanent. But such an isolated Deity we refuse to believe in; He is simply the product of abstract thought. If God be *in* the world, as well as

---

[1] Clifford meant by "eject" the individual human being's inference of consciousness and mind in other human beings. These are not "objects" to him, they are *outside* his own consciousness; they are *ejected* or *thrown out* of his consciousness, and recognized as not being a part of himself.

greater than it, He must work under time's conditions; and the distinction of "actual" and "potential" is, to that extent, relevant to Him. Here, indeed, the philosophical *prius* is the actual, if by "actual" we mean with Aristotle *end* or *purpose;* but in Time-evolution, from which we cannot shut out the Deity, the potential has its meaning and its place.

6. Hence, sixthly, there is little force in the objection that Personality, being conditioned by time, is inapplicable to the Deity, inasmuch as the Deity is out of time—is eternal.

For, first, eternal does not mean "out of time": it means *never-ending.* As applied to God, it means, "without beginning of days or end of life": it is that to which no limit in time can be set.

Then, next, timelessness, in the sense of "out of time," is for us an empty term. Being ourselves in time, we can form no notion of an existence out of time, nor really attach to it a definite meaning. What we know is that, although in time, we ourselves have thought-processes (conception, for instance) into which no consciousness of time enters. And we know, further, that God is revealed to us in time, and not out of it; and on this time-revelation we can build. We have got, somehow or other, to conceive time as an imperfection, a defect; just as some people speak of it as though it were an actual substance, and others as though it were a living creature. But time is no defect. What is a defect is man's ignorance of the real properties and relations of things, and, consequently, his ignorance of how principles will work themselves out in time. What is a defect is man's incompetence to make sure that what he wills against a future day will actually be done when that day arrives, and his impatience with time's delays. There is nothing to lead us to suppose that it is mere time that makes men's judgment to err with respect to the future. The ground of their error lies in the fact that they have only a limited acquaintance with only a limited number of things, and a limited power of controlling them. But given adequate knowledge of the properties and collocations of things, given exact acquaintance with the constitution of the universe and of all the forces therein at work (such as we must ascribe to God), and, even under time's conditions, we obtain a very real meaning of Omniscience and Divine prevision; and we can see how this omniscience should be unerring, while yet it refers to things that will happen many days hence.

Says Jevons: "We may safely accept as a satisfactory scientific hypothesis the doctrine so grandly put forth by Laplace, who asserted that a perfect knowledge of the universe, as it existed at any given moment, would give a perfect knowledge of what was to happen thenceforth and for ever after" (*The Principles of Science*, bk. vi.).

7. But, lastly, another form of the notion that lies at the root of the reluctance to regard God as a Person is the idea that, by so regarding Him, we reduce Him to the position of one individual among a countless number of others. But this does not follow, if the individuals, countless in number, are all finite and are all dependent upon Him. It would only follow, if each had a distinct existence of his own. *Derived* personality is one thing: *self-existent* personality is quite another.

Summary and Conclusion.

We need not, then, find personality an insuperable barrier to our Theistic structure. It may quite legitimately be ascribed to God, because it is not necessarily finite. It would only be necessarily finite, if the correct idea of it were that of an Ego as one reality set over against a Non-ego as another reality, each absolutely distinct and independent. But this is by no means the true conception of Personality, nor is it given by the logical doctrine of Correlation. "It suffices for laying the foundation of personality," as Lotze truly remarks, "if a spiritual being has the faculty of apprehending itself as 'I' in opposition to its own states, which are only its 'states' and not 'I'. A relation to an external reality [a *real* non-ego, of such kind that this *as such* might enter into consciousness and the ego thus be posited in opposition to this perceived non-ego, and thereby become limited] is not necessary ; and, consequently, 'personality' also is not bound to the condition of *finiteness*,—to wit, to that of being limited by another reality of the same kind " (*Outlines of the Philosophy of Religion*, Prof. Ladd's transl., pp. 64, 65).[1]

(II.) From the Personality of God, let us pass next to His UNITY : God is ONE.

" One " here is opposed to " many ". It is the antithesis of idolatry and polytheism, in its widest sense, as the worship of " gods many and lords many," as well as of polytheism in that narrower sense sometimes known as " monolatry," which regards heathenism at the stage where the multiplicity of gods becomes specialized into local or national deities—like the patron or protecting saints of mediaeval Christendom.

As opposed, then, to polytheism in its various

---

[1] See also the *Mikrokosmus*, bk. ix. c. iv.

forms, monotheism (or the doctrine that God is one) commends itself to the enlightened reason; and, as the rational alóne is true, we cannot refuse to accept it. Anything like a hierarchy of deities, such as the ancient Greeks had, with Zeus at the top and perhaps Dionysus at the bottom, does not meet the deepest requirements of the case; much less does the Roman deification of the Emperors, which simply marks the decadence of Religion.

The doctrine of one God, or Monotheism, is easily traced to its springs in human nature. There is, first, the sense or feeling of dependence on some Being who is competent to meet our wants—those of them that we ourselves are unable to cope with. There is, next, the rational necessity superinduced on this feeling, which drives us (half-unconsciously, it may be) to the conclusion that this Being must be one and supreme; for, as the deepest wants of one human being are found to be precisely those of another, and as no man can supply his own wants, much less those of his fellow, the ultimate resting-place is *one* God, the Author and Father of mankind, whose care for His own creatures is unbounded and whose tender mercies are over all His works. *Many* deities, with different and conflicting interests (like those of the Greek pantheon), would, obviously, not be the final resting-place; while a plurality of deities, each with the same goodwill and intention towards us, and each equally powerful to supply our needs, would, no less clearly, be a wasteful and perplexing reduplication of agents. Taken any way you please, Polytheism, although not actually absurd, is indefensible. A tutelar deity, tribal or national, would simply be a local protector, a magnified patron, alike susceptible to his client's flatteries and jealous of the claims of competitors ; and, so, outrages the fact of the solidarity of the race. A hierarchy of divinities is an unmanageable conception, if the divinities themselves are not in unison ; and it is an unnecessary conception, if they are. As, moreover, we need the element of unchangeableness in the Deity, this is not likely to be got in a hierarchy : it is given securely only in the conception of a being One and Supreme.

But, further, the human want that secures God to man is of a peculiar kind. It holds a unique position among natural wants—namely this, that it is not a want of one particular part of our being, but of every part of it. We need a God to whom we shall give an undivided attachment and obedience –a God who shall meet our intellectual, our emotional, our volitional, and our moral requirements ; a God who shall uplift us, and, in uplifting, shall ennoble us wholly,—one in communion with whom we shall find ourselves bettered, and by attachment to whom we shall attain rest.

But the gods of polytheism and idolatry cannot thus affect us. Instead of elevating, they have a tendency to degrade us, and in serving them we should dissipate our energies, instead of concentrating and conserving them. The Object of worship, in order to exalt us, must Himself be high,—neither the work of a man's own hands, nor the mere creation of his fancy. To worship stocks and stones is to abnegate reason, and that can never raise us ; and to put fictions in the room of the Great Reality can only end in disastrous consequences.

Nevertheless, although polytheism (including idolatry) is thus an abnegation of reason, the forms of it are not all equally degrading. The lowest form is when a man takes a stock or a stone and makes it his personal fetish ; when he accepts it simply as a temporary deity, suited to serve a particular purpose and after that to be disowned, and when he looks upon it simply as *his* god. This is really the religion of selfishness. The worshipper here regards himself as the sole object of concern, and his own interest as the sole actuating principle of his obeisance. Considerably higher is the conception of a *household* god, of a god protecting a home or family (*lares* or *penates*) ; for, the worshipper now regards himself, not as an individual, but as the member of a group, and feels his own interest to be (partly or wholly) bound up in the interest of the group. It is higher still when the tutelar deity becomes tribal or national; for, with every advance in the widening of the conception, comes a corresponding widening in the individual worshipper's human sympathies (in his sympathy for his fellow-men) and a corresponding merging of self-interest in the interest of others. Still, until you reach monotheism, you cannot attain the idea of universal brotherhood or cosmopolitanism. Only when you look upon God as One, can you conceive Him as Father of the race, and all men as "made of one blood". Polytheism, even at its best, is narrow and cramping, and is tainted with selfishness. Monotheism alone can adequately recognize the solidarity of man, and, at the same time, fully conserve the place and the rights of the individual.

This is the same thing as saying that polytheism, although it may rightly enough be spoken of as a religion, is incompetent, under any form, to give the highest and purest conception of Religion. Religion, in its most general signification, may be defined as men's sense of dependence on a being or beings higher and greater than themselves, affecting them for evil or for good, in union with whom blessedness is found, and to whom allegiance is due. But, though this be religion in its most general meaning, the specific content wherewith it is filled up, as civilization advances and man's spiritual insight and spiritual experience increase, makes an enormous difference. Nature-worship, or the recognition of natural forces as mighty powers needing to be propitiated, is one thing; it is quite another thing when the Object of worship is looked upon as one, gathering up in Himself all power and using the forces of nature only as His instruments or agents. It is a further thing still when you endow Him with the highest wisdom and the purest love,—conceive of Him as one supreme righteous Being, who, while all-powerful is also all-good, and whose dealings with mankind are prompted by a Father's affection and directed by a Father's wisdom. The conception is now fully justified both to the heart and to the reason.

Monotheism, then, has its root in man's sense of dependence on a Higher Power, and it is safe-guarded by rational considerations. Polytheism, however it may rest on man's sense of dependence, is lacking in the support of reason.

Historical.

1. The non-rationality of polytheism was early seen in cultured Greece. As far back as the days of the Eleatics, the gods of the popular pantheon

were strenuously attacked. We have already seen (Lecture III.) how Xenophanes assailed them. His example was eagerly followed by others. Not only did Parmenides and the rest of the Eleatic school strike at the heathen worship through philosophy, but they attempted to establish its irrationality on purely metaphysical grounds. To them, *unity* was the interpreting term of the existent, and such unity, divine and all-embracing, as excluded the possibility of change or becoming in any absolute sense. Their doctrine, therefore, was pantheism,—which absorbed polytheism. From a different standpoint, Democritus and the Atomists generally pursued the attack, and they were joined by the Epicureans. Neither of these sects denied the existence of the gods, but both of them excluded the gods from the world, relegated them to a sphere outside nature, and thereby practically ignored them. It was the Sophists, however, who really initiated the era of efficient criticism, and generated among the Greeks a spirit of scepticism which went far to undermine the popular religious convictions. They were, in this respect, ably seconded by the poets. They had, on the one hand, the aid of Euripides,[1] who "represents the

---

[1] Of Euripides, Mr. James Freeman Clarke says:—"His is the anti-religious tragedy. It is a sneering defiance of the religious sentiment, a direct teaching of pessimism" (*Ten Great Religions,* p. 285).

reaction against the religious tragedy"; and, on the other hand, the help of Aristophanes, who, though himself a *laudator temporis acti*, does, by the way in which he brings the gods on the stage, expose the popular religion to public ridicule. Paradoxical though it may seem, the Sophists were also seconded by Socrates. Whatever quarrel Socrates had with the Sophists, he was here fully at one with them. Not, however, in the *spirit* of his attack. While *they* were essentially sceptical, *he* was reverentially inquisitive; and, though he ultimately suffered death as an "atheist," his atheism, as he himself well knew, was the worthiest theism. After Socrates, came Plato and Aristotle, —whose whole systems were pronouncedly anti-polytheistic, each on its own lines; and the contest did not cease when they were gone. Whether with high-toned purpose (as among the Cynics), or with less spiritual penetration and from lower motives (as among the Cyrenaics and the Epicureans), polytheism was effectually disowned by the educated and the thoughtful. Sometimes a near approach to positive monotheism was put in its place,—as when Antisthenes opposed to the many gods of Greek heathenism one pure God, invisible to sense, unpicturable to the imagination, unrepresentable by symbol; who was best served, not by outward homage, not by sacrifices and ceremonies, but by righteous living. Sometimes the result was negative—that God there is *not*, in any proper sense of the term, but that Nature (as with Democritus), with its atoms, its uniformity, and fixed laws, is all. Sometimes (as with the Peripatetics) it was a qualified theism, what was known in Britain in last century as Deism,—the doctrine that God *is*, and that He brought the world into existence, but that, having done so, He retired beyond its circle, leaving it to work out its own destiny. Sometimes, again, it was pantheism—as with Parmenides in earlier days. But, whatever was the substitute, philosophy in all its sects and schools was done with polytheism : native Greek intellect had been strong enough to overthrow it. For, undoubtedly, when the idea of the divine unity was reached in Greece, it was arrived at, as Zeller very justly says, "less by way of syncretism than of criticism ; not by blending the many gods into one, but by combating the principle of polytheism" (*Pre-Socratic Philosophy*, Eng. transl., vol. i. p. 65).

What happened among the Greeks happened also among the Romans. Progressing intelligence saw that the popular theology was irrational, and the conscience felt that a doctrine that fostered immorality could not be true. The final result was greatly aided by Rome's intercourse with Athens—whence, as we know, Greek philosophy was transported as a living power to revolutionize Latin thought and Latin manners.

2. Considering the part that philosophy thus played in effecting the downfall of polytheism, it is interesting to observe what were the kinds of argument that availed in this great work.

(1) One chief method of attack was *sarcasm.*

This was the method of Xenophanes. Other Greeks followed in the same vein : though it must be allowed that the Greek philosophers as a rule, knowing what the end of determined and too outspoken opposition to the popular theology would be, were more cautious and reserved. They found it best not to pose as so-called "atheists" but to countenance the popular religion, while they taught a philosophic doctrine that really subverted it.

It was different, somewhat later, when the popular theology was visibly losing its hold. Sarcasm then became a very powerful weapon—as in the hands of Lucian, "the satirist and wit, the prose Aristophanes of later Greece".

Sarcasm, too, in early Christian times, was the great Patristic instrument of aggression. It is wielded with much dexterity by Justin Martyr;

17

and other early Apologists are quite alive to its importance.

The forms of Sarcasm, however, have been various. Sometimes (as with Xenophanes) it was founded on the rational objection to anthropomorphism; but more frequently (as with Lucian and the Christian Apologists) it was aimed at the glaring inconsistencies and moral defects of the mythical gods—their amours, rivalries, jealousies, domestic quarrels, and so forth.

(2) But a second mode of attack was, acknowledging the gods in set speech, but ignoring them so far as any real efficient action in the world was concerned. This was the prime method of Epicurus,—best exemplified, perhaps, in the Roman poet Lucretius. There are gods indeed (it is admitted), and they created the world; but it is simply presumption and self-conceit on man's part to suppose that they take any interference in mundane affairs. It would be beneath their dignity to interest themselves in any way in anything so petty and insignificant as man. *There* they are, living in happiness and blissful ease away beyond the created world, and cries and prayers from suffering beings on earth can never reach them. When they formed the world, they gave it its immutable laws, and then withdrew from it, to live in a state of *otium cum dignitate*, allowing it

to go its own way according to the form originally prescribed to it; and man's wisdom lies in studying Nature and its laws, and in conforming to the inevitable as best he can.

In this teaching of Lucretius, do we not seem to be listening to some modern scientist?

(3) Still another method, and possibly the most effective of all, was that of not boldly attacking, but quietly sapping, the popular faith. This was done by inculcating doctrines that, when assimilated, would of themselves produce an alienation from polytheism, and the false would fall away of its own accord, simply from men's lack of interest in it.

This was the philosopher's way *par excellence*. Parmenides adopted it in the interest of pantheism; Plato used it in the interest of a high-toned spiritualistic philosophy; and it was employed by Aristotle in his magnificent efforts to organize human knowledge and to give to thinking a rigorously scientific expression. It was practised, too, by Cicero, who, though outwardly acknowledging the popular deities, did what he could in his philosophical writings to undermine them and to substitute morality for religion; while Varro "does not throw even the decent veil of Cicero over his conclusions, but openly urges his countrymen to maintain the ceremonies and culture of the State religion, while they acknowledge to themselves that such beliefs are false, and such practices futile" (Merivale, *The Contrast between Pagan and Christian Society*, p. 28).

(III.) The third element in the Theistic conception is, that God is ALL-PERFECT.

This follows from the fact that God is a necessity of human nature. For, whatever else He is, He must, if adequate to meet our wants, be the source and consummation of all that is noble and good in ourselves: He must possess all our excellences, with the defects and finite limitations removed. Hence we say that He is (1) Omniscient, and, therefore, Omnipresent; (2) All-holy,—ideally righteous, just, and true; (3) Omnipotent and All-wise; (4) All-merciful and All-good. This is so obvious that we need not dwell upon it.

(IV.) Lastly, God is both IMMANENT and TRANSCENDENT.

The God that man's deepest wants demand is not a bare Creator, who, having brought the world into existence, with its furniture and living creatures, withdrew from it and left it henceforth to itself. Not a God dwelling in a distant region apart, in supreme indifference to all created things, not one simply " sitting upon the circle of the earth," will satisfy our better nature; but a God who, while greater than us, is also near to us: "Closer is He than breathing, and nearer than hands and feet". A Creator is, indeed, required; but not in the abstract sense that is usually accepted. We need a Creator who is also the Sustainer of His own work, and so is ever present in it. Though not confined to one place, God must be also *here;* and, while He imparts life to His creatures, He must also constantly maintain and quicken that life. The world cannot monopolize the Deity; but, at the same time, it cannot dispense with His perpetual presence and His continual protecting power.

This, I take it, was the truth that Anaxagoras in the days of old was aiming to express when he said that "Mind (Intelligence, Νοῦς) is that which set in order and was the cause of all things". For, though he himself does not put this doctrine to its full theistic use, nor indeed apply it rigorously in his rational explanation of the universe, and so comes under the rebuke of Socrates and also of Aristotle, there can be little question that it lends itself naturally and readily to the explanation of the world on the principle of the immanence of the Deity. For, Anaxagoras's Nous was a spiritual essence, itself unmoved but the cause of motion—

in other words, the spiritual force that formed the world, changing the chaos of matter into a cosmos. Given Matter and given Motion, yet Anaxagoras could not see (with Empedocles and Leucippus), nor would he have seen with our modern cosmic theorizers, that you have explained the universe. You have to account for motion itself, and *that* Matter cannot do. Hence, Nous or Intelligence becomes imperative. But here, practically, Anaxagoras stopped. His whole problem was to account for the Cosmos; and, having done this, he seems not to have pushed his inquiries further into the nature of the primitive world-forming mind. It was Socrates's great complaint against him (see the *Phædo*) that, when you came to him wishing and expecting to hear all about this intelligent ordering cause of the universe, you were put off with a discourse about natural and mechanical causes— "air, æther, water, and many other things equally absurd". Nevertheless, Anaxagoras ascribed to the world-forming Intelligence unchangeableness and omniscience, and his own starting-point in philosophy was the human Ego. Does it not thence follow that, as unchangeableness and omniscience are attributes of an Ego, the logical outcome of the Anaxagorean principles was the identification of Nous with God? Moreover, Anaxagoras ascribes Nous, not only to men, but, in a lesser degree, to

animals, and, in a still lesser degree, to plants. Is
he not here groping his way towards an articulate
expression of God's all-pervading presence? We are
unreasonable when we expect absolute clearness,
rigorous logic, and unwavering consistency in the
first originator of a great conception. It is enough
if we can see that Anaxagoras is on the track of a
deep truth, and that he felt, though dimly, that his
mechanical causes are not the ultimate explanation of the universe. His procedure is quite in
keeping with that of great physicists and theists
of later times. Both Sir Isaac Newton and Kant
(the latter, at least, in his *General History of Nature
and Theory of the Heavens*) devoted themselves to
the mechanical interpretation of Nature; but both
also strongly maintained the compatibility of the
mechanical explanation with the *teleological* view,
which regards Nature as dependent upon and
significant of God.[1] Perhaps, of moderns, none is
stronger than Hermann Lotze in maintaining the
same thing:[2] and Lotze has many followers.

But the relation of God to the universe may
be viewed in a one-sided way, giving thereby only
a partial truth.

[1] Kant, however, eschewed teleology in his later works.
[2] This is seen in many parts of the *Mikrokosmus*; but special
reference may be made to bk. iii. chap. v. and bk. iv.

We have already seen that the Atomists and certain others in Greek antiquity located the gods outside the world and left the latter simply to the play of its own inherent forces. The Deists of last century did very much the same thing. This is, obviously, altogether inadequate. God's transcendence does not mean His existence *outside* the world, but is a brief way of expressing the fact that it is on Him that the world is dependent. If God is, He must have a continual interest in that which He Himself produced.

But not less inadequate is it to maintain the immanence of God, while denying His transcendence. This is what is done by Pantheists. "*Deus,*" says Spinoza, "*est omnium rerum causa immanens, non vero transiens*" (*Ethics*, bk. i. prop. xviii.). But this is to assert either of two things, neither of which is competent to explain the universe and our experience. It is either to say that God is only one principle in the universe along with others—and then He ceases to be God, even although we conceive this Divinity as the generically highest principle. Or, it is to say that the universe itself is God—in which case we part with all those distinctions of personality, rectitude, etc., that are of the most vital importance for knowledge and for morality alike. If God be simply the totality of things, the mystery remains pre-

cisely where it was : the word "totality" explains
nothing. If He be merely a principle enclosed in
this totality, He is a subordinate Deity needing to
be referred to something higher.[1]

III.

We have now seen the meaning of the position
that God is a necessity of human nature ; we have
seen what, psychologically determined, is the Idea
of God ; and we have also emphasized the fact
that, as human nature is progressive, this implies
a corresponding progressiveness in the revelation
of the Divine character and attributes. It only
now remains to complete this branch of our subject by casting a glance at what Bunsen called
"God in History," and Lessing "the Education of
the Human Race," or what may be otherwise
denominated History's testimony to the being and
nature of God.

If God is, He must have a distinct connexion
with the creatures of His own hand, and His contact and relations with them must be discernible
in their lives and history. Not only must the
individual man bear witness to His power and

---

[1] For an interesting historical account, briefly put, of the transcendence of God in both Greek and Christian Theology, see Lecture
ix. of Hatch's *Hibbert Lectures.*

presence, but human history must testify to His over-ruling providence and paternal care. Not, indeed, that we may find ourselves able to trace His workings there save in broad and general outline the field is too large and the matter too complex to admit of anything more. But this general outline must at any rate be possible. This at least we must be able to say, " Lo, these are parts of His ways," even though we may have, at the same time, to confess, " But how little a portion is heard of Him !"

The idea of the historical testimony here dealt with, practically originated with the Hebrews. The Jewish national government was explicitly theocratic. When Moses desired to see the " face " of God, it was not permitted him; he was allowed simply to see His " back ". That revelation to the Jewish lawgiver in the cleft of the rock may be taken as an allegory. Even then, it was felt that the Deity could be best discerned by the traces of Him discoverable when He had passed by. Indeed, the Jewish history was itself conceived as a theophany: and, in this light, the historical books of the Old Testament (such as *Joshua* and *Samuel*) were classed by the Jews themselves among the books of *prophecy*. Belief in human progress and in an over-ruling Providence was of the very essence of the Hebrew faith : and, thereby, it stands contrasted with all other ancient teaching. Perhaps, it might have been expected that ancient Greek and Roman thought would have approximated to it here; but (with the partial exception of the Greek tragic poetry and of Herodotus's tentative generalizations) it did not. "In Greek authors of classical times," says Professor Butcher, "there is no trace of the thought that the human race as a whole, or any single people, is advancing towards a divinely appointed good : there is nothing of what the moderns mean by the 'Education of the World,' 'the Progress of the Race,' 'the Divine guidance of nations'. The first germ of the thought is in Polybius (*circ.* 204-122 B.C.), whose work illustrates the idea of a providential destiny presiding over the march of Roman history, and building up the imperial power of Rome for the good of mankind. Diodorus Siculus, again (*circ.* 59 B.C.), speaks of the gratitude due to those historians who, seeing men bound together by natural kinship but separated in place and time, have attempted to bring them together in one ordered whole (ὑπὸ μίαν καὶ τὴν αὐτὴν σύνταξιν ἀγαγεῖν), therein making themselves the ministers of Divine Providence (ὥσπερ τινὲς ὑπουργοὶ τῆς θείας προνοίας γενηθέντες). The notion of a universal history is here based on the sentiment of the unity of the human race and of its hope for the future" (*Some Aspects of the Greek Genius*, pp. 155-6).

But, although the doctrine of God in history may be said to have been characteristic of the Jews, neither the philosophy of this doctrine nor the systematic attempt to exemplify it from general history is,[1] of course, to be found with them. Indeed, these were hardly possible till Christianity arose, with its bold insistence on the Fatherhood of God and the solidarity of the race; and, even then, we have to wait for St. Augustine with his *Civitas Dei*, before we get them in a really distinct form. In their present guise, however, they are of modern birth, and may, without much departure from truth, be said to owe their existence to the Germans (beginning with Lessing), but are specially associated with the name of Hegel; while, in recent years, they have been cultivated in our own country, with marked results, by Bunsen, Buckle, Mr. Lecky, and Professor Flint.

According to Hegel, the philosophic value of human history is, that it shows us in concrete form the development or evolution of Rational Freedom,

[1] We have the germ of this, however, in the prophecies concerning the nations,—which look upon the nations from the point of view of their relation to the kingdom of God.

as part of the working out of the Idea, in the well-known threefold manner of the Hegelian dialectic. Beginning simply as the Idea, it starts in an abstract and impoverished fashion having no real content and being indeed equivalent to non-being. It, next, objectifies itself by passing over into Nature, where it comes into contact with the concrete and the particular. And, lastly, disengaging itself from Nature, it returns upon itself as free Spirit fraught with meaning and content, rich with the treasures of self-consciousness—like the rewarded bee returning to its hive laden with honey ; not, however, "before it has gone through all the stages of individual life, and realized itself in many outward forms, with which stages and forms the philosophy of spirit is conversant. One of the forms in which the concrete conscious spirit realizes itself is the State, and the philosophy of history is that part of the philosophy of spirit which traces the evolution of reason manifesting itself as the State" (Prof. Flint, *The Philosophy of History*, p. 497). " Philosophy," says Hegel, "concerns itself only with the glory of the Idea mirroring itself in the History of the World. Philosophy escapes from the weary strife of passions that agitate the surface of society into the calm region of contemplation ; that which interests it is the recognition of the process of development which the Idea has passed through in realizing itself,—*i.e.*, the Idea of Freedom, whose reality is the consciousness of Freedom and nothing short of it. That the History of the World, with all the changing scenes which its annals present, is this process of development and the realization of Spirit,—this is the true *Theodicæa*, the justification of God in History. Only *this* insight can reconcile Spirit with the History of the World, *viz.*, that what has happened, and is happening every day, is not only not 'without God,' but is essentially His Work" (*Lectures on the Philosophy of History*, Eng. transl., p. 477).

Now, this Hegelian "Idea": how to understand it has been the great difficulty—more particularly in its relation to personality and in connexion with the Divine. Theistic, pantheistic, atheistic interpretations have all been given. But, interpretation apart, what is valuable for us all is, that herein Hegel clearly recognized that the world is not blindly ruled by chance, but is informed with thought; and so he taught the propriety and the necessity of reading history with an intelligent regard to the development or unfolding of rational tendencies or ends.

Accepting this teaching, we approach History with intelligent regard; and what, I think, we find is :—

That the rational tendencies are really the
disclosures of a Divine plan : in other words, that
God rules in the world, and that His purposes
with man are, in part, unambiguously declared.

1. First, we find that human actions, on the
large scale, or on the stage of history, do show a
tendency, with many fluctuations, towards progress, righteousness, and freedom. This is particularly seen in such a case as that of Political
Liberty, which, through much struggle and after
many vicissitudes of fortune, has at last achieved
success in the leading nations of the civilized
world, and is, obviously, on the road to universal
victory. It is shown, again, in the case of Slavery :
where emancipation was long indeed in coming,
yet it came at last : and it too is on the way to
universal victory. Again, it is shown in the
vindication of the rights of Conscience, in the
emancipation of Women, in the development of
the Universal Brotherhood of men, and in many
similar movements, which have for their impelling
motive the conviction of the sacredness of personality and the worth of man, and which find their
justification in the maxim, " Be a person, and
respect others as persons ".

2. But the way in which these momentous and

far-reaching results have been wrought out impresses us with a second principle,—namely this, the presence of a guiding or over-ruling Providence : or, if you prefer to express it so, the fact of an immanent Deity.

This is best felt when we consider the surpassing vastness of the spiritual issues that mankind have achieved, in the face of apparently insurmountable difficulties, and at moments when failure seemed to be entire and final. Human progress has not been a straight line, but a complex curve ; and, out of man's weakness, strength has been extracted. There is no question that the present supremacy of some of the noblest and most dearly cherished principles—such as Freedom and Humanity -were not gained by men, in all ages and in every land, banding themselves together and deliberately setting these principles before them as objects of pursuit, consciously and determinedly striving after them, harmoniously supporting each other in the effort to secure their triumph, working shoulder to shoulder or hand in hand. On the contrary, the great, and sometimes perhaps the sole, hindrance to the earlier success of great principles was just the opposition, temporary yet intense, of men themselves. The dead resistance came, not from opposing fate or from untoward environment, but from human wills doggedly resolved to withstand innovation and to maintain the *status quo*. Yet this dead resistance was ultimately broken through, and men's fatuous behaviour, even their barbarism and lawless exercise of brute force, their selfishness, their cruelties and their acts of injustice, were over-ruled for good. This over-ruling for good, so often unexpected, and in ways and by means contrary to all expectation, taken in connexion with the onward flow of righteousness (temporarily obstructed, indeed, yet never permanently impeded), its irresistible continuous march to final victory, unhasting yet unresting, this, I say, testifies to the thoughtful of the presence and the guidance of One who manifests Himself in history, because history deals with human beings and eternal interests, and human beings and eternal interests are His: in other words, it shows that, on the large scale, "judgment is laid to the line and righteousness to the plummet," and that man's true place and destiny are not problematical.

Note, particularly, the point of our argument. It is shown by history that, measured on the vast scale, human actions have been on the whole in the line of freedom, righteousness, and progress. But this ultimate pointing of corporate human action (including, of course, all the great institutions—social, political and religious—in which corporate action has embodied itself) towards a great end can, under the circumstances, only be fully accounted for on the supposition of an over-ruling Providence or an immanent Deity, and of man's being under a Divine education. For, sometimes the darkness and corruption on the earth have been so great and so long continued that movement onwards, after such a prodigious check, seemed impossible ; and sometimes the final result has been so much vaster and immeasurably better than men themselves expected, and has been effected by instruments so humble, that we are driven by an irresistible logic to the conclusion that a greater than man is here. The argument is, that a purpose and a plan are discernible in human history, wrought through man and in accordance with the principles of human nature, yet higher than what man, with his limited prescience, his faltering judgment, his vacillating morality, his intellectual and other weaknesses, could consciously have intended or effectually achieved. It is inductively proved that there is God in history. As Hegel, in the *Logic*, puts it : " Reason is as cunning as it is powerful. Cunning may be said to lie in the inter-mediative action, which, while it permits the objects to follow their own bent and act upon one another, till they waste away, and does not itself directly interfere in the process, is nevertheless only working out the execution of its own aims. With this explanation, Divine Providence may be said to stand to the world and its process in the capacity of absolute cunning. God lets men direct their particular passions and interests as they please ; but the result is the accomplishment of— not their plans, but His, and these differ decidedly from the ends primarily sought by those whom He employs" (Wallace's transl., p. 302). Long before this, Shakespeare had said :—

> There's a divinity that shapes our ends,
> Rough-hew them how we will.

But, even if there were less inductive proof of God's presence in history than there is, we should still be bound to believe that human history manifested God, though we might fail to perceive it, if, *on other grounds than those of history*, we were convinced of God's existence. For, if God exists, He cannot simply be the God of men as individuals ; He must have to do with them in their corporate condition—as families, tribes, nations, yea, as a race. Man as an individual, as distinct from man as a *social* unit, is an abstraction, a nonentity. A man is essentially the member of a community, the part of an organic whole ; and the individual and his good are inseparably bound up in the existence and the good of the whole.

Grant, then, that God is, and you must also grant that His presence and His action are marked in human history, though you might not yourself be able clearly to discover it, or though you doubted the alleged discovery, in some particular cases, on the part of others.

So, God in history is only part of the doctrine that God is a necessity of human nature. The one follows from the other, or the one supplements the other. A Deity inattentive to His own creatures, or indifferent to their ultimate destination, would not meet our deepest spiritual wants. If He is *my* God, He must also be *yours*; if He has a purpose for *me* as being one of "His offspring," He must have a purpose for the whole offspring also; and, if I can discern His purpose in my own case, His purpose must be discernible (to some extent) in the case of the race. The premisses are given, and the conclusion follows :—

> One God, one law, one element,
> And one far-off divine event,
> To which the whole creation moves.

THE SECOND COURSE OF LECTURES.

1893.

LECTURE VII.

IN my last Course of Lectures, I laid down as explicitly as I could, and developed to the extent that the time at my command allowed, the doctrine of the psychological basis and logical grounds of Theism. It remains for me now to carry forward the argument into the various mental provinces of emotion, volition, and intellect. I make the commencement to-day with the Emotions.

Lord Kames, in his *Elements of Criticism* (vol. i. c. iii.), has said: "It is the province of a writer upon ethics, to give a full enumeration of all the passions; and of each separately to assign the nature, the cause, the gratification, and the effects". By "passions" here is to be understood "emotions" (for, that was the signification of the term in Kames's day, as it was also in Aristotle's); *i.e.*, those complex, secondary, and derived feelings which go considerably beyond bare sensations, and of which the intellectual characteristics are parti-

(277)

cularly pronounced, thereby marking them off pre-eminently as the "higher" feelings. They are essentially "ideational or representative," but involve representation of the vague, indefinite kind; and, on the physiological side, they are *centrally-*initiated feelings, - as distinguished from most kinds of sensations,[1] which are *peripherally*-initiated. And, thus regarded, Lord Kames's statement may be accepted as correct, with certain obvious and necessary qualifications. These qualifications are: (1) That the Passions or Emotions, though properly falling to be handled by the ethicist, do not by any means constitute the whole of his province; and (2) that, although he must enumerate and classify the emotions, and, to a large extent, assign their "nature, cause, gratification, and effects," nevertheless, an absolutely complete enumeration is not necessary, even if it were possible –the great *typical* instances being, in most cases, all that is required; while, of many of the Emotions (Beauty, for instance), the "causes" are so numerous that he may well be excused if he contents himself with less than a *full* enumeration of them.

From the point of view of emotional theism, far less will be demanded of us than what is expected of the systematic ethicist. It will be sufficient if we deal simply with those great uni-

---

[1] The exceptions are found among the Muscular feelings.

versal emotions that give a distinct psychological basis to the religious sentiment.

I.

(i.) The first that I shall mention are of an aesthetic character,- *viz.*, Awe, Sublimity, and Beauty.

1. In order to understand Awe, we must bring it into direct comparison with Fear; for, fear and awe are often confounded, and many anthropologists and not a few philosophers (led by Hume, echoing Lucretius) ascribe the beginning of Religion to Fear.

What, then, is meant by Fear? Socrates, in the *Protagoras* (§ 119), has defined it as "a certain expectation of evil". But this, though so far true, is not enough. Two differentiæ are required; for (1) not only is Fear the sense or feeling of impending evil, it is also (2) loss of nerve, or want of self-confidence, in view of the expected evil. It has an unhinging and deranging effect both on the body and on the mind, and, in its perfected form, paralyzes action. Moreover, when past, it is found to have left behind it *dislike*, or even *hatred*, of the object that generated it, prompting to retaliation and revenge. In this way, it is seen to be essentially a repelling, not an attractive, force.

But if so, then obviously Fear cannot be the ground or originator of Religion, though it may have to do with the moulding and development of the religious disposition, and with the creation of superstitious rites and ceremonies. For Religion, as facing the objects of fear— whether natural and real (earthquakes, storms, etc.), or merely mental and fictitious,— reposes on the notion that the object feared may be propitiated and its malign or disastrous consequences averted. But what is this but saying that the terrifying object has also a beneficent or milder side? And it is to this idea of the beneficence that is in it that Religion really attaches. Evil, maleficence, and harm simply stir in us aversion, and arouse in us reaction against the causes of them. It is only release from terror that gives us the joy of rebound, and begets gratitude and affection, and thereby elicits religious regard.[1]

Turn now to Awe. If in fear we have a paralyzing, in awe we have a quieting, or soothing, emotion. Both mind and body are here composed. This arises from our consciousness of being in the presence or in the power of superior might,—yet, might *not* of the maleficent kind. There is the

[1] Hence religion could not have originated in mere *terror* of dead ancestors.

feeling of impotence (for, the awe-inspiring is necessarily the mysterious); but there is also the sense
of security. Appeal is made to the serious side
of our nature; and the appeal inspires trust, not
fear.

Now, this gives, clearly, a psychological theistic
foundation. In the Deity, there must be the
mysterious, the unfathomable. Yet, this unfathomable must impress us as beneficent and good, and
thereby create confidence. There is an *attractive*
force in this, which fear altogether wants: and
reverence, veneration, and adoration spring from
love. Even when the sense of unworthiness works
in us, it has, as the sustaining background, the
consciousness of privilege and admiration of the
exalted object; and the felt honour of being
allowed access to the High and Holy One, together with the gratitude ensuing, is the impulsive
force that characterizes the situation.

2. Nearly allied to Awe is the Sublime. Both
are elevating and ennobling feelings, and both are
the foundation of some of the highest qualities in
man's nature. But the sublime has a certain
stimulating and stirring energy about it that is
absent from awe. This is the result of the sympathetic imagination, by which we are led to
identify ourselves with sublime objects, and so to

feel as though *their* power were *our* power. As, however, sublime objects overshadow us, there is frequently an element of uneasiness or dissatisfaction entering into our contemplation of sublimity; and there is not always that marked sense of security or privilege that distinguishes Awe.

The nature of the Sublime is clearly seen in the leading examples of it. Through the Eye, we get the three kinds known as magnitude, elevation, and depth: illustrated by extended space, the starry heavens, an abyss. Through the Ear, we get sublimity, but in more limited quantity: as in the roar of a great cataract, the sublime silence of a vast still desert. Everything that manifests strong power in action, unless it be associated with the coarse and vulgar, is of the nature of the sublime: the violence of a hurricane, the eruptions of Vesuvius, the destructive energy of an avalanche. Everything that impresses us with the idea of power *pent up*, more especially, when we see conspicuous effects produced by small apparent expenditure of energy, easily and without effort, is also of the nature of the sublime: *e.g.*, the creation of the world by the Word of God ("God said, Let there be light, and there was light"), the gentle dashing of the rock-tossed wave in a calm sea in a rising tide. There is, further, the sublime of magnanimity and valour: seen in a unique figure defying opposition, standing alone in solitary grandeur (Athanasius against the world), or in a handful of men maintaining a contest in the face of fearful odds. Sublimity, too, may belong to social rank or official station (an august personage, a king, a despot), as well as to venerable institutions (the Papacy, the law-courts). In the intellectual genius of Shakespeare, in the diplomacy of a great statesman, in the strategy of a great general, we have examples of the sublime in mental qualities and mental achievements. Furthermore, thoughts and conceptions(including imaginations)may be sublime: Newton's conception of gravitation, or Mr. Norman Lockyer's Meteoric theory of the formation of the universe. Finally, there is a sublime in Ethics: seen, for instance, in moral heroism or self-sacrifice, in force of character and lofty virtue (as in Sir Galahad), in moral retribution and moral indignation, in unselfish disregard of personal reward or public appreciation.

The sublime is thus, in a manner, omnipresent. No wonder that it should have a religious application. It has to do, like Awe, with that side of piety that is concerned with reverence and veneration, and it is also productive, in many circumstances, of self-abasement. But, further, the notion of the Infinite is obviously generated here; and the fault that one has to find with Prof.

Max Müller and those who think with him is, not that they lay stress upon the Infinite as an important religious element, but that they will have religion to originate therein, and the Infinite to be the first religious conception of primitive man, fabricated by a special religious faculty. *That* position is both philosophically unsound and historically unsubstantiated.

. 3. But what now of Beauty ?

We have hitherto been dealing with emotions that associate themselves with the idea of power, and that have an elevating or exalting effect upon us. Here we have an emotion of the soft refining order, always pleasurable, fitted to hold and entrance us distinctly quiescent, therefore : beginning with sensuous experiences through the eye, and extending only by degrees to intellect, morality, and the social relationships.

In its primary form, as connected with the Eye, and, again, in its first secondary form, as related to the Ear, Beauty rests on an original susceptibility of the organ to certain sights and sounds : light, colour, lustre, on the one hand ; musical harmony and melody, on the other. But, in more complex cases, intellectual elements and associated effects come in. This introduces unity in diversity, constancy in change, fitness of means to ends, and so forth ; as also the beauty of morality, seen most conspicuously in the exercise of the amiable virtues —mercy, generosity, humanity.

Now, in the intellectual aspect of this emotion. as well, of course, as in the ethical aspect, religion finds a distinct psychological impulse. Lotze has very felicitously compared beauty in Nature to the beauty of a painting. If this comparison is just, then it follows that, however true it be that there are optical and other physical conditions of Natural beauty, yet our admiration of the Natural world is conditioned by the supposition that it is, like a painting, the production of an Artist's imagination, and that the unity it displays is the unity of an end bodied forth in this very painting by the Artist himself. As it is the artist's *idea* that gives meaning to the materials of which a painting is composed, it is the Artist's idea that affects us in our love for the beautiful in Nature.

This, no doubt, was very much what Berkeley meant when he represented Nature as a Divine visual language,—the world so arranged that God speaks to man by natural signs, just as men speak to each other by words symbolically significant.[1]

And the conception is, unquestionably, that of

---

[1] Dialogue iv. of *Alciphron ; or, The Minute Philosopher.* Berkeley should be studied in Prof. A. Campbell Fraser's splendid edition, or, at any rate, in his *Selections from Berkeley.*

the religious consciousness. Beauty has in it more
than what is merely natural: and the power that
Nature has of chaining and holding fast the en-
raptured individual, and of drawing him forth into
itself, is felt to bespeak the attractive influence
of Him who supports nature and in whom alone
both it and the individual have their being.

(ii.) The next group of Emotions comprises
Love and Sympathy. These are essentially unselfish feelings ; leading one out of oneself, making
one transcend oneself, and impressing one, ultimately, with a sense of personality greater and
higher than the finite.

1. Love is distinctly unselfish, and, even in the
form of self-love, is the direct opposite of selfishness. Selfishness is egoism *debased*,—egoism, when,
instead of having regard to the good and interest
of others, it uses others simply for its own ends,
when it turns them into means for effecting its
own purposes or instruments for procuring its own
gratification. The ego now, instead of accepting
its place as one individual among many, has made
itself the centre and final end of the whole, and
demands that all shall be subordinated to its
pleasure.

Self-love, on the other hand, is founded on self-respect ; and self-respect implicates altruism, and is the ground and indispensable condition of every virtue : —

> To thine own self be true :
> And it must follow, as the night the day,
> Thou canst not then be false to any man.

But Love, in its altruistic form, is insatiable. It is, therefore, like knowledge, centred in the Ideal. This capacity gives it its theistic function. A God that could be only a little loved would be no God, and the soul that has not a capacity for more than human love is not the human soul. "Religion," says Channing, "answers to the deepest want of human nature. We refer to our want of some being or beings, to whom we may give our hearts, whom we may love more than ourselves, for whom we may live and be ready to die, and whose character responds to that idea of perfection, which, however dim and undefined, is an essential element of every human soul. We cannot be happy beyond our love. At the same time, love may prove our chief woe, if bestowed unwisely, disproportionately, and on unworthy objects ; if confined to beings of imperfect virtue, with whose feelings we cannot always innocently sympathize, whose interests we cannot always righteously promote, who narrow us to themselves instead of breathing universal charity, who are frail, mutable, exposed to suffering, pain, and death. To secure a growing happiness and a spotless virtue, we need for the heart a being worthy of its whole treasure of love, to whom we may consecrate our whole existence, in approaching whom we enter an atmosphere of purity and brightness, in sympathizing with whom we cherish only noble sentiments, in devoting ourselves to whom we expose great and enduring interests, in whose character we find the spring of an ever-enlarging philanthropy,and by attachment to whom, all our other attachments are hallowed, protected, and supplied with tender and sublime consolations under bereavement and blighted hope. Such a being is God" (*Remarks on the Character and Writings of Fenelon*). Thus it is true, what Pascal says, that "the heart has its reasons, which reason knows not".

2. But, if this be so, Love must go hand in hand with Sympathy. The affection that craves for Deity implies a sense of fellowship or communion with Him; a living interest, therefore, in all that interests Him, and an acceptance of His ends and objects as one's own. The one sentiment is the necessary complement of the other: and the fellow-feeling that pours itself out in sympathy with finite beings finds its consummation in Him who is greater than the finite, and in whom the finite seeks repose.

(iii.) Sense of Dependence, Benevolence, and Gratitude, are the last class of emotions to be considered.

1. Benevolence and Gratitude are the counterparts of each other. Good-will shown towards me, especially if it issues in good deeds done to me, naturally makes me grateful. Good feeling reciprocates good feeling, and the receiver of gifts is bound in thankful attachment to the giver.

2. But this is not necessarily Sense of Dependence. We may have a sense of dependence without the idea of benevolence in the object whereon we are dependent : and gratitude hardly emerges (though feeling of satisfaction does), unless benevolence enters, with the consequent beneficence.

Hence the impossibility of laying the sole foundation of Theism in Sense of Dependence.

(1) In the first place, that is to make religion a wholly passive thing ; and the logical outcome is Quietism. (2) In the next place, it is to forget that the sense of dependence that is concerned with religion is only such as generates *gratitude* in the recipient. But, before gratitude is begotten, there is implied the conception of a benefactor, of the being on whom we are dependent treating us in a benevolent fashion. (3) Lastly, it is to ignore

19

the fact that, sense of dependence is not the only emotion that has to do with religion. There are Awe, Beauty, the Sublime, and so forth, as we have already seen; but, chief of all, there is Sympathy or sense of fellowship and communion—an Emotion that enters as an essential element into the religious conception, and without which Religion can hardly be said to have a connotation.

II.

Feeling is an important factor in Religion, but it is not the sole factor. It was Schleiermacher's leading contention, as laid down in the *Discourses on Religion*, that Religion is independent both of knowing and of acting— of intellection and of volition, "it resigns, at once, all claims to anything that belongs either to science or to morality," and is primarily a sentiment, an affection, a feeling, "sense and taste for the Infinite". He said, further: "If man is not one with the Eternal in the unity of intuition and feeling which is immediate, he remains, in the unity of consciousness which is derived, for ever apart". This last is an obscure doctrine: and so, in the *Glaubens-lehre*, he tried to give definiteness and precision to his position by laying stress on the sense of "absolute dependence" on the Infinite as the fundamental religious experience.

Now, waiving the question as to the precise meaning that Schleiermacher attached to the Infinite (sometimes he describes it, pantheistically, as "the universe," and sometimes he denominates it "God"), the objections to basing religion solely on feeling are very great, and seem to me to be insurmountable.

1. In the first place, not every feeling is religious, although Schleiermacher was driven to maintain the opposite: "There is no sensation," he says, "that is not pious, except it indicate some diseased and impaired state of the life, the influence of which will not be confined to religion". We have only to look over a list of the Emotions to see that many of them have no religious implication whatever, while many of them are absolutely anti-religious. On the one hand, there are emotions that are mainly physical (such as timidity); there are intellectual emotions (novelty, incongruity, knowledge); there are emotions associated with power, and emotions associated with impotence. On the other hand, there are purely selfish emotions (vanity, avarice, jealousy); but, above all, there are emotions of the strong malevolent type (hatred and revenge).

2. Next, if feeling be identical with religion, then thought must be, not only unessential, but positively injurious to religion the cause of error

and degeneration. Whence it follows that the lowest races, being the least reflective and the most impressionable, would be the most religious; while highly cultivated peoples and great religious thinkers would be farthest removed from the religious ideal : to be "wise and pious at the same time" would then become a kind of paradox. Whence, also, it follows that subjective feeling is the standard of objective truth.

What, no doubt, Schleiermacher is aiming at in his doctrine of Feeling is, to emphasize what has been appropriately called the *inwardness* of religion —its living subjective spontaneity, as distinguished, on the one hand, from the acceptance of religious truth on mere external authority, and, on the other hand, from the bare intellectual acquiescence in religious propositions, in theological formulæ or dogmas, which never touches the heart or creates enthusiasm : "from within, in their original, characteristic form, the emotions of piety must issue". But, though it be true that dogmatic formulæ are not in themselves religion, nor mere formal acceptance of them or bare intellectual adherence to them sufficient for piety,—although it is quite the case that truth, in order to be effectual, must be appropriated, assimilated, lived,—it does not follow that either dogma or intellect vitiates religion, or may, without detriment, be dispensed with. On the contrary, religion, like every other spiritual discipline, must be mediated through notions; and it is only by thought that we can ascertain what is pure and true in the original religious consciousness, and how far, and in what way, spontaneous religious feeling needs to be purified and corrected. Philosophy comes in, when we try to determine the object of religious devotion; and Logic comes in, when we set to systematize our religious experiences: and neither of these is unimportant, nor is either of them really absent even in the religion of the plainest man.

3. But there is a third religious element, which we dare not omit. Taken at its best, Feeling is only part of religion. Besides emotion, Religion implies intellectual perception and moral activity. It has a cognitive side and a conative side, as well as an affective side: and these three are by no means the same. It is one thing to experience gratitude or to feel attachment: it is another thing to apprehend the object to whom the gratitude is shown or the attachment felt: it is still another thing to submit oneself in cheerful and full obedience to this apprehended object. Feeling, intellection, volition, all enter into religion. You cannot resolve any one of the three into any one of the others; neither from one can you evolve the other two. What is possible is to show that

all three are mutually dependent. Gratitude is generated through the intellectual perception of a benefactor dispensing gifts; and gratitude, in turn, produces a readiness and disposition towards active obedience.[1]

III.

But, granting the fact of the Religious emotions in man's nature, and granting the necessity of an object on which to exercise them, it may, nevertheless, be maintained that we are yet far from emotional *theism*. We have not exhausted the possibilities. There are two alternatives, at least, that ought to be considered—each of which seems very formidable. In the first place, it may be said that the situation is fully met by emotional *pantheism*; in the next place, it may be said that, not God, but *Humanity* is the satisfying object.

These two positions we must now examine.

1. That Pantheism finds its most plausible support in the emotions, I fully admit. The

[1] There are several very good succinct accounts of Schleiermacher accessible in English translations. One may be found in Lichtenberger's *History of German Theology in the Nineteenth Century;* another in Pfleiderer's *Philosophy of Religion,* vol. i.; still another in Ueberweg's *History of Philosophy,* vol. ii. For a compact statement of the Idea of Religion, see Liddon's *Some Elements of Religion,* Lecture i. Schleiermacher's Discourses themselves have been recently translated by Mr. John Oman, B.D., under the title, *On Religion : Speeches to its Cultured Despisers.*

closeness of connexion between subject and object in the tender feelings is universally acknowledged. There is a union here that is not achieved either in intellectual apprehension or by conative endeavour. Even the beauty of External Nature, not to speak of the affection between persons, has this cementing and difference-obliterating attraction about it. Much more must this be the case, then, with deep religious devotion, when the soul of the worshipper goes out of itself (as it were) and holds intimate communion with the Object of worship.

But this is by no means equivalent to saying that the difference between subject and object is ever actually effaced in the emotions, or that the one ever literally becomes the other. Outward nature and the individual spectator remain two, even when spirit goes forth to greet spirit; and the attachment of one human being to another always involves in it the distinction of separate individuals.

This I tried to point out, as clearly as I could, in my first Lecture, on " Theistic Doubt "; where, also, I endeavoured to appraise mysticism and to give the exact rendering of religious devotion. I need not repeat myself here; but will only say that what I have now called emotional pantheism is simply the highest form of a very general mental experience,—namely this, that, when a person is deeply interested or deeply absorbed in anything, he loses consciousness of his own existence—he and the absorbing object seem identified. But we are not at liberty to infer from this that the two are really one,—that there is reached a point where difference is not, and where identity alone obtains. That would be a total misreading of the psychological facts ; and it is on such a total misreading of the psychological facts that emotional pantheism, or emotional mysticism, is based.

2. Let us pass on, then, to the second substitute for theism, namely, Worship of Humanity.

This is the Positivist's religion, initiated by Auguste Comte. There is no God but Man. Yet, not any individual man although some men show far higher and nobler qualities than others. but man *collectively.* The human race, with certain limitations, according to Comte, is the object of worship. Society in its collective life (says Littré) is the *Être Suprême ;* and the individual's highest duty is to further, as best he may, the progress of humanity, and to devote himself in ungrudging effort to the service of mankind. This is the central idea, which must have justice done to it : the idiosyncrasies, inconsistencies, and aberrations of " the Priest of Humanity," especially in his later days of feeble health and shattered nervous system, may well be left out of account.

Now there is here, clearly, a noble end : and rich possibilities of emotional fervour are not wanting. The end is far too great to permit of my using, regarding the worship of Humanity, any such contemptuous language as was employed by Prof. Huxley when he designated it " the incongruous mixture of bad science with eviscerated papistry," and vehemently declared : " When the positivist asks me to worship 'Humanity'— that is to say, to adore the generalized conception of men as they ever have been and probably ever will be I must reply that I could just as soon bow down and worship the generalized conception of 'a wilderness of apes'". Criticism, to be effective, must be calmer and more sympathetic than that. Humanity, even in its generalized form, has for me, and, I suppose, for most other people, a quite different interest from what attaches to " a wilderness of apes " : and the positivist cult must have a worthy element in it before it could have proved attractive to ardent souls. It is not dependent for its power alone on the rhetorical setting given to it by such masters of eloquence as Mr. F. Harrison and Mr. Congreve ; it is effective through the sentiment of the heart embalmed in its chief conception. *Homo sum: humani nihil a me alienum puto.* Altruism has undoubted absolute value, and naturally exerts an elevating, broadening, and stimulating influence.

But, notwithstanding, I cannot believe that Humanity is either a fit or an adequate object of worship. For :

1. First, Humanity is an abstraction : and to worship an abstraction is for man impossible. It is only the concrete that can enlist our feelings, and so draw forth our adoration.

" Take it then," you say, " in its Ideal form, and regard positivism as devotion to this Ideal,— the Ideal humanity." Well, in that case, you achieve morality, but not religion. Your Ideal needs embodiment, before it can be worshipped.

2. But, next, even when we take Humanity as a name for men regarded *collectively*, worship is still impossible. For, worship is *worth*-ship : and the worth that is discernible in mankind generally is a limited quantity, and is so spoilt by sins sins often of the grossest, most revolting character that anything rather than devotion is here appropriate. Not even savages (so ethnologists insist) worship each other. While they pay their homage to stocks and stones and animals and plants, man himself, of whom they know so much (*because* they know so much), is, with rare excep-

tions, left scrupulously aside. It is only in mythology that heroes are deified: it is only after myths have grown around beings that are believed to have lived in a distant past—a past (as Grote so happily phrased it) that never was present—that apotheosis takes place; or only under circumstances of the decrepitude of faith, such as we find in the days of the decline of the Roman Empire. And, after all, mythology may not be a case in point: it *will not* be so, if (as is probable) myths had for their primary objects, not human beings, but the forces and powers of Nature.

What earnest energetic people may contract towards Humanity is *enthusiasm:* they may become fired with a zeal to elevate and benefit mankind, to raise them out of the mire and to help them on the way to progress. But enthusiasm is not worship: philanthropy is different from anthropolatry. The two things are essentially distinct, and by no alchemy can the one be transmuted into the other.

3. Nor, lastly, is Humanity in itself complete. It is finite and presupposes an Infinite,—an Infinite that shall be to it complement, completion, perfection. Taken at its best, it has not self-sufficiency; and its very lustre goes, the moment it claims to be all in all. Perhaps, we may look to China for a corroborating example, on the large scale. If

you wish to see morality divorced from religion,
you find it in Confucianism: and Confucianism is
the State religion of China. It is a kind of huge
experiment of taking man as the self-sufficient.
Well, what is the result? "Chinese society," says
M. Edgar Quinet, "makes man the final end, and
so humanity finds its goal in its starting-point. It
is stifled within the limits of humanity. In this
dwarf society, everything is deprived of its crown.
Morality wants heroism: royalty its royal muse;
verse, poetry: philosophy, metaphysic: life, immortality; because, at the summit of everything,
there is no God" (*La Genie des Religions*, pp. 224-
5, quoted by Aubrey L. Moore). Water cannot
rise above its level; and we may depend upon
it that, if the level of religion be low, all other
departments of human interest will suffer propor-
tionately. We may depend upon it, also, that
love to man will not be strengthened by removing
love to God. It is only when the fifth Commandment is placed, in true Jewish fashion, upon the
First Table of the Law, and regarded as concerned
with *piety*, that the succeeding Commandments
find effective sanction.

IV.

We have, up to this point, been dealing with
those who admit that the emotions do afford a

psychological basis for religion, though how far this basis is *theistic* has been matter of dispute. But now we must take account of those who deny the validity of the religious emotions altogether, and who, on the fact of *counter*-emotions and the painful experiences of life, coupled with certain ethical data, arraign Providence and base an atheistic conclusion. I am not going to occupy time with an account of ancient Buddhism, or with telling *in extenso*, once again, the oft-told tale of Schopenhauer and Hartmann ; nor am I to reproduce the criticism so effectively made by Prof. Sully in his *Pessimism*.[1] I must assume that as known, or as easy of access. I am merely to face the pessimistic position as it concerns the emotional and ethical parts of the argument here laid down.

Life, says the pessimist, is in its very nature an evil. So far is it from having worth and from being something to be cherished, that it is radically worthless and is to be deplored. "The *evil of the world*, according to Schopenhauer," I am quoting, for convenience, Prof. Pfleiderer's abstract, "is to be accounted for ultimately by the fact that the will in its individual manifestation, as the indi-

---

[1] See, also, Prof. Flint's *Anti-Theistic Theories*, lecture viii. How Prof. Sully's criticism is viewed by pessimists themselves, may be seen by referring to Fran Olga Plumacher's article on " Pessimism " in *Mind*, 1st series, vol. iv.

vidual will of every living being, and also of man,
is nothing but egoistic desire for individual self-
assertion, desire of pleasure for pleasure's sake.
These egoistic individual wills naturally come in
perpetual conflict with each other and with the
order of the world, and the result of these conflicts is a great preponderance of pain over pleasure : pain indeed forms the real positive content
of life, while pleasure is a mere episode when pain
is occasionally quieted, and therefore merely something negative, an accidental feature in the positive tissue of life. But as the will only aims at
pleasure for pleasure's sake, this world, so full of
pain, is the opposite of its ideal, is bad through
and through. The existence of the world is itself
the greatest evil of all, and underlies all other evil,
and similarly the root evil for each individual is
his having come into the world. This is not only
the root evil but the root sin, since the existence
of each being in the world is based on a first act
in which the will to live, which is also his will,
received individuality and bodily form. This first
act of the will, its entrance upon existence as a
separate will, is the 'original sin and original
guilt' of our race" (*The Philosophy of Religion*, vol.
ii. p. 233).

Now, this gives us very clearly the ground-prin-

ciple of the pessimistic teaching, and may be taken
as fairly representative of serious pessimistic
thought. In so far as pessimism is not grounded
in "disappointed egoism," or in a man's upbringing
and environment, or in natural temperament and
physical constitution, and in so far as it is not
a mere passing mood arising from momentary
dissatisfaction with life and the world, it centres
in the doctrine of Pain. Life is evil, because the
real positive content of it is pain, and pleasure is
only negative and accidental.

The criticism of this is threefold.

1. In the first place, the doctrine of Pain that is
here laid down is psychologically erroneous. The
normal fact of human existence is Pleasure, not
pain: Evolution itself being witness. Evolution
as interpreted, for instance, by Mr. Herbert
Spencer and by Mr. Leslie Stephen is essentially
non-pessimistic: for, its fundamental doctrine is that
conduct is good when it subserves life and bad
when it impedes or destroys it. This means that
Life itself is the good, by reference to which other
things called good are to be tested: in other words,
life and happiness are convertible terms. The same
implication of the normal character of Pleasure is
contained, but without reference to Evolution, in
the laws of Stimulation and Conservation of

Pleasure as formulated by Professor Bain in *The Senses and the Intellect* (3rd ed., pp. 282-295).

But, further, Pleasure is not mere relief from pain, but is itself a positive state, towards the attainment of which we are prompted, altogether apart from considerations of pain, and for the continuance and increase of which we crave. It is not, as some maintain, mere equilibrium, out of which we are driven by the intervention of pain (which is conflict and unrest). It has a distinct quality of its own (although, of course, relief from pain is one way of giving pleasure), and rises and falls in quantity independently of painful conflict. Anticipated enjoyment may initiate activity, as much as present discomfort. Moreover, we may pass from one *kind* of pleasure to another, or from a lower *degree* of pleasure to a higher, no pain intervening. *Negative* pleasures, indeed, there are, or pleasures that may be described as repose after conflict ; but, out of this state of repose, pleasure has itself the power of prompting us—it can, of its own motion, and with a view to realizing itself, originate action. Thus is the pessimistic conclusion seen to be psychologically illegitimate. Pain is not, in an unqualified fashion, the *primum mobile* of human endeavour.

2. But, next, the pessimist's conception of pain is ethically inadequate. Pain is not, in the Ethical sense, an unmitigated evil. On the contrary, it

refines the affections and strengthens character ; it is a means of bracing man's moral fibre. No just appreciation of its moral value could ever eventuate in pessimism, nor can pessimism logically lead to a just appreciation of its moral value.

3. Lastly, Pessimism, in its endeavour to weigh pains against pleasures, attempts a fruitless task ; and, when it gives preponderance to the former over the latter, it seems to underestimate or to ignore some of the most patent facts of human life and to exaggerate others.

In the first place, it minimizes the fact that life is a progress, and that there is such a thing as pleasure in *pursuit*, even when there is not complete attainment. There is scant room for Ideals in pessimism ; and yet Ideals give to life its zest, and are a standing witness to the worth of human existence. There is scant room for enthusiasm ; and thereby pessimism compares most unfavourably with Worship of Humanity, which, however defective in other respects, does not err by ignoring the value and the needs of man's heart.

In the next place, it exaggerates man's selfishness. It lays stress on cupidity, ingratitude, inhumanity, on the clashing of individual wills in the struggle for existence, to the comparative neglect of the unselfish and generous side of human nature —of mercy, philanthropy, and the other social and

cementing forces. But this last side is a most
significant one. Take the fact of Mercy or Forgiveness among men, and what is implied in it?
Before mercy, in the form of forgiveness of injury
or remission of debt, is possible, there is implied
a natural readiness on the part of a man to love
and befriend his fellow; for, the only return that
the injured or offended person gets for his forgiveness is the penitence or repentance of the offender
—in other words, is the removal of the feeling of
estrangement. But how comes the removal of
the feeling of estrangement to be regarded as
adequate compensation? It can only come from
this, that the love of man to man is the natural
order of things, and mutual hate, with the accom-
panying pessimism, is unnatural. Hence the fallacy in Schopenhauer's contention that, as a man
cannot be in full accord with any one but himself,
he ought to confine himself to his own society.
Surely there is here a gross paralogism. For (*a*),
even granting that a man cannot be in *full* accord
with any one but himself, it does not follow that
he must wholly eschew the society of others; even
partial accord may be productive of much good
to him. But (*b*), next, it is not granted that a
man may be in full accord *with himself:* his egoism
is no more perfect than his altruism; indeed, there
are cases where a man is in fuller accord with

others than with himself. (*c*) Thirdly, there is an ambiguity in the word "self," which may mean either a man's higher or his lower self, his better or his worse nature. Asceticism, when it arises from misanthropy, is not likely to be productive of real and lasting self-satisfaction.

Lastly, too great prominence is given by pessimism to the pains of circumstance and of environment in life,—to the pains of conflict with the order of the world ; and too little weight is put on man's power to counteract these or to rise above them, and on the force of human will. External Nature is not the inexorable Juggernaut-car that morbid pessimism supposes, and robust human nature can maintain its own in the universe and yet not find life intolerable. Man has a happy gift of subduing Nature by submitting to her : *Natura enim non nisi parendo vincitur*, as Bacon aphoristically puts it (*Novum Organum*, Lib. i. Aph. 3).

If, then, we would sum up the criticism, it amounts to this :—There are misunderstanding and misinterpreting of the facts of experience in pessimism ; there is, also, undervaluing of experienced facts, and there are exaggerating and ignoring of experienced facts : in a word, there are *suggestio falsi* and *suppressio veri.* [1]

[1] As German pessimism had its origin in pantheistic soil, it has been said that pessimism is the natural outgrowth of pantheism.

V.

A word, now, as to our subject in its historical aspect.

1. First, Emotional Theism.

Emotion, as a factor in religion, is, of course, as old as religion itself; but the definite insistence on it as a theistic basis is of recent date. Indeed, the schools of philosophy, from old Greek days to quite lately, and similarly the schools of theology, still imbued with scholasticism and under the influence of the formulating intellect, laid the foundation of theism almost wholly in Reason. When philosophers like Hume did take account of Feeling, it was usually with the intent of disparaging religion—of warning off the wise, on the plea that feeling and fancy are an unstable foundation on which to rely. Exception must be made of the mediaeval mystics (such as St. Bernard of Clairvaux), who regarded Love as the very being and essence of God, and as the quality in which man's perfection also consisted, inasmuch as man is formed in the image of God. Yet, in the present

This, however, is a mistake. Pantheism is not atheism; and, as a matter of fact, the great pantheists of history were not pessimists. In ancient Greek days, when Pantheism was frequent, pessimism existed only as a mood of the poets (Sophocles, for instance), and was not theoretical at all. In more recent times, the greatest of all the pantheists, Spinoza, never dreamt of pessimism, nor, if he had, would pantheism, with its privative theory of Evil, have seemed to him to be in any way necessarily pessimistic.

connexion, Schleiermacher, through his keen perception of the deep religious wants of man, may be said to have been the first to emphasize the importance of the *heart*, as distinct from the head, and to have given the great impulse to theistic consideration on this line, an impulse that has not yet expended itself. Nevertheless, Schleiermacher has not been followed implicitly. Even those who are in fullest sympathy with his main position have not failed to see that it is not wholly satisfactory,—that the emotions are not competent alone to bear the weight of the theistic structure. They have, accordingly, combined it with the intellectual and the moral arguments—more especially, with the latter. Thinkers like Mansel, who, following Kant, are chary in invoking the speculative reason, are yet emphatic in insisting on ethics and *the sense of dependence*. While they underestimate the cognitive process, they are fully awake to the importance of the emotive.

2. Secondly, Emotional Pantheism.

This is a quite intelligible position, if Emotion be the sole originator of religion ; and the pantheism of Schleiermacher is more than apparent. " Offer with me reverently," he says (though how far he rightly interpreted Spinoza may be questioned), " a tribute to the manes of the holy, rejected

Spinoza. The high World-Spirit pervaded him; the Infinite was his beginning and his end; the Universe was his only and his everlasting love. In holy innocence and in deep humility he beheld himself mirrored in the eternal world, and perceived how he also was its most worthy mirror. He was full of religion, full of the Holy Spirit. Wherefore, he stands there alone and unequalled; master in his art, yet without disciples and without citizenship, sublime above the profane tribe" (*Discourses* ii., Mr. Oman's transl.). Pantheism of the same type may be traced clearly in sentimental writers like Rousseau, whose appreciation of and sympathy with objective Nature are intense; and the pantheism of the poets reflected in some pieces of Wordsworth and of Tennyson is very much of the emotional stamp.

To the same category is to be referred the modern scientific pantheism known as Pancosmism, where the conception of Force takes the place of the Deity, and man's immortality is identified with that of this imperishable force. Constance Naden has thus given expression to it in poetry:—

> Yes, thou shalt die; but these Almighty forces,
> That meet to form thee, live for evermore:
> They hold the suns in their eternal courses,
> And shape the long sand-grasses on the shore.

Be calmly glad, thine own true kindred seeing
  In fire and storm, in flowers with dew impearled,
Rejoice in thine imperishable being,
  One with the Essence of the boundless world.

3. Thirdly, Worship of Humanity.

This originated in the atmosphere of Christianity, and under its influence. I refer not alone to the Comtian ritual, which avowedly imitated the Roman Catholic custom, but to far more important matters. Positivist Altruism is but the spirit of the Saviour stript of the Divine impulse, and the Golden Rule writ small. It is only in a *theistic* setting that the story of Abou Ben Adhem can be felt to represent the truth of the situation.

4. Lastly, Pessimism.

This had an Oriental source in far-back Buddhistic times; but, in the Western world, it sprang up, less than a century ago, with Schopenhauer. Its greatest hold to-day is in Germany, though Schopenhauer's followers there are by no means at one with the master on primary and important points. Some dispute the doctrine of the negative character of pleasure; some (like Hartmann) attempt to improve upon the metaphysical foundation of Will; later disciples have quarrelled with the ground-principle of the conflict of separate individual wills as motived by pleasure. Its strongest ally, however, is Secularism; where it takes a practical turn, and enters the arena of politics.

This same secularism has invaded France; but philosophic (as distinguished from literary) pessimism is there at a discount.

In Britain, the interest in pessimism, in so far as it is not secularist, is mainly literary. " Is life worth living?" has been a subject for the pens of brilliant essayists like Mr. Mallock; but, outside the covers of Reviews, there is little enthusiasm. A sound psychology, coupled with a general appreciation of the doctrine of Evolution, has kept Philosophy untainted; while the vigorous, healthy instinct of the nation, combined with a living faith in the Supreme, has been sufficient to resist the canker in its social inroads. It is felt that pessimism has a value as against a too roseate Theodicy— an extreme Optimism (such as that of Shaftesbury, of Leibniz, or of Pope in his *Essay on Man*) : but, in itself, it is morbid and irrational.

LECTURE VIII.

THE introduction to Ethical theism will best, I think, be made by a consideration of Ethics regarded as science of the Ideal, and of the nature of the Ethical Self. These two topics will, therefore, form the subject of to-day's lecture.

I.

Ethics, taken in its proper signification, includes two things. On the one hand, it consists of an investigation into the nature and constitution of human character; and, on the other hand, it is concerned with the formulating and enunciating of rules for human conduct: as Schleiermacher puts it (*Discourses* ii.), " it teaches what man should be for the world, and what he should do in it". In the first case, it is theoretical Ethics; in the second case, practical. The practical is necessarily dependent on the theoretical; for, in order to be a sure and trustworthy guide to conduct,—ere ever it can lawfully claim the authority of a counsellor and help to man,—Ethics must repose on a well-considered analysis and investigation of man's

(313)

mental and moral nature, as well as of his social conditions. It is, therefore, in the closest manner allied with psychology and with sociology ; and the methods of these two sciences are precisely those that stand us in good stead here.[1]

As compared with kindred sciences, however, Ethics has a complication peculiar to itself. It deals essentially with the " ought," as distinguished from the " is"; it is the science of human character and conduct *as they should be*, and not simply as we actually find them : in other words, it applies to them a standard of *worth*. Nevertheless, as the ideal, in order to be of any true value, must be founded on the real, the starting-point for all ethical speculation must be human nature as it falls actually within our ken. We must analyze and study the " is," if we would discover the "ought to be"; and, however far forward our theorizing may carry us, it must both begin from, and return again to, actual experience.

But the word "ideal," as applied to Ethics, is somewhat ambiguous. It may refer simply to an idea present in the mind, and not em-bodied in fact : or it may signify a highest or best conceivable state of things, partly indeed

---

[1] I have given a brief statement of the relation of Ethics to the allied sciences in an article on " The Logic of Classification," in the first series of *Mind*, vol. xii. pp. 246-251.

realized, but the full realization of which is still future. It is in the second sense that the word is here employed ; and, though this sense includes the other (for, in so far as the ideal has to be *won*, it may be denominated an idea), it goes considerably beyond it. An ideal is also an idea, though an idea need not, by any means, be an ideal.

Further, it must be observed, regarding the ideal, that ethical relations are essentially rational relations. "So," you say, "are other relations—such as those of knowledge." Yes, but ethical relations have as their distinctive feature the fact that they are relations between *persons*,—*i.e.*, between rational beings having community of interests. Hence the foundation of "rights" and "duties". These exist, strictly, only between persons— between conscious beings sharing in the same nature ; they exist between me and my fellow-men, but not between me and dead unconscious matter. Matter is that which I *use*, which I turn to my own and others' profit, but not that which can claim of me any particular right. Hence, also, the ground-principle of Ethics,—*viz.*, that of *equality between men*,—is a rational principle, and thereby finds its justification : it is what Bentham expressed in the formula, " Every one to count for one, and no one for more than one ".

The full definition of the science, therefore, will

be : Ethics, the science of human character and conduct as they ought to be, founded on the knowledge of what human character and conduct have been and are. Or, in order to bring out the ideality more clearly :—Ethics, the science of the ideal with a view to conduct. Or, still again, in order to emphasize the fact that Ethics has to do alone with persons :—Ethics, the rational determination, with a view to the guidance of life, of the right (ideal) relations of persons to each other.[1]

Now, objection to a science of the ideal may be taken on two different grounds. It may be objected that there cannot be a science of the ideal, because there is no valid distinction between the ideal and the real; or it may be objected that there cannot be a science of the ideal, because, although there is a valid distinction between the ideal and the real, the ideal is (from the very nature of the case) unknown and therefore undefinable.

---

[1] That Ideals are not mere imaginations, has been clearly shown, with regard to Ethics, by Prof. J. Grote, in the fourth chapter of his *Treatise on the Moral Ideals.* Reason and imagination are not contradictory of each other, but are mutually helpful. " I look upon imagination as the active portion of the intelligence, that in which the life of the intelligence consists, and from which, as the intelligence advances, new deposits are ever made of actual knowledge, which thenceforward loses a portion of its interest, and becomes for some purposes dead." In a like spirit, Novalis says,—" To be eternally poetical is to be eternally true ".

1. The first of these objections is Ferrier's. In a note in the second volume of the *Remains* (p. 206), he puts it very pointedly thus :—

"Sir James Mackintosh, and others, have attempted to establish a distinction between 'mental' and 'moral' science, founded on an alleged difference between fact and duty. They state, that it is the office of the former science to teach us *what is* (quid est), and that it is the office of the latter to teach us *what ought to be* (quid oportet). But this discrimination vanishes into nought upon the slightest reflection; it either incessantly confounds and obliterates itself, or else it renders moral science an unreal and nugatory pursuit. For, let us ask, does the *quid oportet* ever become the *quid est?* does *what ought to be* ever pass into *what is*, or, in other words, is duty ever realized as fact? If it is, then the distinction is at an end. The *oportet* has taken upon itself the character of the *est*. Duty, in becoming practical, has become a fact. It no longer merely points out something which *ought to be*, it also embodies something which *is*. And thus it is transformed into the very other member of the discrimination from which it was originally contradistinguished; and thus the distinction is rendered utterly void; while 'mental' and 'moral' science, if we must affix these epithets to philosophy, lapse into one. On the other hand, does the *quid oportet* never, in any degree, become the *quid est*, does duty never pass into fact? Then is the science of morals a visionary, a baseless, and an aimless science, a mere querulous hankering after what can never be. In this case, there is plainly no real or substantial science, except the science of facts, the science which teaches us the *quid est.* To talk now of a science of the *quid oportet*, would be to make use of unmeaning words."

To this it may be answered :—(*a*) First, there are a great many mental phenomena that bear no *moral* implications whatever ; they are simply facts of consciousness, and, therefore, may very well be separated from those other facts of consciousness that *do* have a moral implication. Thus, on tasting sugar, I experience the pleasant sensation of sweetness. This sensation is a simple psychical fact, without ethical significance ; and there is no sense in classing it along with compunction or remorse, in which the ethical significance is everything. (*b*) Secondly, we may very well grant that, to a certain extent, the "is" and the "ought" are identical, and yet not be driven to Ferrier's conclusion. For, unquestionably, there is much in human character and conduct that "is" as it "ought to be". But the peculiarity of the case is, that, even when the

two are identified, the " is " will not let us rest in
itself, but urges us on to the conception of the
" ought," and forces us (as it were) to give the fact
an *ethical* interpretation. (*c*) Then, thirdly, human
character and human conduct, as actual fact, have
much in them that *ought not* to be. They fall short
of an ideal standard, and are thereby differentiated
from contiguous or allied phenomena. (*d*) Lastly,
we know, because we have seen it—it is determined
by a wide induction of particulars,—that the ethical
ideal does influence mankind; and when we ask
the reason, we find it to be, because the ethical
ideal is adapted to man's better nature and higher
aspirations, and because it is believed to be ultimately realizable by him. And the ground of this
belief in its ultimate realization is an unquestioned
fact of experience,—*viz.*, that man has power,
within limits, of working out his ideals, of working
towards them or of bringing them to pass. Although conditioned by his environment, he can, so
far, change or transform his environment—he has
a certain ability of moulding or bending circumstances to his will; and this ability is what renders
Ethics possible, and answers objections against its
ideality.

Put shortly, then, Ferrier's fallacy lies in an
equivocal use of the word " reality " or " fact ". A
thing actually experienced is a fact, and a thing

merely anticipated or possible may be denominated a fact also. But the second is not a fact in the same sense of the word as the first is, although it may, by and by, become an actuality in that sense of the term too. So, the "is" and the "ought" may both be designated facts; but, while ideality is of the essence of the latter, it does not necessarily enter into the former. The "ought" appeals to man's endeavours and aspirations; the "is" has reference to his mere acquisitions and actual attainments.

2. The second objection takes a somewhat different form. "Granted," it may be said, "that the ideal of Ethics has existence; still Ethics cannot be a science, because this ideal cannot be defined." And if we ask, "Why cannot this ideal be defined?" we receive for answer, "Because it is only in process of realization".

Now, is this a valid objection? I think not. For, obviously, it overlooks the fact that Ethics rests on a basis of experience, and that it is quite possible to gauge *tendencies* and to interpret them correctly. Shall a knowledge of the hyperbola be denied us, because the asymptote is ever approaching that curve but never reaches it? On the contrary, the very circumstance that you can lay

down the doctrine of the asymptote proves you to
have a knowledge of the hyperbola ; and the very
circumstance that there is such a thing as *improvement* in human character implies that you have a
knowledge of that something in whose direction the
improvement takes place. Indeed, the word "ideal"
has no meaning unless on the supposition of a
higher and a lower, a better and a worse ; and from
higher we pass to highest, and from better to best.
It is fallacious to try to shut us up between two
alternatives, as though these exhausted the possibilities ; and it is misleading in the extreme to
make a total break between the realized as the
known and the unrealized as the unknown. The
unrealized is *not* the unknown, unless it be of a
kind in every way different from the realized and
known. It is equally the known, if it proceed upon
the lines of the realized ; and so long as we examine
human nature and generalize upon the knowledge
thence derived, we are on sure ground and may
legitimately claim for our procedure the character
of being scientific.

This point, amid much that is admirable, has
been somewhat obscured, and needlessly so, I
think, by Green in his *Prolegomena to Ethics.*
Strong in the opinion that the idea of a better
implies a best, he, nevertheless, when treating of
the formal character of the moral ideal, so em-

21

phasizes the unknown character of this "best" as almost to reduce its value to zero. Here is what he says :—

"Man can never give a sufficient account of what his unconditional good is, because he cannot know what his capabilities are till they are realised. This is the explanation of the infirmity that has always been found to attach to attempted defini- tions of the moral ideal. They are always open to the charge that there is employed in the definition, openly or disguisedly, the very notion which pro- fession is made of defining" (p. 204).

If this were so, in all the rigour of the statement, Green's own ethical teaching would certainly not be what it is, and would not have that stimulating power which it unquestionably possesses. But this is not so, in all the rigour of the statement, nor does Green in other parts of his work conceive it so; for, man *can* know what his capabilities are *before* they are realized. And it is precisely this knowledge that reflection on what is disclosed by ethical introspection, by examination of a man's own conduct, by careful scrutiny of the conduct of others (as revealed personally to ourselves or as declared to us in history), by study of social usages, institutions, and the like, is competent to give. In a very real sense, the limits of man's faculties are given in a knowledge of their nature, taken in con-

nexion with a knowledge of their environment:
and we can as surely tell the end towards which
righteousness is tending, and the lines on which it
must work, as the astronomer can tell the future of
a heavenly body, or the naturalist the character of
an extinct animal from the print of its cleft foot.
We have here, as Cuvier would say, "a surer mark
than all those of Zadig".

Dr. Martineau has put it better than Green.
He says (*Types of Ethical Theory*, Pref. xiii.):-
" The possible also *is*, whether it happens or not ;
and its categories, of the right, the beautiful,
the necessarily true, may have their contents defined and held ready for realisation, whatever
centuries lapse ere they appear".

He says also (*Id.*, vol. ii., p. 151):-" In order
to appreciate a type of character, it is not necessary
that we should have personally passed through it :
be it only possible to us, the key is within us ; on
the principle that we intuitively interpret the natural
language of every human emotion, though we should
see the sign ere we have felt what is signified".

The characteristic of Ethics, as science of the
ideal, may be put in a few words.

It is the testimony of experience that men *do*
have a conception of the "ought," as distinct from
the "is," and by this conception test their own

character and conduct, as well as the character and conduct of others. It is, further, the testimony of experience that this conception of the "ought" emerges when the principles of man's being—the various springs of action by which he is moved - are in conflict. Further still, it is testified by experience that there is among men the recognition of an ideal unattained, yet presumably attainable, in which the "ought" shall rule, in which the elements and principles of man's nature shall all be harmonized, and peace and happiness shall reign within. Whence it follows that a man is, not what at any particular moment he may here happen to be, but what he is capable of ultimately becoming; and his "perfection" means, not the absence of development or the absolute cessation at some point of all further extension of the range of his faculties, but the entire unison and full exercise of all his powers.

It is these facts that give to Ethics its justification and its meaning. It is because of its ideal, proved inductively to be a reality, and with a view to stimulating towards its attainment, that Ethics has existence ; and it is in the examination, explanation, and interpretation of this ideal that Ethics finds its highest function.[1]

---

[1] The greater part of this section appeared in *Mind*, 1st Series, vol. xiii., pp. 89-93.

II.

We pass now to a consideration of the Ethical Self.

A man's ethical self is what is usually known as his Character. Now, what is meant by Character?

The word "character" (Greek χαρακτήρ) signifies, strictly, a graving instrument; then, a stamp upon a coin or seal; then, the impress of a seal upon wax. So that a man's character is, properly, the stamp or image that he bears; and a great writer like the author of the Epistle to the Hebrews, when he wishes to express our Saviour's nature on its Divine side, can find no term more suitable than this very χαρακτήρ: "the brightness of His glory," he says, "and the express image (χαρακτήρ) of His person". It is, therefore, a standing witness to two things:—(1) first, that man is an impressible being, capable of being moulded according to a particular plan or pattern; and (2), secondly, that, being so, his acts and conduct are amenable to law. And, indeed, were this not the case, there could be no such thing as a science of Ethics. Science exists only where laws are discoverable; and a science of the arbitrary and capricious would be simply a contradiction in terms.

It is quite on the lines of the original signification when the word "character" comes to denote the letters of the alphabet, or any picture or symbolical representation of an idea. Either way, it is something expressive—something engraved or inscribed,—something, therefore, that we have the power of reading and interpreting—a distinctive mark.

> Angelo,
> There is a kind of *character* in thy life,
> That to the observer doth thy history
> Truly unfold . . .
> In our remove be thou at full ourself;
> Mortality and mercy in Vienna
> Live in thy tongue and heart.
>
> *Angelo.*   Now, good my lord,
> Let there be some more test made of my metal,
> Before so noble and so great a figure
> *Be stamp'd upon it.*
>
> (*Measure for Measure*, Act 1. sc. 1.)

Etymologically, then, the word bears testimony, so far, to the nature of the thing. But no exposition of Character would be regarded as satisfactory that rested simply on an etymology. Let us proceed, then, to consider the subject in its various details. In doing so, I ask the following three questions:—(1) First, what are the Elements of Character? (2) Secondly, in what manner is Character formed? (3) Thirdly, what is the special Force that is implied in the formation of Character?

I. First, what are the elements of Character?

Human nature consists of a multitude of principles, variously classified, but in general so well understood as to justify me in dispensing with any very elaborate grouping of them. According to current psychological analysis, they arrange themselves around the three centres of Intellection, Feeling, and Conation. The intellectual side of our being is concerned with knowledge or truth, in all its forms and departments—it is the dry, clear light of Reason ; and, as no one can pass through life without having his interest aroused in knowledge at many points, intellectual regard must of necessity enter appreciably into his character. So, no one can pass through life without being deeply stirred on the side of emotion. Loves and hates are naturally strong with men, and the social element is one from which none of us can escape. Will, again, represents activity, and expresses the side of our character that is concerned with our leading avocations and pursuits : it, also, frequently appears as impulsiveness or energy. To these inward endowments, we must add a man's physical constitution, which has a marked share in making him to be what he is, and which determined the old classification of Types of character, or what was formerly known as the Four Temperaments— the sanguine, the melancholic, the choleric, and the phlegmatic.

These are the various parts of human nature, covering collectively the whole of it. But, for our present purpose, it will be convenient to group them somewhat differently. It will be convenient for us to regard man as the subject of various principles, each of which is operative to some extent in every individual, but any one of which may in any given case predominate. Of these principles, some are interested and egoistic, centring in the individual's self (such as self-love, vainglory, etc.); others are disinterested, not having an immediate reference to the individual's self, yet not leading him to take account of other living beings (such as love of knowledge); others still, while disinterested, are also extra-regarding or altruistic, having other human beings than oneself for their object (such as sympathy, compassion, friendship). It is also to be observed that, of the egoistic principles, some are decidedly malevolent (such as jealousy, revenge, vindictiveness); others not.

Now, human Character, taken in its proper sense, denotes, not the absolute annihilation of any one or more of these principles, but the degree of strength that obtains between them. Butler has caught this very well, when he says (*Sermon* xii.): "There is greater variety of parts in what we call a character, than there are features in a face: and

the morality of that is no more determined by one
part, than the beauty or deformity of this is by one
single feature : each is to be judged of by all the
parts or features, not taken singly, but together. . . .
From hence it comes to pass, that though we were
able to look into the inward contexture of the
heart, and see with the greatest exactness in what
degree any one principle is in a particular man ;
we could not from thence determine, how far that
principle would go towards forming the character,
or what influence it would have upon the actions,
unless we could likewise discern what other principles prevailed in him, and see the proportion
which that one bears to the others. Thus, though
two men should have the affection of compassion
in the same degree exactly : yet one may have the
principle of resentment, or of ambition, so strong
in him, as to prevail over that of compassion,
and prevent its having any influence upon his
actions ; so that he may deserve the character of an
hard or cruel man : whereas the other having compassion in just the same degree only, yet having
resentment or ambition in a lower degree, his
compassion may prevail over them, so as to influence
his actions, and to denominate his temper compassionate. So that, how strange soever it may
appear to people who do not attend to the thing,
yet it is quite manifest, that, when we say one man

is more resenting or compassionate than another, this does not necessarily imply that one has the principle of resentment or of compassion stronger than the other. For if the proportion, which resentment or compassion bears to other inward principles, is greater in one than in the other; this is itself sufficient to denominate one more resenting or compassionate than the other."

Just so: Character is a certain proportion amongst the various elements of our nature, and our ruling trait is determined by its strength in relation to the other features. This does not, however, prevent the *kind* of character that a man will have from depending, not only on his possessing such and such elements of human nature, but also on the various influences in life to which he may be exposed. On the contrary, these influences have their own part to play— physical surroundings, race, nationality, social customs, etc.; and, when we sit as moral judges on a man's character, these must all be taken into account.

II. Such, then, being the material of which Character is composed, the next question is, How is this material to be manipulated? In what way is Character formed? By what steps is it built up?

This introduces us to the nature and tendency of Habit,—to the psychological laws of acquisition, in their application to morals.

It is here as elsewhere: "practice makes perfect". Moral habits are formed by a continuous process of repeated acts.

The main points to be attended to are the first start of a habit, and the repetitions necessary to secure its final stability.

1. The management of the first start is determined by the end in view. As the great object in moral education is, not merely to arouse attention, but also to engage the affections, much depends upon one's power to seize the favourable moment, when the mind, for one reason or another, is in the best disposition towards moral things. Success is further conditioned by a knowledge of the individual's leading propensities or inclinations, and by the necessity of presenting morality, as much as may be, on its winning or attractive side. Nor must the physical conditions of Habit be neglected: bodily fatigue can never be favourable for beginning any acquisition. If the initiative must be taken under feeling, if it is only when deeply moved or keenly interested that an effective impression can be made, a lethargic state of the body is not conducive to successful training.

2. Repetition demands the same attention to the physical conditions that the start of habit does. But let this attention be given, and the effects are very conspicuous.

(1) First, Repetition produces pleasure in doing an act, and also facility or ease in doing it. Facility and pleasure go together,—at any rate, in cases where initial distaste has to be overcome. The limitations are evident. (*a*) In the first place, the pleasure is a notable feature only in certain instances, or at certain stages in the formation of moral habit. If there be no primary distaste or disinclination to be overcome, it may not be conspicuous even at the commencement: but, even when there is a primary distaste, the pleasure obviously becomes less intense as the habit approaches the position of a fixed and settled thing. Once it reaches the stage when it acts automatically, when it becomes to us "a second nature," the pleasure attaching to it is little obtrusive,—it is similar to that of a bare instinct ; we may, indeed, be unaware of it until we try to break away from the habit, and then the pain attaching to the wrench impresses us with the potentiality of pleasure that this habit contains. But (*b*), next, pain may be the result of repetition, not pleasure. This is so in all cases where indulgence breeds satiety, or where a want has been created without

the corresponding power of satisfaction. More-over, even pleasures will pall, if there be no inter-mission.[1] Then (*c*), lastly, there is a particular relation between active habits and passive impres-sions, which Butler, with his wonted insight, was the first to see and to formulate, although his mode of formulating it needs a certain correction. It is a law verified in our every-day experience that, the more we give ourselves over to mere feeling, the less disposed to action do we grow: whereas, the more we accustom ourselves to act upon emotion, the more does our ability to act increase, and inversely. The sick-nurse and the doctor may be taken as examples. Repeated experience of suffering does, no doubt, to some extent blunt the acuteness of their sensibility to distress; but then there comes, instead of it, the active habit of relieving, the prompt response in practical assistance, the instinctive rising up to help. This is the amended form of Butler's doctrine, that "passive impressions by being repeated grow weaker," whereas "practical habits are formed and strengthened by repeated acts,"—[2] "active prin-ciples, at the very time that they are less lively in perception than they were, are somehow wrought

---

[1] Voluptates commendat rarior usus (Juvenal, *Satires* xi., 208).

[2] Connect this with Maine de Biran's fundamental law of Habit, —*viz.*, "that it weakens sensation and strengthens perception".

more thoroughly into the temper and character, and become more effectual in influencing our practice" (*The Analogy of Religion*, part i., chap. v.). " What is tenable in Butler's position," as Professor Bain remarks (*The Emotions and the Will*, 3rd edition, pp. 458-9), " seems to be this, that the repeated indulgence of pity as a sentiment, without any corresponding action, grows into a sentimental habit. The sentimental pleasure does not [necessarily] diminish, as his doctrine about passive impressions would make us suppose : what diminishes is the *active tendency*, which belongs naturally to our impulses of pity, and would be strengthened by exercise, while in the absence of exercise it may become feebler than it originally was." Add to this, that the habit of acting on an emotion reduces our perception of the emotion itself.

But there is such a thing as the slavery of *routine* in morals : repetition may produce that. Hence the necessity, if moral progress is to be made, of every now and again awakening a fresh interest and creating an enthusiasm. No doubt, Enthusiasm is in bad favour with many. Even Kant sets it down as a passing excitement, or fleeting emotion, not to be countenanced but discouraged. And, unquestionably, if man were pure reason, his ineradicable attachment to virtue would be of an equable kind and would not admit of higher and lower in feeling. But man is not pure reason, and the tendency of moral habit is to check his moral vivacity, to take away the "spirit" from his moral efforts, and to render him "wooden" in his performance of duty. Hence the value of enthusiasm as a moral factor. You must lay captive the heart, before any great moral change is effected; and it is not too much to say that, if you wish to divert the current of habit, nothing but enthusiasm will do it. The full truth seems to be,— that enthusiasm, or strong feeling, is valuable for the *start* of a moral acquisition, and it is necessary, afterwards, in order to save us from the *deadening* effect of repetition. Enthusiasm just means a burst of feeling, in the form of an awakened interest, that carries one beyond the bounds of the conventional, that enables one to burst the fetters of custom, and to strike out a new course or attach oneself to a new cause or idea.

(2) But, next, Repetition produces, not only facility and ease in doing an action, but also a predisposition to do it.[1]

This is largely explainable on physiological

---

[1] Hence Hume's definition of Custom. "Wherever the repetition of any particular act or operation produces a propensity to renew the same act or operation, without being impelled by any reasoning or process of the understanding; we always say, that this propensity is the effect of *Custom*" (*An Enquiry Concerning Human Understanding,* Section v.).

grounds. Every thought, feeling, action leaves its effect on the nervous system and induces a pre-disposition to its recurrence. And, as this is vastly aided by Heredity, or transmitted experience, the physiological side of habit is seen at once to be a most important one.

(3) Lastly, Repetition, when sufficiently long continued, insures the stability of a habit. This means that it blunts our sensibility to solicitations to break it, and so gives us a certain power to resist successfully.

But the exposition would be incomplete, did I not touch upon another point in reference to moral habit. Moral habit is inseparably connected with moral progress.

This arises from the fact that Morality is concerned with the ideal: what "is" needs always to be tested by what "ought to be," and present attainment, either in character or in conduct, is only at best an approximation to perfection.

What, then, moral habit effects is this :— Not only does it produce facility in doing certain actions, not only does it create a tendency and wish to do them, it also impresses us with the necessity of doing certain other actions which were concealed from us before. In other words, it widens our vision, increases our faculty, and serves as a motive-spring to perseverance. Here, as elsewhere, one step forward secures another,—acquisition leads on to acquisition ; and ever and anon as we reach a higher level, it is not to find a final resting-place, but to see greater heights rising up before us, and to be stimulated to the achievement of greater things than we have yet essayed.

III. So much, then, for Habit, or, what I may call, the *mechanism* of Character. But Character is not all mechanism. On the contrary, the very action of the agencies we have been considering, the cohesions and associations under repetition, imply the reaction of a non-mechanical something ; and this may be least ambiguously denominated Spiritual Force.

Such force is necessarily presupposed in the fact that habit can get a commencement at all ; and it is still further involved in the possibility of breaking off an old habit and contracting a new one. It is presupposed in moral awakening, when the dead or lethargic soul is stirred up to fresh life and vigour. It lies at the root of moral enthusiasm. But it is in moments of great temptation, when we summon up from the depths of our being the whole moral strength that is in us, that we best appreciate and realize its meaning. We are now at the very centre of the ethical self, and are introduced to a twofold power—(1) first, the power of regulating

22

our desires and inclinations; (2) secondly, the power of beating down aberrant tendencies. Or we might express it under a single formula as, the power of moral progress, in the face of resistance, under the influence of an ideal. There is no doubt that we are so constituted as to identify our better self with the ideal, whereas the baser nature swamps us.

And this is really what is meant by " moral freedom". Moral freedom does not mean "absence of rule," " lawlessness," " the power of doing what we like "; it means freedom *from* something, security against *enslavement*— against the enslavement of our baser nature,— vice. It reposes, therefore, upon self-respect—upon the perception or conviction that morality, not immorality, is the law of man's nature ; and if it were possible, without a contradiction, to conceive a man absolutely devoid of self-respect, you would then conceive a being to whom moral freedom is entirely inapplicable, for he would be devoid of the fundamental quality on which alone moral freedom can rest.

Now, where does this ethical force particularly manifest itself?

1. We see it, first, in the battle with the two selves. For, in the warfare that continually goes on between the two parts of our nature, the higher

and the lower, it is a fact that we can raise ourselves in this struggle only by self-crucifixion. The upward progress is always a wrench—it costs us pain and effort; and we gain our life by losing it. Not Goethe and Tennyson alone attest it, but the whole of human experience—

> That men may rise on stepping-stones
> Of their dead selves to higher things.[1]

2. Another sphere of its manifestation is that of unfavourable environment or adverse circumstances.

It is unquestioned that man has a power of moulding circumstances to his will, of transforming them to his ends, and of rising superior to them when contrary: through the hard discipline of life, demanding pertinacity and patience, he realizes his true self. He is only in part, therefore, the "creature of circumstances," and all moral heroism assimilates him to Prometheus and attests his worth. Character transcends condition; and so far the Stoics, with their contempt for external discomforts, were right.

> Men at some time are masters of their fates:
> The fault, dear Brutus, is not in our stars,
> But in ourselves, that we are underlings.
>
> (*Julius Cæsar*, Act I. sc. 2.)

---

[1] De vitiis nostris scalam nobis facimus, si vitia ipsa calcamus (St. Augustine, Ser. III., *De Ascensione*).

3. Once more, we have a case in point in self-realization through self-effacement or the service of others.

No fact in human nature is more wonderful than that of self-sacrifice, or devotion to our fellows' good. It is not simply that self-abnegation is action in the face of pain, but also that, in this way, Character itself is so marvellously transformed. The development of Self through unselfishness is the supreme mystery of ethics.

Such, then, is the nature of the Ethical Self—its elements, its mechanism, and its spiritual energy. We are now ready to advance to a consideration of Conscience.

LECTURE IX.

I. *The Analysis of Conscience.*

CONSCIENCE is defined by Butler, in the *Sermons*, as "a principle of reflection in men, by which they distinguish between, approve and disapprove their own actions": also, as "rationality, including in it both the discernment of what is right, and a disposition to regulate ourselves by it": also, as "reflection, that principle within, which is the guide of life, the judge of right and wrong": more fully, as the "superior principle of reflection in every man, which distinguishes between the internal principles of his heart, as well as his external actions: which passes judgment upon himself and them; pronounces determinately some actions to be in themselves just, right, good; others to be in themselves evil, wrong, unjust: which, without being consulted, without being advised with, magisterially exerts itself, and approves or condemns him the doer of them accordingly: and which, if not forcibly stopped, naturally and always of course goes on to anticipate a higher and more

(341)

effectual sentence, which shall hereafter second and affirm its own". It is also in the *Sermons* that he gives utterance to the famous sentence :—" You cannot form a notion of this faculty, conscience, without taking in judgment, direction, superintendency. This is a constituent part of the idea, that is, of the faculty itself : and to preside and govern, from the very economy and constitution of man, belongs to it. Had it strength, as it had right : had it power, as it had manifest authority, it would absolutely govern the world."

In like manner, in the Dissertation *Of the Nature of Virtue* (written ten years after the Sermons, and appended to the *Analogy of Religion*), Butler says of Conscience : "It is manifest great part of common language, and of common behaviour over the world, is formed upon supposition of such a moral faculty; whether called conscience, moral reason, moral sense, or divine reason ; whether considered as a sentiment of the understanding, or a perception of the heart ; or, which seems the truth, as including both "· where, of course, he uses the word "sentiment" in its popular meaning of intellectual apprehension or opinion, not in its philosophical sense of higher feeling or emotion.

Now, putting these passages together, we obtain a succinct and accurate view of Butler's doctrine of Conscience. He regards it as having both an intellectual and an emotional side : it is both a species of reflection and a kind of feeling : it is intellection touched by emotion,—just as emotion touching morality constitutes Religion, according to Matthew Arnold. He regards it as eminently practical : acting as a magistrate issuing commands, and regulating conduct. He regards it as dealing with men's internal purposes, thoughts, and dispositions, as well as with their external actions. In other words, Butler conceives Conscience as a Judge, discharging also the various other offices of a court of justice. First, it brings a man's character or acts to the test of the moral law ; this law, however, being (unlike that of the civil judge) internal, self-imposed, and not external or enforced from without. Next, it instantly recognizes the true nature of acts, and pronounces a judicial sentence of acquittal or of condemnation —gives the verdict "guilty" or "not guilty". Lastly, it rewards or punishes accordingly—cheers by its approbation, stings by its remorse. Whence it follows :—

(1) First, that Conscience has "authority," or "supremacy," attaching to it—the authority or supremacy of a judge delivering sentence, without the power of appeal, except to that same judge in cases where fresh light has been thrown upon an

act. This exception is an important one, though
not duly emphasized by Butler. We must never
exclude the possibility of fresh light; for, although there is no higher tribunal than that of
Conscience itself, nevertheless, owing to the complexity of man's nature and the difficulty of
disentangling motives and the fact that insight and
knowledge come by experience, it may be necessary
for Conscience from time to time to review its own
decisions—to revise its judgments. This has been
admirably put by Professor Fowler, in his *Principles of Morals* (part ii., pp. 205-6). "The Conscience," he says, "or Moral Sense or Moral Faculty
is sometimes called *authoritative*, or *absolute*, or
supreme. As none of these attributes could possibly be applicable to an uncompleted process [not
to the state of conflict preceding a moral judgment, not to the moral judgment itself, not to the
consequent feeling of approbation or disapproba-
tion], it is plain that, so far as they apply at all,
they apply to the final act of judgment and the
feeling inseparable therefrom. But we must exercise great caution in the employment of these
terms, and in the associations which we connect
with them. The final decision, as it is the total
result of reflexion, is, of course, authoritative. But
it can only be called absolute and supreme in the
sense that there is no appeal from it to any other

tribunal than to the subsequent action of Conscience itself. But there always is, or ought to be, an opportunity of making this appeal back to the Conscience itself, as guided by better information and further reflexion. We are, therefore, quite justified in using these attributes as exclusive of any external authority, but we are not justified in using them as exclusive of the subsequent and more matured judgments of the Moral Faculty, sitting, as a court of appeal, on its previous decisions."

(2) Secondly, Conscience controls. By which is meant that, when reflection has done its best to set an act in its clearest light, and when an unhesitating decision has been pronounced, a rational man necessarily accepts the verdict: and, were man strictly rational, he would always guide himself accordingly. This is, obviously, what Butler means in the second of the definitions already given, when he ascribes to Conscience "both the discernment of what is right, *and a disposition to regulate ourselves by it*". It is irrationality that explains the inconsistency between men's conduct and their better judgment. Present impulse, present passion, is frequently too strong for our higher resolves : hence the anomaly.

Kant saw this, as he saw so many other things, and emphatically expressed it. Referring to the

Categorical Imperative, he says: " But why then should I subject myself to this principle and that simply as a rational being, thus also subjecting to it all other beings endowed with reason? I will allow that no interest *urges* me to this, for that would not give a categorical imperative, but I must *take* an interest in it and discern how this comes to pass; for this 'I ought' is properly an 'I would,' valid for every rational being, provided only that reason determined his actions without any hindrance. But for beings that are in addition affected as we are by springs of a different kind, namely, sensibility, and in whose case that is not always done which reason alone would do, for these that necessity is expressed only as an 'ought' and the subjective necessity is different from the objective" (Abbot's transl., p. 68).

(3) Thirdly, Conscience is an enlightener and revealer to us. Whether it always controls *de facto* or not, it always enlightens us; for it is a species of reflection, and reflection is an illuminative process, bringing character into clear view, showing us the true nature of our acts, and leaving us without excuse if we refuse obedience. Moreover, by exercise it habituates us to moral perception and produces ease in forming decisions,—according to the well-known principles of Habit, the reward to those who "by reason of use have

their senses exercised to discern both good and evil".

Now, with all this as a just analysis of Conscience in its ordinary workings, as actually experienced, we may unhesitatingly agree. Whatever be our theory as to the origin of Conscience and of the moral ideas, whatever opinion we hold as to the ultimate basis of the moral law, whatever be the name we prefer to call the Conscience by, we need have no difficulty in admitting that Conscience is pre-eminently a judge, and that its main functions are to enlighten or reveal, to recompense or reward, and to control or guide. Whether, however, we shall go farther and maintain, with Butler, that the sentence of Conscience is that of the Divine Law, and its authority derived from the Supreme, is the great metaphysical question that will meet us in next lecture.

II. *Moral Judgment.*

For the sake of clearness, what has now been said may be regarded from another point of view: it may be taken in connexion with Moral Judgment.

Judgment is a word having various significations; meaning one thing in Logic, another thing in Psychology, another thing in popular usage, and still another thing in Courts of Justice.

In Logic, judgment stands for the mental process of coupling or disjoining two ideas, one being subject and the other predicate : it designates the subjective side of what, when expressed in words, is known as a "proposition". Psychologically, judgment is simply the mental act of understanding or apprehending the meaning of a statement ; no matter whether the statement be true or false, sense or nonsense. In common parlance, "to form a judgment" is to draw a conclusion from premisses, or to come to a definite decision after deliberation and reflection : and "to express my judgment" is to state my opinion. Finally, in Courts of Justice, judgment means weighing evidence, bringing actions to the test of Law, and punishing or rewarding accordingly.

Now, obviously, it is to the last of these senses of the word that judgment in morals assimilates itself. A moral judgment is different from the mere affirmation of union or disjunction between two ideas. It is different, also, from the simple understanding of a proposition—although this, of course, is implied in it; as well as from the process known in vulgar phraseology as "making up one's mind". It presupposes a law by which we test character or conduct ; it implies bringing an agent and his acts to the tribunal of strict justice, and condemning or acquitting him, as the case may be.

Moral judgment, then, I define as the verdict that we pass upon an agent (oneself or others), acting out of a conscious or intended motive that has a definite relation to the moral law.

Regarding which it has, first of all, to be observed that it is the agent himself, rather than his outward action, that is the subject of a moral judgment, and the agent only in so far as he acts from a conscious motive. The propriety of this is obvious. For, oftentimes, a man's outward action is no real test of his inward character. An outwardly good deed may be done out of a very reprehensible motive; and a disastrous deed may, through lack of wisdom, be the consequence of what was intended by the doer only to lead to good. "Not every one that bears the thyrsus is inspired." Hence the command is "*Be* good," rather than "*Do* good"; it refers to character, and only in the second place to conduct.

Again, a man can hardly be regarded as having acted rightly who simply does the right thing by chance, without ever meaning it; while a man cannot justly be denominated an evil-doer who, without willing it, commits a blameworthy deed. Hence the distinction between formal and material rectitude. An act is materially right when it is outwardly such as would flow from a regard to the moral law ; it is formally right when, in addition to this, it actually proceeds from a conscious regard to that law. It is with formal rectitude, thus defined,[1] that the moral judgment properly deals ; and the material, standing by itself, is morally valueless.

Nevertheless, we cannot, except each one for himself, get directly at people's motives. We can merely infer them from their outward actions. Hence it is that, by a not unpardonable latitude, we frequently speak of the morality or immorality of an outward action. But, when we do so, it is always on the supposition that the inward spring from which it flowed was right.

Thus is *morality* differentiated from bare *legality*. The mere judgment of overt acts from the side of legality is a comparatively easy and a comparatively unerring thing. Certain actions are forbidden by the law, and the doing of them is, therefore, wrong, and entails punishment. Here is a man who has been proved to have infringed the law ; he is, consequently, amenable to the proportionate condemnation and punishment. But it is different when we try to apply the standard of morality to his act. All moral judgments are essentially hypothetical : they are conditioned by the tacit assumption that we have correctly interpreted the

[1] The words " formal " and " material " have a variety of significations ; but their *history* cannot find place here.

motives of the actor. But this is a large assumption.
Motives are extremely complex; they are, indeed,
the man, and are not easily accessible. Hence the
infinite possibility, in our moral judgments, of error
and of injustice.

This being understood, let us return to our
definition of Moral Judgment. Plainly, moral
judgment consists of four distinct elements. It
is, first, a perception of the moral character of the
act,— *i.e.*, of its rightness or wrongness, of the
fact that it conforms or does not conform to the
moral law. It is, secondly, a perception and
acknowledgment or admission that, according as
the act is right or wrong, the agent deserves well
or deserves ill. It is, thirdly, the feeling (and
perhaps outward expression) of approbation or of
disapprobation consequent on these perceptions
and admissions. It is, lastly, the perception of
moral beauty or of moral ugliness.

The first of these perceptions is intuitive, in the
sense to be presently defined. But that does not
forbid that there shall be acts (possibly, many in
number) that shall demand, on the part of him
who would judge them, a great deal of preliminary
investigation and clearing from extraneous circumstances, before it is possible to perceive their exact
character. They are complex in a high degree ; and

difficulties and error with regard to them are due, not to a false perception, but to the mistake of supposing that we have taken account of all the circumstances, when certain of them have been ignored and others (it may be) have been misunderstood.

From the perception of desert which constitutes the second element—must be distinguished the actual apportionment of reward or praise, of punishment or blame,—which may or may not be in accordance with merit or desert, but which, even when justly apportioned, is a logically separate consideration. The perception of desert is one distinctively ethical: it is applicable to persons and to persons only. An inanimate object, a machine, may wholly conform to the physical and mechanical laws under which its existence is possible, and, conforming to these, may continue to serve its purpose or fulfil its end; but, in doing so, it does not acquire merit or come under the category of reward or punishment. But a human being, possessing a character and the power of forming and transforming character, is essentially meritorious or demeritorious: he has an ideal standard of right and wrong by which to test his acts, and, according as he has approached the requirements of this ideal standard or allowed himself to fall below them, he feels himself deserving of approval or of condemnation—a feeling which itself would remain as reward or punishment, although all outward reward or punishment were withdrawn.

The third and fourth elements in moral judgment are moral approbation and disapprobation, and the æsthetic feelings of moral beauty and sublimity or moral ugliness and baseness; of which this alone need here be said, that the two must not be confounded. Moral beauty or sublimity is merely the feeling of pleasure or of awe that the individual derives from the contemplation of moral acts (especially acts like generosity and heroic virtue), while moral approbation is his feeling of sympathetic appreciation of the doer of such acts: the one is subjective and individual (although dependent on objective conditions); the other is objective, social, and disinterested. Moreover, I approve of a moral act because I conceive it to be right, not because I feel it to be beautiful: in other words, moral approbation has its roots direct in the perception of rectitude; and, though we may perceive the rectitude of an act and yet fail to be impressed with its beauty (for, men differ greatly in susceptibility to beauty), we cannot perceive its rectitude without also approving.

III. *The Intuitive Character of Conscience.*

Many modern advocates of Conscience lay stress on what they call its "intuitive" character; and, inasmuch as its pronouncements are intuitions, they regard them on this account as eminently binding. We may best discuss the matter of intuition in connexion with such ethical notions as Right, Wrong, and Ought.

Right and Wrong.

Right and Wrong properly denote a *relation*— the relation of conformity or the want of conformity of an act to the moral law. So that, when it is said that right and wrong are qualities intuitively perceived, the only meaning can be that, given the law and given an act, we at once perceive that this act does or does not come under the law,—just as we immediately perceive, when two rods are laid alongside each other, that they are equal in length or unequal. But this does not explain to us either the origin or the validity of the moral law itself; nor does it help us in getting an act into that simplified condition in which it can be brought into immediate reference to the moral law, any more than does the perception of the equality or inequality of length in two rods help us to procure the rods whose lengths are to be tested. Yet, one of the greatest difficulties in morals often is, to get the complex simplified; and a stiff problem in Ethics has reference to the validity of the moral law.

The moral law itself is in form universal, and rests on the rational basis, " That whatsoever is good for me is good for all other similar beings in the same circumstances ": in other words, it eliminates the idea of individuality, and legislates for man as man; as Bentham pithily puts it, in words already quoted, " Every one to count for one, and no one for more than one ". This is just the philosophical way of expressing the Christian precept, " All things whatsoever ye would that men should do to you, do ye even so to them "; and this universality of scope has rationality as its basis and its justification.

But, although thus universal in form, the contents of the system of moral precepts have grown, are growing, and will continue to grow. As men's circumstances change and experiences increase, as the range and the relations of life are expanded, fresh aspects freely come to view and new additions are made to the already existing code. Although there is little fear that men shall ever outgrow the Ten Commandments, yet a richer and ever richer interpretation will, with widening experience, be given to them, and every age and every nation will have to make its own application of them.

The result of all which is, that right and wrong designate an act viewed in relation to a universalized principle of conduct, taken in connexion with all the circumstances of the case.

Ought.

But it may be said, "Not only do I perceive that such or such an act is right or wrong, but, at the same time, I perceive that it is such as ought or ought not to be done". Now, what is meant by this?

Take a non-ethical instance of "ought". I work a sum in arithmetic, but find that the result is incorrect. On revising my work, I discover that I *ought* to have carried two at some point, but did not. Now, what is the meaning of "ought to have carried two"? It means that, if I wish the operation to be correct, in accordance with the rules of arithmetic, that is the thing necessary to be done.

So, in making for a particular place, I lose my way, and am told that I *ought* to have turned to the right at a certain spot. What is meant by this? It means that, if I desire to reach a particular destination, I must pursue a particular direction.

So, when I tell a man that he *ought* to avoid danger, or that he *ought not* to run his head against a post, my meaning is that it would be contrary to reason—contrary, that is, in this case, to his own self-interest—to act differently.

In like manner, when I say in Ethics, " I *ought* to do so and so," it can mean nothing else but this, —wishing my conduct to conform to moral rule, that is the course necessary to be taken, or the act necessary to be done.

Where, then, lies the difference ? It simply lies here : *not* in the " ought," for, the ought in all the four cases means the same thing ; *but* in the objects of the ought and the inducements that lead us to conform to it,—*i.e.*, in the sanctions—sanctions not imposed from without or arbitrarily enforced, but working themselves out from within. If I refuse to conform to the rules of arithmetic, I simply fail to get the sum correct ; if I will not pursue the road that leads to a place, I simply never reach that place ; if I run recklessly into danger, I am punished. But if I refuse to conform to the law of Conscience, I suffer in the severest way of all. Character and conduct are here at stake ; and, as the consequences of good and bad conduct are of infinitely greater moment to me than those of right arithmetic (regarded simply as an intellectual discipline), or those of reaching a certain place by a certain route, or even those of bodily safety, the " ought " comes to me with the authority of the highest blessing or of a curse. Hence, its binding force is the binding force of serious consequences.

This does not, of course, mean that these consequences are merely external or necessarily of a materialistic kind. On the contrary, it includes all the effects on Character, egoistic and altruistic, and emphasizes the phenomenon of Remorse. Nor does it mean that we are constantly to act out of a conscious regard to consequences. It is quite compatible with a love of the "ought" for its own sake (as we shall see presently), and with the well-known experience of acting purely out of a sense of duty. But it shows that, in the ultimate analysis, Consequences (understanding the term broadly) are what give validity to the moral law; just as their ability to maintain health is what gives validity to the laws of hygiene, or their efficacy in promoting the happiness and prosperity of a people is what gives validity to the laws of a land.

If this be so, we are at once furnished with a satisfactory answer to the question, Why ought I to obey the moral law?

To this question, some are fond of making answer, Because it is right to do so. But, obviously, if "right" be, as has just been explained, a relation, —if it expresses the relation between an act (or, rather, the doer of it) and the moral law,—if it has no meaning except as saying, Here is conformity or non-conformity to the moral law,—the answer, "Because it is right to do so," is simply a vicious circle: it is equivalent to saying, "This is right because it ought to be done, and this ought to be done because it is right"—a way of reasoning which, certainly, does not advance us far.

The way to escape the vicious circle is to lay the foundation of "ought" in the consequences attached to, or, rather, inherent in, action; and to see in these the real force and authority of conscience.

"Oh, but," some will still persist, "you thereby lose the real *ethical* value of 'ought'. The real ethical maxim is, Follow right. whatever be the result ; or, as Tennyson puts it,--

> Because right is right, to follow right
> Were wisdom in the scorn of consequence."

But what does this really mean ? It just means, "Follow right, whatever be the damage to your immediate prospects in life, to your selfish or temporal interests"; or, "Follow right, whatever present pain it may cost you". It is either the pitting of temporal pleasures against character, or of the temporary against the permanent; and, in either way, it is at most but an estimating or weighing of consequences. And even when we are grandly told, *Fiat justitia, ruat caelum* ("let justice be done, though the heavens should fall"), we need not be greatly troubled ; for the *caelum*

that is here put in jeopardy is simply the *material*
heavens, to the passing away of which we could
readily enough assent, if that be the condition of
" *new* heavens and a *new* earth, wherein dwelleth
righteousness ".

But moralists of all schools are ultimately driven
to Consequences as the real test of morality.   For,
let us take such a principle of human nature as
Malevolence, and let us seek to assign its ethical
place as a spring of action, and, if we are not to
locate it arbitrarily and capriciously, we must
rationally appraise it by its consequences.   Butler
himself admits this, in the classical distinction that
he draws between instinctive and deliberate resentment.   The former he regards as legitimate.
Why?   As being necessary to our preservation.
The latter he condemns.   Why?   Because it is
merely a refined luxury, unnecessary to meet the
circumstances of the case, and disastrous in its
results.   Consequences, again, give us the principle
of determination as between legitimate egoism and
illegitimate selfishness, as also between egoism and
altruism.   That both egoism and altruism have a
rightful place in human nature, I take for granted.
But how are we to determine the limits of the
two?   Obviously, by the rational estimate of the
consequences of each.   Egoism, we say, is natural

to man in the form of self-love, because a man, as
one among others, has his equal rights with any
other man; and, as I myself am nearer to myself
than any other person can possibly be, my first
attention is properly to myself. But Selfishness is
a different matter; and when I pit egoistic self-
love against egoistic selfishness, and determine in
favour of self-love, it is on the ground that selfishness, when pronounced, much more when paramount, is destructive of my whole nature. So, when
I limit a man's altruism by his egoism, it is on the
ground of consequences. A man wholly altruistic,
if such could be supposed to exist, would be a
curse to the world. For, if I myself were wholly
to spend myself in serving others, that would be
simply to breed *selfishness* in them, to turn them
into selfish exactors of my service, to teach them
to look upon me simply as an instrument for their
own gratification; and that would be suicidal to
the object of altruism (which is *mutual benefit*), and
so is condemned. Once more, how but by consideration of consequences—consequences to a
man's own self, consequences to the community at
large—can you determine the immorality of the
principle, " It is lawful to do evil that good may
come " ?

We need not be frightened, as many have been,
by the word " consequences " in Ethics, if con-

sequences be adequately interpreted. It has application to character, and to all that conduces to
the formation of character; it looks to the welfare
of the individual and to that of his neighbour
too.

What, then, is intuitive in Conscience is precisely what is intuitive when we draw a certain
conclusion from certain premisses, or when we
form a judgment after deliberation and weighing
of evidence. Given a clear understanding of the
moral law, with experience in morals, and given a
clear knowledge of the exact nature of a given act,
and we at once declare: "This is, or is not, con-
formable to the law; this ought, or this ought not,
to be done": but, on what the validity of the moral
law itself depends is a thing to be determined by
philosophical investigation and reflection.

IV. *Virtue its own Reward.*

Some think that they get over difficulties by
maintaining that "Virtue is its own reward";
understanding by "virtue" well-doing in general,
right living, acting from a sense of duty.

This is a very true or a very erroneous proposition, according to the sense we give to it. If (1),
in the first place, it simply means that there is
such a thing as the *pleasure* of virtue (in other

words, that a good conscience, or a conscience void of offence, is a source of happiness),—if it means that the reward of virtue is not, strictly speaking, something imposed from without, but something necessarily resulting from the virtuous disposition itself, not an extraneous prize but an inward felicity,—this is a very true proposition, to which we may unhesitatingly assent ; just as we assent without difficulty to the proposition that eating is its own reward, or even that forbidden pleasure is, to the eupeptic man, little troubled by remorse or the monitions of conscience, its own reward. If (2), on the other hand, it means that the pains and wrongs of life, if taken in the proper spirit, have a *disciplinary* value, if it means that the virtuous man, by the injustices that he is here called upon to suffer, learns patience, meekness, humility, and all the heroic qualities that we are wont so to admire and laud,—if it means that thereby he has his character strengthened, elevated, and refined, whereas to the vicious man grossness and deterioration of character is the inevitable consequence of vice and wrong-doing,— that, too, is a proposition to which we may readily enough assent. But if (3), thirdly, it means (as most assuredly it must, if it is to have distinctive value) that virtue is always duly recompensed here,—if it means that there is always a just proportion between the reward it brings and the self-abnegation it costs, —this is a proposition so entirely contrary to experience that we must at once reject it. The virtuous man is essentially a self-sacrificing and self-denying man, and essentially a sympathetic man. But the more sympathetic he is, the more sensitive he becomes to the sufferings of others, the more intensely does he suffer himself. His pity's recompense is that of Prometheus :-

> A silent suffering and intense ;
> The rock, the vulture, and the chain,
> All that the proud can feel of pain,
> The agony they do not show,
> The suffocating sense of woe,
>   Which speaks but in its loneliness,
> And then is jealous lest the sky
> Should have a listener, nor will sigh
>   Until its voice is echoless.

(Byron, Prometheus.)

So that, even if we went the length of admitting with Bacon, in the *De Augmentis*, that "all virtue is *most* rewarded and all wickedness *most* punished in itself," we must yet confess the indisputable fact,

> Of what while life still lasts will still be true :—
> Heaven's great ones must be slandered by earth's little :
> And God makes no ado.

And it is just because Virtue is *not* its own reward, but, on the contrary, oftentimes brings

misfortune and discredit to its possessor, not only
loss of worldly goods and station, but also pain
and misery,—it is just because it does so that men,
from Job downwards, have been so greatly puzzled
and perplexed. Then, if Virtue were its own
reward, what room would there be for disinterestedness and self-sacrifice? These would simply
be reduced to a form of selfishness. But disinterestedness and self-sacrifice are facts of human
nature, and facts that give to human nature its
nobility and grandeur. And just because these
are facts of human nature, and because experience
shows them to be insufficiently rewarded here,
therefore, have men been driven to the conclusion
that there is a Future Life, where disinterestedness
shall be valued at its proper worth, and where
merit and desert shall receive their just recompense
of reward.

But note what kind of future it is that Conscience thus postulates. It is a future life under
the reign of Righteousness; and, as such a reign
of Righteousness is inconceivable except as under
a Righteous Person, it is a future life under God.
But is it a future life in which all wrongs shall be
righted and all injustices redressed? It must be
so, when correctly understood; but we must be
careful not to misunderstand it. Future righting
of wrongs and redressing of injustices must not be

so conceived as if it were *then* that the few pounds
or pence that our grasping neighbour has dishon-
estly kept back from us shall be paid down, or the
little patch of land of which a fellow-man, stronger
and more tyrannical than ourselves, has deprived
us, shall be restored. If the present life with its
experiences teaches us anything at all on the moral
side of our being, it is this —to be generous as well
as just; and the real ground of a future life,
disclosed in the conscience, is not the necessity of
giving to each of us our pound of flesh, which we
have failed to get here, but the necessity of giving
righteousness the absolute supremacy, and, in particular, the necessity of rendering something to us
for our having to gain perfection through suffering.
Suffering in itself, even when it refines the character, is a thing so terrible, and seems to us so ill
recompensed by any present compensating consideration that we are driven on by it to the thought
of a great hereafter, when it shall be found that
the blessing of security and of a perfected character
is more than compensation for any present pains
and hardships, and an eternity of bliss more than
overbalances the threescore years and ten of
mixed pain and pleasure here.

V. *Reward.*

But, although it is not true that Virtue is its

own reward, in the sense just now considered, it is, nevertheless, true that Virtue *has* reward or *brings* reward. And it may be well for a moment to consider this.

The rewards of virtue, like the penalties of vice, are of many forms.

1. In the first place, there is inward peace—the *positive pleasure* of virtue, and the support to a man in the face of discouragements.

2. Secondly, there is good reputation with those best qualified to praise,—the natural consequence of upright living.

3. Next, there are temporal advantages that naturally follow the practice of the virtues.

4. Lastly, virtue elevates and refines the character, and is the promoter of social unity, concord, and peace.

In striking contrast to all this is Retribution or the recompense of vice.

1. First comes the haunting fear of guilt,—the pain and terrors of Remorse. Says Schiller: "The world is perfect everywhere, wherever man does not come with his torment. This one thing I feel and know clearly: that life is not the highest of goods, but guilt is the greatest of evils." And it is evidently guilt that Socrates has in his mind, when he maintains the two famous paradoxes: (1) first, that it is a greater evil to do ill than to suffer

ill; and (2) secondly, that it is a greater evil to remain unpunished for wrong done than to suffer punishment.

2. Next comes the irony of seeming success; when the object of desire is attained, but, being reached, fails to satisfy, while the craving for satisfaction continues.

3. Then comes Deterioration of character; when the evil that a man does reacts upon himself, —when his interest in the good diminishes, and the slavery of vice grows upon him.

4. Lastly comes the influence of a man's vicious conduct upon others; the consequences of which may be appalling.

VI. *Moral Motive.*

But, what, now, about the doctrine of Moral Motive? *Is* there such a thing as a purely moral motive? Is it possible for a man to do good just because it is good; to do right simply from regard to right?

Most unquestionably (as I have already admitted); and this is the best thing, on the side of morals, that he can do. No high ethical achievement, indeed, is possible without it; just as it is impossible for the artist to excel unless he has enthusiasm for art on art's own account, or for the student of science unless he be carried away with a love of science for the sake of science, or for the scholar unless he be "soul-hydroptic with a sacred thirst" for learning.

Yet, there is no opposition between this and the position I have just assigned to Consequences in Ethics,—though undiscerning people often think there is. Consequences are the foundation of Morality,—what *justifies* it to the reason, what we see to be the ultimate ground of it on calm and serious reflection. Acting out of a purely moral motive is the end that the moral man *consciously* sets before him. But between the end that a man consciously aims at, and the reason that justifies him (if he feels the need of justification) in aiming at that end at all, there needs be no antagonism; and *here* there is none. The only difference between the two things is that, of the one he is directly conscious, of the other he becomes aware (if at all) through thought and reflection.

A testing example may be found in certain casuistical reasoning,—in all such reasoning as proceeds upon the principle, "It is lawful to do evil that good may come". Against this principle the healthy conscience at once rebels. Now why? Let us take a concrete instance, and we shall see. In Shakespeare's *King John* (Act iii. sc. 1), at the point where the two Kings, John of England and Philip of France, have warmly pledged their friend-

24

ship and sealed it with a sacred oath, Cardinal Pandulpho appears upon the scene direct from the Pope, with excommunication for King John, and calling upon Philip to renounce his alliance with England, to take up arms against it, and to prove himself the champion of the Church. Nobly Philip pleads his pledge, his oath, his sincerity :—

> This royal hand and mine are newly knit,
> And the conjunction of our inward souls
> Married in league, coupled and link'd together
> With all religious strength of sacred vows ;
> The latest breath that gave the sound of words,
> Was deep-sworn faith, peace, amity, true love,
> Between our kingdoms and our royal selves.

But all to no purpose. Pandulpho answers :—

> That which thou hast sworn to do amiss,
> Is not amiss when it is truly done ;
> And being not done, where doing tends to ill,
> The truth is then most done not doing it :
> The better act of purposes mistook
> Is to mistake again, though indirect,
> Yet indirection thereby grows direct ;
> And falsehood falsehood cures ; as fire cools fire
> Within the scorched veins of one new burn'd.

Now, from this casuistry we instinctively recoil. We feel that truth is too sacred to be thus juggled with, and we take up arms against the cardinal. But is our antipathy a mere instinctive feeling, or has it not also a rational foundation ? When we probe it to the bottom, we find that it has a rational foundation—namely this :--That, if a doctrine such as that here taught were carried into practice, Society could not exist. If one dishonest act is allowed to be a proper ground for indulging in another, and if deceivers are to be justified in going on deceiving, then social order and mutual trust are at an end. Our revulsion is really grounded upon consequences ; and moral motive is, in ultimate analysis, rational.[1]

" But," you say, " it is a man's acting from a moral motive that we praise, not his regard for consequences ; and, even if we knew all the consequences, and if these consequences were all such as we thoroughly approve of, yet, if he acted with a view to these, we should not pronounce him virtuous."

Should we not ! What ordinarily makes consequences an *inadequate* moral test is the fact that we usually can trace them but a very short way ; and what makes them *distasteful* to us is the fact that we are apt to identify regard to them with selfishness. But the union between selfishness and consequences is purely incidental ; it is not

---

[1] Another fine example of the principle under consideration is found in the reasoning whereby Odysseus tries to overcome the scruples of Neoptolemus in the *Philoctetes* of Sophocles.

at all necessary or essential. Why should it be thought a selfish thing in me to take account of the likely results of a particular act ? There is no reason whatever ; save perhaps this, that the selfish man is naturally one who does try to gauge the likely results of his acts, but it is the likely results *solely to himself.*

In like manner, Consequences are apt to be distasteful to us because of our tendency to identify them with bare *utility;* and utility is a word, in common usage, associated mainly with the material, commercial, and prudential side of life, with its less dignified and lofty aspects.

Yet, further, Consequences can hardly be made by us the direct test of morality, because they are often of such a kind that the immediate conscious pursuit of them would fail of its purpose. This is in line with the Hedonistic paradox,—That you cannot find pleasure if you make it the immediate object of your quest ; if you are to obtain it, you must seek it indirectly. Health, for instance, comes to us through work ; but work, not health, is the thing that immediately engages our attention. So, knowledge has its pleasures ; but they come mainly when knowledge is sought for its own sake.[1]

[1] See Professor Sidgwick's *Methods of Ethics*, 4th edit., bk. ii. chap. iii. Also, Professor Bain's *Practical Essays*, pp. 19-26.

This paradox is but part of a greater; reposing, as it does, on the law of Transference (which is but a form of Contiguity), according to which we frequently transfer our affections or our dislikes from a given end and concentrate them on the means,—as when the miser gloats over his hoarded wealth, or the author cherishes the pen with which he wrote his book, or the sufferer who has been operated on comes to dislike the beneficent operator. In its highest ethical application, it means the impossibility of the individual attaining Virtue if he imports into the pursuit of it a conscious reference to self. No man can ever be really virtuous if he goes about perpetually saying to himself, "How very virtuous I am!" The whole merit of a self-sacrificing act is removed, once it is ascertained that it was done with a view to self-interest. This is the same thing as saying, that self-realization, in the highest sense of all, is attainable only through self-effacement : in losing our life, we gain it. "But my future fate?" "Yes, thy future fate, indeed?" "Thy future fate," says Carlyle, "while thou makest *it* the chief question, seems to me—extremely questionable! I do not think it can be good" (*Past and Present*, bk. iii. chap. xv.).

But the Hedonistic paradox must be carefully limited and guarded. Not every kind of pleasure comes under its sway. In point of fact, there are many pleasures that are *directly* obtainable. Thus, we directly obtain pleasure in the hot bath, though we make that pleasure the immediate end of our taking the bath ; and our pleasure in eating is not diminished by our consciousness that we are enjoying the meal, nor our pleasure in a friend spoiled by our sense of satisfaction in his company. The paradox holds good conspicuously in the case of a particular class of pleasures,—*viz.*, in the case of those that are consequent on disinterested action (as in knowledge, self-sacrifice, benevolence) ; and what prevents my attaining pleasure here in the direct way is the fact that I seek it as *mine*, the fact that I am morbidly self-conscious about it, that I thrust the shadow of the ego between myself and the object of my quest. Indeed, I try to combine two contradictories—to act disinterestedly, while at the same time the thought of self is uppermost in the action. And this intervention of self, this personal intrusion, is what inevitably makes me lose the desiderated pleasure : for, the pleasure of disinterested action (from the very nature of the case) is not something superadded to the action, is not something tacked on to it from without, but its own natural result, something in which itself necessarily eventuates.

Moral Motive, then, there is ; and, practically,

it determines the value of a man's Character. A morally good act is an act good *in itself*, if you rightly understand the expression "in itself". It is an indispensable phrase, in certain contexts: (1) first, when a man is likely to place his own selfish interests against the good of others; and (2) secondly, when he thinks that he can achieve morality by consciously aiming at the pleasure of it. But, in neither case, are we shut out from an ultimate reference to consequences: rather, in both cases, such a reference is necessary for the complete explanation.

LECTURE X.

VII. *Rational Implicates of Conscience.*

IT is time now to turn to the origin of Conscience, with its rational implications.

That Conscience is not a simple but a complex thing will, I think, from what has been already said, be clearly seen ; and that it has undergone development is not likely to be disputed. The civilized conscience, for instance, is one thing ; the uncivilized conscience is quite another. Time was, in our own country, when many actions were looked upon without rebuke or reprehension which are to-day sternly condemned : many practices were tolerated by our forefathers which we peremptorily disallow ; and, within the present generation, we have seen a marvellous growth of people's sensitiveness to the barbarity of unkind and cruel treatment of their fellows and of the lower animals. It is, obviously, one thing when people take as their highest moral ideal the giant warrior—coarse, brutal, and unsparing, "with whom revenge is virtue,"—whose chief delight is in blood-shed and the cruelties attaching to war, and whose leading recommendation to admiration and honour is the malignity and bitterness he has shown to-wards enemies and the sufferings he has inflicted on them. It is a totally different thing when they take as their ideal the humane enlightened man, whose chief delight is to further unity and concord on the earth, and to practise mercy, generosity, and love. The difference is usually expressed as "an advance in civilization"; but this just means an advance in moral consciousness, for enlightened views and refinement of nature go hand in hand.

This, however, admitted, it does not follow that we must be able to trace historically every step in man's moral advance, from the first germ of the moral conception to its highest development at the present day; nor, even if we could, would it alter, for the ethicist, what I have called the origin of conscience. By "origin" is not here understood *historical* beginning, but logical or rational implica-tion. Fascinating, indeed, and valuable are all anthropological investigations, all ethnological study of savage peoples and extinct races; and we can hardly have too much of them. Intensely interesting are all Darwinian facts and speculations; and we give them a hearty welcome. But, even if it were positively established that man is developed from the ape, or that the lower races of men now existing on the earth are the real type of primitive man, it would in no way injuriously affect the conclusions that I am now about to mention. Our inquiry does not rest on any theory, however plausible, of the actual steps through which man has passed, historically, before he reached his present position. It is concerned with another, and a more important, matter. Taking Conscience as we find it, it asks : " How can we explain it ? What is implied in the fact of there being a conscience at all ? "

To this, I give the following reply :—

1. First of all, there is implied that Conscience is a *social* thing. By which I mean that it is not explicable except by a distinct reference to Society,— in which it originated, and without which it clearly never could have been.

The attempt has often been made in philosophy to take the *individual* as the moral unit, and to explain a man's moral nature as though it were a strictly private possession, something exclusively his own—starting up somehow within him, following its own *laws and development*, and manifesting itself outwardly in his conduct, yet altogether independent of other men. But, plainly, this attempt is destined from the beginning to utter failure. The primary moral unit is not the individual, but *individuals*; and, if we can suppose a man devoid of hereditary tendency brought up from his birth a solitary, without ever coming into contact with any other human creature or social being (and, of course, unconscious of the Deity), it is quite inconceivable how Morality could ever arise within him. Morality implies a relation to moral law, but moral law equally implies the relation of one *person to other persons*; and the leading ethical conceptions of virtue, justice, altruism, self-sacrifice, as well as the leading ethical emotions (sympathy, generosity, friendship, mercy), involve a distinct reference of the individual to other individuals, sharing with him the same nature and having (to some extent at least) identity of interest. No matter whether, in actual history, the beginning lay in the Family (as a past generation thought), or in the Tribe (as recent anthropological research seems to countenance), or in the State (as in old Greek conception, Spartan and Athenian alike). Whatever the primary form of Society, it was of the nature of a community, the members of which were bound to each other by distinct ties. However great the differences, there was a unity; and the mutual contact of living beings was what gave birth to and kept alive the ethical regards.

Nor does this obliterate the individual, as some

would have it : on the contrary, it gives him room for development and growth. He is *there*, one among many, born into society, with his nature adapted to the situation, and ready to expand under social influences. He comes into existence a social being, the child of parents who were themselves social products. And, even if we go back with the Darwinian to pre-human times, Sociality is still regarded as a quality of the creatures from whom man is supposed to be descended ; and the strictest Evolutionist, who carries us to the primitive protoplasm, must still conceive that protoplasm as containing the germ of what, when the time comes, will unfold into sociality and ethics.[1]

Hence the mistake that Hobbes made, when he conceived men as first living apart in mutual enmity and then brought together through the mutual need of protection against each other's ferocity. The men in the first part of the theory are mere abstractions, products of the logical understanding, and not at all the beings whom we know as men : they want the social element, without which man would not be man : or, rather, this element is presupposed in the very fact of their

---

[1] The two chief English works, apart from Mr. Spencer's writings, on Evolutionary Ethics are—Mr. Leslie Stephen's *Science of Ethics* and Mr. S. Alexander's *Moral Order and Progress*.

existence in mutual opposition, and then illogi-
cally let slip in Hobbes's explanation.

Hence, too, the fallacy in Rousseau's theory
that society originated in a "social contract,"—in
the formal agreement of men who had formerly
been at deadly strife to band themselves together
for self-interest. Before you can get men existing
in bitter feud, you must suppose them to be, to
some extent, and in some relations, social beings.
Each man is begotten of parents; and each man
is dependent, in early years, from the very neces-
sities of the case, on the care and nurture of others.

Conscience, then, is, in the essence of it, social :
and its dictates have reference to the relations of
men with men, or with other intelligent or sentient
beings.

2. The second characteristic is that of *generalization.*

If morality is nothing apart from a *law*, then
it is possible only when men have reached the
stage of being capable of formulating and understanding law.

I put it thus guardedly, because there is no
need here to foreclose the question, whether there
ever was a time, historically, when men were without this generalizing power. That must be settled
for us, if at all, on anthropological and philological

grounds. But, whatever the ultimate settlement, it can only affect the *time* when morality began to appear in the history of mankind, *not* the fact that, when it did appear, generality was a necessary element in it.

3. Lastly comes the fact of *authority* — the authority of a sovereign, of a lawgiver, of an arbiter and judge.

This is clearly implicated in Sociality. But that does not mean that it originated solely and simply from the *external* authority of civil government and local institutions. These, no doubt, aid greatly in the confirming and extending of it; but they cannot of themselves account for it. For, *their* authority is external; the authority of conscience is internal. And although, indeed, it be true that an external authority may be said to become internal when a man makes it his own— acquiesces in it, willingly and cheerfully accepts it, —nevertheless, this very power of cheerfully making an external authority our own presupposes rational and social elements in our nature which are not themselves the product of anything external. It presupposes the perception (at first, perhaps, a vague feeling) of the good obtainable from submission to authority—a perception of the identity of one's own good with the good of the community;

and it presupposes social emotions, binding one being to another, and thereby acting as a spiritual force of an authoritative kind (internal, not external)—an attractive influence that *constrains*, without coercing.

True it is that, when we take the individual and watch the development of morality in him, we see that first of all he is a creature *under* authority, helpless in the hands of parents and guardians, and only by degrees comes to realize the full nature of obedience and submission. For several years, he is subjected to the control of others; and, all his life through, being a citizen of some country, he is put under certain restraints and has to curb himself in a thousand ways, which, but from social necessity, he might not be inclined to do. But, even at the earliest stage, he is also *in* authority; for, those in whose hands he is feel him to be a possession, or a charge entrusted to their care, and his needs or wants call forth their active ministration, and his person and his helpless condition bind them to him in the bonds of affection. And this fact he himself is not long in discovering. The tyranny of infants over mothers and nurses is proverbial; and all the time that the child is learning the value of being obedient, he is also experiencing the power of his own personal influence in extracting obedience.

It is impossible, indeed, to determine at what precise moment the first dawn of self-consciousness begins in infants. But it is reasonable to suppose that, when it does begin, consciousness of *putting forth power* is at least coeval with consciousness of external compulsion; and, in the case of the *moral* consciousness, it is reasonable to suppose that the sense of self-direction or self-control is not posterior to that of control by others.

What, then, does this mean? It means that external authority is only one element in the training of a child; and that the real process can only be understood and explained when you take into consideration the circumstance that both he and his trainers are social beings, and both are centres of influence. To ascribe everything in the first instance to *external* authority, is simply to suppose that the infant comes into existence a non-social being, with no original adaptability to his surroundings, and no pre-dispositions, and to ignore the fact that he and his educators are in nature one : in other words, it is to regard him as a bare mental abstraction, and not as a human creature.

But, further, the authority of Conscience is the authority of Reason, directed to a particular kind of relations; and men may act contrary to conscience on the very same ground that they may act irrationally ; *viz.,* because the lower nature may overpower the higher, because present pleasure may be more pressing than the idea of future good, because the passing may thrust out the permanent from our view. Hence, if Reason is binding on man, so is Conscience ; and of each it may be said, —"Had it strength, as it had right : had it power, as it had manifest authority, it would absolutely govern the world".

VIII. *Ontological or Theistic Implications.*

This explains at once the view I take of the ontological and theistic implications of Conscience.

So far as the argument for the existence of God arising from the necessity of a future life in the interests of Righteousness is concerned, *that* was touched on in last Lecture (pp. 364-366), and may be here dismissed. But, so far as the proof of God's existence is dependent on the *Authority* of Conscience, that may seem to be entirely swept away by the doctrine of conscience as essentially a *social* faculty. But is it? Not so. The argument from the Authority of conscience is,—That, conscience being by its very nature a sovereign issuing a command, as well as a judge delivering a verdict (just as the king of old—Solomon, for instance,—besides being clothed with regal power,

25

was also the dispenser of justice), this means that
its authority issues from a *person*, for no conception of authority is possible save as that of a person over persons ; and, as this personal authority
has *universality* attaching to it, this means, in the
last result, that it is gathered up in God : its
approbation, when we do well, points us up to
Him as to our Friend ; its disapprobation, especially as seen in the intensest form of remorse, its
warnings and its reproofs, point us up to Him as
to our future Judge.   Yea, Remorse is particularly
striking, and eminently God-referring ; for, being
the harrowing feeling consequent on our consciously breaking the moral law, its testimony is
specially noteworthy.   Obviously, we cannot have
remorse towards a mere abstract law.   We might
regret breaking a law, we might be *annoyed* with
ourselves for breaking it ; but we should not feel
that we had done any *injury* to the law, so as to
blame ourselves reproachfully for transgressing it.
We can have remorse only on the consciousness
of our having injured a *person*.   And hence, ultimately, Remorse runs up into an acknowledgment
of the being and authority of the Head of all
persons—God.

   But, it may be said : Is not this simply the
reflection of the authority that Society, *an aggregate of persons*, exercises over the individual ?

The obvious answer is, that this would be so, only if the fact of social authority did not itself implicate the authority of the individual. But this it does. For, if the individual is nothing abstracted from society, society itself is only a collection of individuals; and the individual is part of society, not simply as an item necessary to the completion of the whole, but as a portion organically connected with it, like the limbs of a body or the branches of a tree. In other words, the authority that Society exercises over the individual—whence comes it (seeing that it is neither mere brute force nor crude coercive power) but from the fact that the two are sharers in the same nature; that the whole is an organism, not one of whose members may rightfully say to another, "I have no need of thee"? The whole lives in the parts; and the parts are lifeless, if detached from the whole.

But the arguments for God's existence, from the side of Conscience, are not exhausted either by the fact of Virtue's not being adequately rewarded here or by the supremacy of the moral dictates. They are supplemented by two others, of a pregnant kind.

The first of them emphasizes the circumstance that the hold that Conscience has over us is, not the hold of ethical perfection fully attained by us, but the hold of an *Ideal* binding upon us because believed to be ultimately realizable. Now, this Ideal moves us in a living way; it has superior motive force in it. But this, we feel, it could not have if it were itself a bare abstraction. Its power arises from its connexion with personality. And this, when pushed to the extreme issue, just means that One lives in whom perfection is centred, who elicits the Ideal in man, and to whom the ideal points as man's ultimate source. We have here the drawing power of Person on person, alike infusing energy and sustaining effort.

But, next, the nearer a man approaches the ethical ideal, in his endeavours and aspirations to live the highest life, the more sensitive grows his conscience,—*i.e.*, the more intense the pain at transgressions on his part. Hence, the extreme of self-upbraiding is found in the most upright and conscientious men.

This, no doubt, is in part explainable by the laws of Association, and in part it arises from the fact that every breach, however small, of the law of holiness by a good man opens his eyes to the infinite possibilities of future breaches: it affrights him, because it discloses a boundless *potentiality* of evil in him, because it arouses in him the suspicion that it may be only the index in his nature of untold alienation from righteousness. But, when all is said that may be said in the way of accounting for it in this manner, there still remains the patent fact that there is a glaring want of all proportion between the offence and the pain produced by it ; and this, to my mind, can be accounted for only by the supposition of its bearing testimony to a future life and to the existence of an All-holy God.

These arguments appeal very strongly to myself,—although I do not forget that they are only parts of the more general argument that the *whole* of human nature presupposes God. They have the speciality of dealing with a region of man's being where the stratum of the Divine (if I may be allowed a geological term) crops up more strikingly and conspicuously than it does anywhere else. The pressure of Character is ever upon us ; and it occupies and interests us far more continuously than either intellectual or any other pressure. Knowledge is, in comparison, a luxury ; ignorance the majority of men could bear. But character (conduct, as Matthew Arnold, viewing it from without, designates it) is three-fourths of life ; and the issues involved therein are constantly obtruding themselves on our attention. Whatever may be absent, the call of morality is unceasingly importunate. Herein lies the special significance of ethics, and what gives it peculiar value to the theist.

IX. *Objections.*

Against the Ontology of ethics, there are several current objections. These must here be met.

1. First, it is maintained that the so-called ontological implications are not there till we ourselves put them there ; in proof of which (it is said), we have only to note the fact that they were never drawn forth till quite recent times, and by men to whom ethics was subordinate to religion.

Now, let us grant for the moment (what, however, may be very justly questioned) that the metaphysics of ethics is of recent date. What then ? Truth is not to be gauged by the date of man's knowledge of it. It may have been there from the beginning,—wrapped up, involved, or contained in Ethics,—though it were drawn forth, evolved, extracted from it, only yesterday. A seed of wild mustard has been known to lie in the ground for years without germinating, and then to have germinated after a certain period. We should never think of saying that there was no life in that seed until the season in which it germinated : we are reasonable in this instance and say, that it had lain dormant all the term of years, and was brought forth only when the circumstances became favourable. So with the ontological truths of conscience. The time when they were first laid hold of by man and dragged into clear consciousness is not, of necessity, the time when they first began to be : the discovery of them is not the origination of them.

Nor has any one class of men a monopoly of truth. Suppose, again, for the sake of argument, that it was *religious* men that first insisted on theistic ethics. Why should it be thought a disparagement to a truth to be associated with Religion ? If religion has simply opened men's eyes to the full implications of the deliverances of Conscience, while it did not create these implications, ought we not rather to be indebted to religion than unthankful to it ? Whatever furthers our insight, or stimulates us to discovery, ought to be welcomed and gratefully accepted ; and, if you object to an ethicist that he is a religious man, then with equal reason must you object to the physicist—the astronomer, the chemist, the optician —that he is a man with a good pair of eyes.

2. But, secondly, it is argued :—" The so-called ontological truths of conscience are worthless because Conscience is itself derivative, it is a

growth: you can explain it on the principles of the experientialist or of the evolutionist".

Well, suppose it *is* derivative or *is* evolved: how does this militate against its value? We are not usually in the habit of reasoning that, because a thing is acquired or because it grows, it is, therefore, of less worth than if it were original or came at once full-blown into existence. On the contrary: in the case of judgment, for instance, we are in the habit of placing more trust in the opinion of a full-grown man than in that of a boy. And why? Because the faculties of the one are *matured;* those of the other are not. Again, we do not despise the intellectual achievements of the present generation because, through the lapse of time and the accumulated experiences of ages, they have only now become possible. Again, our manual or lingual dexterities—say, one's power of writing or of reading—are none the less valuable because they had to be acquired through much pain and labour,—by the " strait gate " of the alphabet and the " narrow way " of the spelling-book and the Royal Readers. These abilities have grown, or they have been built up, according to the laws of association and acquisition ; and it is certainly no discredit, nor does it detract from their worth, that they are not innate but acquired, not original but derivative. Why, then, should it be different with ethical and moral facts? Why should the fact that they grow or are acquired *not* detract from intellectual or physical abilities, and yet be held to throw discredit on the development or acquisitions of the Conscience? Surely there is something unreasonable in this, and men's minds have got warped by some great prejudice.

No truth seems more needful to be insisted on at the present moment than this,—That no theory of the *origin* of the moral ideas can tell against the import and the value of those ideas themselves. Even if, with some thinkers, we evolve the moral from the non-moral, or, with others, suppose that man's present mental and moral capacities have developed by a natural gradation from the rudimentary mental and moral capacities of the lower animals, —so far would this fact be from shaking our faith in their present trustworthiness and worth, that it would tend to increase it. For, the one great principle of Darwin is, that, in the struggle for existence, the *fittest* survive; and Mr. Spencer's great principle runs, that life and vigour mean the *adaptation of organism and environment.* So that, the very fact that Conscience has survived the the struggle proves its fitness; and what greater guarantee of its truth need be desired than the circumstance that it is in harmony with its environment?

3. But, now, let us face another type of objector. Granting that religion is inseparably connected with ethics, the full requirements of the case, it is maintained, are met by *pantheism.*

This Ethical Pantheism has been widely favoured in Germany, and it has also had distinguished advocates in England. By Fichte, at least in his earlier days, God was identified with the Moral Order of the world ; and the same thing was done by Matthew Arnold, when he defined God as " the stream of tendency whereby all things strive to fulfil the law of their being," and as " the Eternal not ourselves that makes for righteousness ".

(1) Fichte's position has been put in few words by Lichtenberger thus :—

" During the first part of his career, Fichte attached himself in religious matters to Kant. He guards his disciples against the subtleties of dogma. He teaches the necessity of a moral order of the world, which he calls God ; but he expressly denies personality to it, and finds himself not incorrectly accused of atheism. Faith is the accomplishment of what duty orders us to do, without hesitating and without giving regard to consequences. All good actions succeed, for the world is organized for the good ; bad actions fatally fail. All Fichte's philosophy is a masculine appeal to action" (*History of German Theology in the Nineteenth Century*, Eng. transl., p. 12).[1]

Now, regarding this view, it may be at once said, that a "moral order" is an unmeaning expression, unless it implicate personality : for, Morality itself, as we have just seen, has no significance except as between *persons*. Mere "order" in the universe is neither moral nor immoral : the most that we can say about it is, that it is either the condition of morality or the generalized expression of how morality disports itself in fact. No doubt, the good, like the beautiful and the true, needs an ordered mechanism for its development and realization ; and no doubt the world is so constituted that sin "will out," that the consequences of evil acts inevitably work themselves out to the bitter end—as, obversely, the consequences of righteous acts cannot be arbitrarily checked. But this does not in itself constitute the order of Nature moral. The morality lies, not in the world-order, but in that higher personal relationship to which natural order only gives the means of expression.

(2) Neither, on the other hand, has "stream of tendency" any moral implications, if regarded

---

[1] For a succinct account of Fichte's views, see Pfleiderer's *Philosophy of Religion*, vol. i. (Eng. transl.), pp. 275-301. See, also, Professor Seth's *Hegelianism and Personality*, lecture ii.

as impersonal. It has only then a just meaning
when conceived as expressive of the ascertained
drift of men's conjoint actions, guided by an Idea,
and determined by a preconceived end. It is a
felicitous expression for God's moral government
of the world, *so far as men have been able to
discover it in actual experience,* and might very
well stand as the motto for a philosophy of history.
But it is not adequate, nor is it even felicitous, if
the implication of "God" and "government" be
removed from it. Moral *tendencies* are, indeed,
all that we can discern in the history of the race ;
but a "stream of tendency," if it flow at all, must
come from some*where* and be going some*whither*.

It is needless to say, further, that neither a
moral order nor a stream of tendency could enlist
the highest religious veneration, nor satisfy the
deepest devotional feelings of mankind. We may
admire "order," or we may *submit* to it, but we
could not *worship* it ; nor would our worship be
very real, or very lasting, if the object of it were
merely a flowing "stream". Worship can be real
and lasting only when we have a definite conception
of the goal towards which the stream is tending.[1]

X. *Historical.*

I conclude with a reference to the *history* of
Ethical Theism.

[1] See, also, lecture vi. pp. 239, 240.

1. The feeling of the connexion between ethics and religion must have been a very old one in the history of mankind; but it comes first into prominence in the monotheistic faiths,—which is the same thing as saying that it is distinctively Semitic. We saw, in Lecture II., how the Hebrew Scriptures represent it; and we saw there, too, the precise attitude of Christianity. It is hardly necessary to add that Mahometanism follows, in this respect, the Hebrew and the Christian teaching. Considering its origin, it could not do otherwise. The God of the Koran is characterized by high moral attributes, and He is set forth as man's future Judge, who will reward every one according to his deserts.

2. But Tragic Poetry agrees, in this point, with monotheistic religion.

In ancient Greek tragedy—as seen, for instance, in Æschylus,—the workings of conscience are inseparably bound up with the retributive justice of the gods. The "unbending moral order" that is there disclosed as ruling in the lives of men, is a moral order essentially divine. Remove the divine side of it, and the merely moral side lapses or becomes inexplicable. Men are under the supremacy of Zeus, and it is the will of Zeus that ultimately comes to pass; and although, by an unfelt contradiction, Æschylus says, in one place, that—

> Forthwith to mortals God invents a cause,
> Whene'er He wills their dwellings to destroy,—

he more generally, and of set purpose, represents the divine vengeance as the direct result of man's guilt. He does also, in several of his plays, clearly bring out the humane end of punishment, and relieves the sternness of Justice by ultimately unfolding the Mercy it enwraps. Thus does Æschylus blend ethics with religion, and appeal to the one — in the only way that a tragic poet can—as the justification of the other.

Sophocles is in nowise different; except that, with him, the humane side of the Deity comes into greater prominence.

But what is true of Æschylus and Sophocles is true of all great tragic poets—ancient and modern alike. It is truest of all of Shakespeare. Tragedy could never have had existence, had man's life been looked upon as merely under the sway of blind Force; or had the hardships and calamities of human life been regarded apart from any moral import. Mere irresistible misfortune, or crushing disaster, severed from Divine end, might indeed appal us; but it could not impress us with the true tragic sentiment. In tragedy, there must be a fulfilment of the oracle of the gods, and such a fulfilment as brings out some ethical aspect of life's experiences.

3. Not yet, however, have we arrived at the philosophic formulating of the theistic implications of the conscience : neither religion nor tragic poetry gives us *that*.

Perhaps, the germ of it is to be found in Socrates. His teaching, in the *Memorabilia*, about the "oracles" of the gods as intended to guide men as to what they *ought* and what they *ought not* to do; his insistence on the true meaning of man's persuasion of the ability of the gods to make him happy or miserable; his solemn exhortation to his friends to purity of life, both in public and in private, on the plea of God's omnipresence and omniscience; his claim, in the *Apologia*, of Divine sanction to his own philosophizing, and his definition of that philosophizing as the effort to inculcate virtue on the Athenians,—all seem to point in that direction. Again, we have seen [1] the high Ethical conception of the Deity entertained by Plato, and the Platonic doctrine of man's kinship to God through holy living.

But the Moral argument, as explicitly stated, comes much later. It is scarcely even mediæval. For, although great interest attaches to the doctrine of conscience laid down by Abælard, in the twelfth century, and, again, to the ethical teaching

[1] Lecture II.

of St. Thomas, as given in the second part of his *Summa Theologiæ*, in the thirteenth century, neither of these illustrious thinkers does more than indicate the intimate connexion between Ethics and Theology, and prepare the way for theism on the basis of the conscience. If, as Dr. Hutchison Stirling reminds us,[1] there was really no veritable "Natural Theology" "till the work expressly so named" by Raymund of Sabunde, this dates our argument from the middle of the fifteenth century of our era. Raymund laid particular stress on the fact of retribution, and therefrom extracted the necessity of God's existence and of a future life. The name, however, of greatest influence, in Britain and throughout the English-speaking world, was that of Butler; and Kant is the modern starting-point, on the same lines, in Germany. To Butler, Conscience was "divine reason," "naturally and always of course going on to anticipate a higher and more effectual sentence, which shall hereafter second and affirm its own"; and, to Kant, the Practical Reason demanded the Deity as a postulate. Fichte endeavoured to adapt the view to pantheism; Wordsworth, in his *Ode to Duty*, gave it enduring expression in poetry: and the *Christian* setting of it, in its most perfect form, was reserved for Cardinal Newman. Said Newman,

[1] *Gifford Lectures*, p. 24.

in one of the finest passages in the English tongue : "Conscience is not a long-sighted selfishness, nor a desire to be consistent with oneself; but it is a messenger from Him, who, both in nature and in grace, speaks to us behind a veil, and teaches and rules us by His representatives. Conscience is the aboriginal Vicar of Christ, a prophet in its informations, a monarch in its peremptoriness, a priest in its blessings and anathemas" (*A Letter Addressed to his Grace the Duke of Norfolk*, p. 57).

Page after page might be filled with the names of theologians and of philosophers who, since Butler's day, or since Kant's day, have accepted the moral argument, with such additions or modifications as seemed to each to be necessary. The following at once occur to the mind :—Ulrici, Trendelenburg, Lotze ; Rothe, Dorner, Schenkel ; Martensen, Van Oosterzee ; Vinet, Janet ; Channing, M'Cosh ; Sir William Hamilton, Chalmers, Tulloch, Flint ; Sumner, Mansel, Whewell, Bishop Ellicott, Dr. W. G. Ward, Dr. Martineau, and the author of *Agnostic Faith*. Detailed consideration is here impossible. But it may be well to indicate, in a few sentences, the leading points that mark the lines of cleavage among the foregoing writers as ethical theists.

They have reference to three allied questions :—first, the exact relation between ethics and religion:

secondly, the place or importance of the moral argument, as compared with other theistic evidence afforded by human nature ; thirdly, the question of priority as between ethics and religion.

As to the first of these questions, many have held, with Butler, that religion and morality, though intimately associated, are, nevertheless, distinct—there is something in the former over and above what is given by the latter ; many, on the other hand, have maintained, with Kant, that religion is nothing but a kind of morality. As to the second question, a large section of thinkers accept the moral argument as one—an important one—among several ; a smaller section (represented in this country by Sir William Hamilton, for instance) regard it as the only valid argument. As to the third question, Schenkel held that we must begin with religion, for conscience is ethically meaningless till we have experienced a conscious falling away from communion with God ; the vast majority reverse the statement and maintain that religion itself is ethically meaningless except on the presupposition of conscience, as consciousness of moral law.

LECTURE XI.

In approaching the intellectual side of the Theistic idea, it will be well to commence with a consideration of the great historical attempts of the human mind to reach the Deity by logical effort. These are usually known as the theistic "proofs,"—drawn respectively from Design, Causality, and Mental Conception; each necessarily fragmentary, but yet held to be satisfactory, if restricted to its own point of view.

I.

The first of these is the TELEOLOGICAL ARGUMENT, or ARGUMENT FROM DESIGN.

This argument is pre-eminently the popular one, and was, accordingly, in point of history, first in the field; although it would be difficult to say when or with whom it actually originated. In the Hebrew Psalms, we know that the heavens are set forth as declaring the glory of God and the firmament as showing His handiwork; and this language represents a religious mood that must

(403)

have been very early. We know, also, that Pythagoras, among the Greeks, was the first to view the world as an ordered whole—a cosmos ; and that his philosophy dealt much with harmony and numbers. But the distinct formulating of the religious experience and of the intellectual apprehension of harmony in Nature as a theistic proof comes to us later. It is doubtful whether it can be traced to Anaxagoras. No doubt, the sage of Clazomenæ was among the first to recognize with any vividness that Νοῦς or Mind is the ruling principle in the universe ; but whether this intelligence or mind was regarded by him as a Divine Providence is questionable. The theistic step, however, was definitely taken by Socrates, and taken on teleological grounds; and so, with him, practically, the argument from design or from final causes (in Aristotelian phrase) arose. His position, as given by Xenophon in the *Memorabilia*, was this :—" As we know our own mind by its operations, so we know God by His works. As we infer the existence of the artist from his work of art, so we infer from the world as a work of art, and, more particularly, from organized beings as living structures, whose parts all minister to the good of the whole, the existence of the Divine Artist—of an intelligent designing Author or Artificer." This reasoning was accepted by Aristotle, and passed on to the Greek Schools. It was taken up, elaborated, and eloquently expounded in Rome by Cicero, was dwelt upon with satisfaction by Seneca, and became the leading intellectual argument for the Divine existence in the Latin world. In Christendom, we find it occupying a prominent place in the writings of the early Apologists (Marcus Minutius Felix, etc.); and it was a prime favourite with the Church Fathers, both of the East and of the West. In Scholastic days, it still commanded respect; though, from the time of St. Anselm, it was overshadowed by the ontological argument. Frequently, indeed, in all ages, we find dissentients from it : it did not rule unquestioned. Epicurus in ancient Greece, Lucretius in Rome, and, speaking broadly, the Atomic and Epicurean philosophers generally, regarded it as vicious. But, practically, it held its own till the time of Descartes and Bacon, who, though themselves theists, banished teleology from the region of Science;[1] and Spinoza is generally credited with having finally disposed of it in Philosophy. This, however, did not prevent Kant, later on, from first accepting the argument and

---

[1] See Descartes's *Meditations*, iv., and *Principles of Philosophy*, i. 28. For an account of Bacon's attitude towards Final Causes, see Professor Fowler's Introduction to his edition of Bacon's *Novum Organum*, pp. 63-68 ; and for a clear, though brief, criticism of the teleological argument from the side of Logic, see Professor Fowler's *Inductive Logic*, 4th edition, pp. 338-352.

then disowning it, though always speaking of it with respect; and when, in last century, the Deistic tide set in so strongly in Great Britain, and David Hume became the terror of all who rested simply in unreasoned convictions, not only did theologians like Paley come forward to stem the current with a *Natural Theology* on purely teleological lines, but philosophers like Reid refurbished the old weapons and tried to put a new edge on them. The necessity became greatest as the century drew near its close; for, then the French Revolution was in full swing, and religiously minded people were driven, perforce, to find a popular basis for Theism, which had been so violently outraged. This accounts for the prominent place given to Natural Theology by Dugald Stewart in his Moral Philosophy Lectures, and points to one ground of the widespread influence exerted by that eloquent Scottish Professor. But the British intellect is essentially practical and essentially concrete. Hence a further reason for our nation's special and continued favour for reasoning that traced the Deity in the works of Nature. Even Scotland, with its reputation for a love of metaphysics, has been always characterized by cautious sense, which has been interpreted as a synonym for distrust of speculation and distaste for what is visionary and impracticable. Hence, Dr. Thomas

Brown, the successor of Dugald Stewart in the Moral Philosophy Chair in Edinburgh, pinned his philosophic faith in Theism on the argument from Design, and vigorously maintained that this is the only valid argument, and that all others are mere scholastic jargon. He said :—

"God, and the world which He has formed— these are our great objects. Everything which we strive to place between these is nothing. We see the universe, and, seeing it, we believe in its Maker. It is the universe, therefore, which is our argument, and our only argument ; and, as it is powerful to convince us, God is, or is not, an object of our belief. . . . My last Lecture, Gentlemen, was employed in considering the evidence which the frame of nature exhibits, of the being of its divine Author. Of this there appears to me to be only one argument which can produce conviction, but that an argument so irresistible, as to correspond, in its influence on the mind, with the power of him whose existence it forces even the most reluctant to acknowledge. The arguments commonly termed metaphysical, on this subject, I have always re-garded as absolutely void of force, unless in as far as they proceed on a tacit assumption of the phy-sical argument ; and, indeed, it seems to me no small corroborative proof of the force of this phy-sical argument, that its remaining impression on our mind has been sufficient to save us from any doubt as to that existence, which the obscure and laborious reasonings a priori, in support of it, would have led us to doubt rather than to believe" (*Lectures on the Philosophy of the Human Mind*, xcii., xciii.).

It is hardly necessary that I should mention in this connexion the *Bridgewater Treatises*, or the *Burnett Prize Essays*, or Professor Flint's *Baird Lectures:* these will occur to every one. Dr. Martineau's *Study of Religion*, too, and Dr. Hutchison Stirling's *Gifford Lectures* are too recent to need to be more than named. But it may not be amiss if I point out that Aberdeen has always been noted for its attachment to this particular argument; beginning with Dr. Thomas Reid, and coming down, through a long line of eminent moral philosophers and natural theologians—Dr. John Gregory,[1] Principal George Campbell, Beattie, Professor Duncan Mearns,[2] Professor Robert Macpherson, Professor Samuel Trail,—till we reach the subtle and sagacious Principal Pirie, who, however, saw, with that dialectical acuteness which characterized him, the weak points in the ordinary modes of putting the reasoning.[3]

---

[1] See his *Comparative View of the State and Faculties of Man, with those of the Animal World.*

[2] See his *Principles of Christian Evidence.*

[3] See his *Natural Theology*, and the posthumous work published last year (1892) from his MSS., entitled *The God of Reason and Revelation.*

Yet, cherished though the Design argument has been, it is not at this moment so general a favourite, either among philosophers or divines, whether here or elsewhere, as it formerly was. The spread and deepening of the scientific spirit has effected that. But it has been effected, also, by a growing philosophical insight, with the consequent conviction that, as a *proof* of the Divine existence, the argument is not conclusive.

We shall now see how, from the point of view of criticism, the matter stands.

1. Arguing from the structure of living organized beings, such as man, whose parts minister to the wants of the whole, Socrates, in the *Memorabilia*, based his reasoning on the principle that "whatever exists for a use is the work of intelligence"; and the conclusion to be drawn from the argumentation was precisely that which was deduced by Aristodemus, "The more I consider it, the more evident it appears to me, that man must be the masterpiece of some great artificer, carrying along with it infinite marks of the love and favour of Him who hath thus formed it". The Socratic principle extended also to Nature, and embraced within its sphere "this stupendous universe, with all the various bodies contained therein, equally

amazing, whether we consider their magnitude or number".

(1) Now, in the first place, the whole question as to the value of the fundamental principle here stated rests upon what is signified by the phrase " existing for a use" (τὰ ἐπ᾽ ὠφελείᾳ γιγνόμενα).

Does it merely mean " serving a purpose"? Then, the validity of this general principle may very justly be disputed; for, many things are serviceable to us that cannot be affirmed to have been brought into existence for the very purpose of this service. Reasoning from "uses" may land us in triviality; and Hegel has very properly warned us against " first of all treating of the vine solely in reference to the well-known uses which it confers upon man, and then proceeding to view the cork-tree in connexion with the corks which we cut from its bark to put into the wine-bottles" (*The Logic of Hegel*, Wallace, § 205).

Or, does the phrase mean, "Designedly brought into existence for the very use that we see the thing serving"? Then, here you presuppose a knowledge of Nature's uses that is only compatible with the supposition that you first know God and are acquainted with His purposes, or, at any rate, are certain that, in all the uses that things in Nature serve, He has a purpose : in other words, you start with taking for granted the Divine exist-

ence, which it is your object in the argument to
prove.

(2) But, next, the representation here given
of God is that of an artist or artificer shaping
or moulding a given material—a mere Demiurge,
working at the universe according to a Divine
pattern, such as we see in the *Timaeus* of Plato.
He is, moreover, only a finite and imperfect artist,
for flaws and imperfections mar the work. Nor
will it avail to say, that these flaws or imperfections are only apparent,—that, if we knew all,
they would be seen to be no imperfections. For,
then, we lay ourselves open to the retort that, if
that were so, it may be argued on similar grounds
that the so-called perfections may turn out to be
no perfections : if we knew all, we should discern
them to be very faulty. The appeal to our ignorance, under the seemingly modest phrase "if we
knew all," is quite inadmissible in an argument
that proposes to reason merely from what we see
and find.

But, worst of all, the Artificer conception is
not one that modern science can countenance.
Evolution forbids it. Nature is a process, a development ; and it is felt that the hard and fast
lines of a definitely fixed mechanism would not
give scope for the energies that we actually find
at work. Teleology there is ; but it is inherent,

not extraneous. As Leibniz clearly saw, "everything has its end just in its own nature, and realizes it by developing its own constitution. And the end of the world as a whole lies in nothing but the greatest possible sum of the perfection, or inner conformity to their ends, of all its parts" (Pfleiderer, *The Philosophy of Religion*, Eng. transl., vol. i. p. 94). And Lotze, in times nearer our own, has perhaps done more than any other man (especially in bk. iv. of his *Mikrokosmus*), to give just philosophical expression to the idea of teleology in Nature.

2. Let us, then, select another typical way of putting the argument, and see if it fares better.

Reid formulates it thus :

"The argument from final causes, when reduced to a syllogism, has these two premises: *First*, That design and intelligence in the cause, may, with certainty, be inferred from marks or signs of it in the effect. This is the principle we have been considering, and we may call it the *major* proposition of the argument. The *second*, which we call the *minor* proposition, is, That there are in fact the clearest marks of design and wisdom in the works of nature ; and the *conclusion* is, That the works of nature are the effects of a wise and intelligent Cause" (*Reid's Works*, pp. 460*b* and 461*a*).

Reid's major premiss has been otherwise expressed. Paley and many besides say : " Contrivance must have a contriver ; design implies a designer ".

Now, Reid's argument may readily be acquiesced in, if only he satisfy us on two points : if, first, he prove to us that the world is an effect ; and if, secondly, he supply us with some means of determining what in the world, what " in the works of nature," are marks of design, and what not. But just here lies the difficulty. Apart from the first condition (which, however, is a most important one), we naturally ask, regarding the second : Is *every* mere adjustment of means to an end a mark of design ? or, are *only certain kinds* of adjustment marks of design—such adjustments, for instance, as we find from experience result from human skill or contrivance ? or, is it only adjustment *on the vast scale* that is suitable for the teleological argument ?

Plainly, not all adjustments of means to ends, not all adaptations of things to uses, bespeak design—that is, bespeak conscious or intended purpose. Here is a huge boulder, with a large cleft in it, resting on the ground ; and overhanging it is a tree, from which the wind wrenches a branch, and, dashing it with great force into the cleft, rivets it so tightly there as to make the branch thus riveted a useful pole from which to suspend a child's swing. Are we to maintain that this perfect adjustment of stone and branch to the use made of it is a mark of purpose or design, is an index of intelligence, a proof of objective mind? Here, again, is a torrent rushing vehemently down a mountain side and cutting for itself a channel in the earth. Where is the evidence of conscious purpose or design? Not every adjustment of means to ends is significant of design. At what point, then, is our argument to begin? There are *unintended* adaptations in Nature, or adaptations from which we are not at liberty to infer conscious intention. On what grounds are we to determine the adaptations that are legitimate to our argument, and those that are not?

I can imagine only two such grounds. Either, first, we are to use none of Nature's adaptations save such as are analogous to adaptations made consciously by ourselves, and which, from our own experience, we know to be significant of conscious purpose: or, secondly, we are to throw the emphasis upon the *vastness* and complexity of Nature's adaptations, and maintain that this is such as cannot be accounted for by mere Chance.

The first of these grounds is not very satisfactory: we need some specific test to tide us over the difficulties that meet us in practical detail.

The cleft of the rock that riveted the wind-tossed branch of the tree might have been made by human hand : we, not unfrequently, see men cleaving rocks for various purposes. And man might have placed the riveted branch in the cleft, with the very object of using it as the point of support for the child's swing : that is only similar to what we see him doing every day.

The stress of the argument, then, must be placed upon the second of the two grounds : and then the reasoning becomes an application of the mathematical doctrine of Chances.

The criticism may be put in another form. Design certainly implies a designer, or marks of design in the effect prove design in the cause. *That* every one must grant. But, then, we have given our adherence to a mere tautological expression ; for "design" means just such works, *and such only*, as a designer effects, and an "effect" presupposes a sufficient cause. And this does not help us in any degree towards ascertaining whether Nature does actually show marks of design. All that you can legitimately reason regarding the world and design is, That, *if* God is the Author of the world, then the world must be such as we should expect from work emanating from the Supreme Wisdom. And if, on examination, we find it to be such, that is *corroborative* of Theism, but is no primary "proof" of God's being.

3. Perhaps, it will be different, if we take a third typical form of the argument,—the form in which it is presented to us by Principal Tulloch in his *Burnett Prize Treatise*, and endorsed by Professor Flint in his *Theism*. Says Principal Tulloch (p. 12) :—

"The theistic argument may be syllogistically expressed as follows, in a form which appears to us at once simple and free from ambiguity—viz., First, or major premiss,

Order universally proves Mind.

Second, or minor premiss,

The works of Nature discover Order.

Conclusion,

The works of Nature prove Mind."

Now, the advantages in this mode of statement seem to be various. In the first place, by using the word "Order" in the major premiss instead of Design, and "Mind" instead of Cause or Designer, the proposition is saved from being obviously tautological. In the next place, by using "order,' rather than "causation" or "design," you remove the burden of proof from the minor premiss to the major ; for, however much people may dispute as

to whether the works of Nature really discover
design, few will deny that they exhibit *order*.
Lastly, the externality of the Designer, as of a
demiurge or artificer, is, in this form of the argument, got rid of.[1]

But, notwithstanding these advantages, the
demonstration is not without its difficulties. For,
what is Order? and, can we say that Order is
universally the correlate of Mind?

By Order is meant either (1) adjustment of
parts, adaptation of means to ends; or (2) law (in
the scientific sense of that term), regularity of
arrangement and occurrence. But, if so, does this
necessarily or universally involve Mind?

Our former example of the Boulder and the
Branch comes back to us and necessitates an
answer in the negative, so far as the first meaning
of Order is concerned. In that instance, there is
no implication of Mind, —except it be the mind of
the person looking at the boulder and the branch,
or of the person thinking of it or utilizing it. There
is no implication of *objective* mind. And unless
objective mind be involved, the argument for
theistic purposes is useless.

But is it different with the second meaning?

---

[1] This would have met with the approval of Tennyson, who is
recently reported to have said: "I do not like such a word as *design*
to be applied to the Creator of all these worlds, it makes him seem a
mere artificer" (*Contemporary Review*, March, 1893, p. 395).

Nature is indeed *uniform;* we can see that it is a
system. But it was just this fact of system (the
reign of law) that led Spinoza to exclude the idea
of a *personal* God from it, and that seemed to
confirm the doctrine of pantheism. Moreover,
Order, though a mark of Mind, cannot be dogmati-
cally asserted to be the property of Mind alone ;
and, even if intelligence be granted as the exclusive
correlate of order, we are yet a long way from the
demonstration of the *unity* of the ordering intelligence. There is nothing absurd in supposing that
the cosmos may be the result of a conclave of
intelligences, just as the Government of Britain is
the product of the combined wisdom of a Parlia-
ment. The Order argument is not incompatible
with a polytheistic conclusion ; only, the gods, in
so far as the order discernible in the world is concerned, are shown to act in unison. Yea, where
discord, jarring, imperfection, maladjustment are
apparent, *there*, it may be maintained, we have the
marks of a compromise between conflicting intelligences and so a clear argument for polytheism.[1]
Nor, once more, can the intelligence discoverable
in the world be shown to be more than finite, and
there is unquestionable force in Hume's contention
(though we might word it more carefully) : "The

---

[1] The case as against polytheism is psychological, and has been
stated in lecture vi., in connexion with the " Unity " of God.

cause must be proportioned to the effect: and if we exactly and precisely proportion it, we shall never find in it any qualities that point farther, or afford an inference concerning any other design or performance. Such qualities must be somewhat beyond what is merely requisite for producing the effect, which we examine" (*Enquiry Concerning Human Understanding*, section xi.).

The only kind of Order that necessarily implicates objective Mind is *moral* order; for, here "order" means Law, not in the scientific sense of mere uniformity or regularity of occurrence, but in the juridical sense of *authority*— of binding command issuing from a lawgiver. But, then, the argument passes beyond theology, and enters the sphere of Ethics; where we have already considered it (see Lecture x.).

"What, then, after all this criticism," it may be asked, "is the value of the Design Argument? or has it any value at all?" Yes, it has a value. It aims at expressing the *immanence* of the Deity in the world, His permeating presence in the universe. Where it fails is, in attempting to demonstrate this immanence syllogistically. Such a mode of proof is impossible. We start from the idea of immanence, *given in theism as based in human nature*, and should simply claim to *illustrate* it from the world,—to illustrate and to enrich it. That there is a *meaning* in Nature is, in the first instance, taken for granted; and the duty of the teleologist is to spell out this meaning, and his success must be the justification of his procedure. The necessary presupposition is that, if the world were not first interpretable by thought, it could never be seen to have its being *in* thought.

II.

The next of the so-called theistic "proofs" is the COSMOLOGICAL ARGUMENT.

The experiences which this argument claims to formulate are such as must have been coeval with man, though the argument itself is comparatively recent. We have not to live long in the world till we find that all things here are full of change, that experienced facts begin to be and cease, that life itself is evanescent and "nothing continueth in one stay". And the longer we live, and the wider our knowledge, the more strongly is this impression borne home upon us.

This has been eloquently put by Professor Huxley (following Heracleitus), in his Romanes Lecture, delivered at Oxford a few months ago. "As no man fording a swift stream," he says, "can dip his foot twice into the same water, so no man can, with exactness, affirm of anything in the sensible

world that it is. As he utters the words, nay, as
he thinks them, the predicate ceases to be applicable ; the present has become the past ; the 'is'
should be 'was'. And the more we learn of the
nature of things, the more evident is it that what
we call rest is only unperceived activity ; that
seeming peace is silent but strenuous battle. In
every part, at every moment, the state of the cosmos is the expression of a transitory adjustment of
contending forces ; a scene of strife, in which all
the combatants fall in turn. What is true of each
part, is true of the whole. Natural knowledge
tends more and more to the conclusion that 'all
the choir of heaven and furniture of the earth' are
the transitory forms of parcels of cosmic substance
wending along the road of evolution, from nebulous
potentiality, through endless growths of sun and
planet and satellite ; through all varieties of
matter ; through infinite diversities of life and
thought ; possibly, through modes of being of which
we neither have a conception, nor are competent
to form any, back to the undefinable latency from
which they arose. Thus the most obvious attribute
of the cosmos is its impermanence " (*Evolution and
Ethics*, p. 4).

At the same time, along with this conviction of
the impermanence of the things of sense and the
fleetingness of the experiences of life, is begotten

dissatisfaction with the impermanent and the fugitive. But this just means that man's nature craves for something that is permanent and changeless and wholly satisfying; and, as this craving is a "natural want," in the sense that we have already defined natural wants (see Lecture v.), this means, not only that man finds satisfaction in God, but also that his theistic longing could not have arisen apart from Him. This is precisely the doctrine of the psychological basis of theism that it has been the purpose of these lectures to maintain and to develop.

But thinkers have submitted the foregoing experiences to the logical understanding, and have tried to throw them into syllogistic form,—thereby weakening their force and detracting from their value. Sometimes they have reasoned, "The world is an effect and presupposes a cause; therefore, God exists". At other times they have said, "I myself am and began to be; therefore, God, as Supreme intelligence and power, exists". Still again they have argued, "Since something now is, it is manifest that something always was".

The first of these modes of arguing is Hobbes's. In the passage already quoted from his treatise on *Human Nature*, we heard him saying:[1] "The effects we acknowledge naturally, do include a power of

---

[1] See Lecture iii. pp. 103, 104.

their producing, before they were produced; and
that power presupposeth something existent that
hath such a power : and the thing so existing with
power to produce, if it were not eternal, must
needs have been produced by somewhat before it,
and that again by something else before that, till
we come to an eternal (that is to say the first)
Power of all powers, and first Cause of all causes :
and this it is which all men conceive by the name
of God, implying eternity, incomprehensibility, and
omnipotency ".

The second mode of statement is Locke's. In
book iv., chapter x., of the *Essay Concerning
Human Understanding*, he lays down the position
that " man knows that he himself is ". Then, com-
bining this with the further position that " he
knows also that Nothing cannot produce a Being,"
he reaches the conclusion that there must be
" Something eternal ". But this " Something eternal " must also be "most powerful" and "most
knowing," otherwise he could not be the source of
all imparted power and of man's knowledge.
" Thus, from the consideration of ourselves, and
what we infallibly find in our own constitutions,
our reason leads us to the knowledge of this
certain and evident truth, that there is an eternal,
most powerful and most knowing being, which
whether any one will please to call God, it matters

not; the thing is evident, and from this idea duly considered, will easily be deduced all those other attributes, which we ought to ascribe to this eternal being."

The third formula is given us by Samuel Clarke.

Other modes of expression, from Albertus Magnus and St. Thomas downwards, or, farther back, from Aristotle[1] downwards (not forgetting, as we reach modern times, Leibniz, Wolff, Cousin), might be noted; but it is unnecessary to multiply examples.[2] This however, from Hugo Grotius, may be adduced as a final instance:—"That there are some Things which had a Beginning, is confessed on all Sides, and obvious to Sense: But these Things could not be the Cause of their own Existence; because that which has no Being, cannot act; for then it would have *been* before it *was*, which is impossible; whence it follows, that it derived its Being from something else: Which is true not only of those Things which are now before our Eyes, or which we have formerly beheld: but also of *those* out of which *these* have arisen.

---

[1] Aristotle, indeed, is practically the originator of the argument. See his declaration about the Prime Mover of the universe, as given in Lecture ii. p. 46.

[2] Reference may be made to Canon Mozley's Lecture on *The Principle of Causation Considered in Opposition to Atheistic Theories*, and to the chapter on "The First Cause" in Professor Calderwood's *Handbook of Moral Philosophy.*

and so on, till we arrive at some Cause, which
never had any Beginning, but exists (as we say)
necessarily, and not by Accident, and this Being,
whatsoever it be (of whom we shall speak more
fully by and by), is what we mean by the Deity, or
God" (*The Truth of the Christian Religion*, bk. i.
sect. 2, translated by Dean Clarke of Sarum).

Now, clearly, this mode of reasoning is not free
from objection. In the first place, it is not well to
start (as Hobbes does) with the assumption that
the world is an effect. All that is given in experience is the world's changeableness, and its inability
to satisfy man's deepest wants. In the next place,
the argument is from a finite effect to an infinite
Cause: in other words, the reasoning is vitiated
by having more affirmed in the conclusion than is
legitimated by the premisses. When it is said,
"Something now is, therefore something has always been," the reply is ready, "Yes, but what
prevents this something that now is from having
itself always been? The eternity of the world has
been maintained by many philosophers; and, un-
deterred by the mental incapacity to think an
infinite *regress,* many of our modern savants find
the permanent and the eternal in the World-
process—a process ever-changeful, 'in which nought
endures save the flow of energy and the rational

order which pervades it'. But, even if the something that now is be admitted to have had a beginning, its existence does not imply any further cause than just what was adequate to its production; if the effect be finite, the cause need not be other than finite." Still again, the conception of God that this argumentation yields is simply that of a First Cause, as *external* Creator—such a God as Aristotle himself acknowledged, *outside* the world, and, perhaps, like the gods of Epicurus, not interesting Himself in its destiny. Hence, by a kind of unconscious propriety, the Causality argument for the Divine existence was the favourite one, if not the sole one, with the Deists of last century. Instinctively they gravitated towards the kind of reasoning that best suited their theistic notion.

√I   But, now, there *is* a truth that the Cosmological argument seeks, though it fails to give it felicitous form. We have here the assertion of the *transcendence* of God, -of the fact that the Deity is greater than the universe; that the world is dependent on Him; that materialism is inadequate as a full explanation of existence; that matter cannot be

---

¹ The difficulties that Materialism has to encounter will be found clearly stated in Principal Caird's *Introduction to the Philosophy of Religion* (chap. iv.), and in Professor Flint's *Anti-Theistic Theories*.

interpreted in terms of itself, but requires the mediation of a higher category, *viz.*, Active Reason. In this light, its value is great. It may be taken along with the teleological argument—it *must* be so taken, as transcendence and immanence go together,—and each may be viewed as indicating, in a fragmentary manner, the materials suitable for filling up our idea of God. In this way, the two give richness and content to the theistic conception, though they do not achieve a logical demonstration of God. They are simply attempts at *definition*—inadequate, of course, as all such attempts must be, dealing with an exhaustless Object; but serving a great and useful purpose, and even necessary, if we are to steady our thoughts on the Divine Being at all. St. Paul saw this, when he rebuked pagan antiquity for the debased character of its religion. He did not accuse the Gentiles, least of all the Greek and Roman heathen, of being ignorant of God. On the contrary, he acknowledged that they possessed the idea of Him. But what he blamed them for was their failure to fill in the idea with a worthier content,—which they might very well have done, if only they had cared; "for," said he, "the invisible things of Him, since the creation of the world, are clearly seen, being perceived through the things that are made, even His everlasting power and divinity " (*Romans*, i. 20).

III.

We now reach the last of the three "proofs,"—the ONTOLOGICAL ARGUMENT.

This argument, which infers from our conception of God to His actual being, may be said to have originated in the eleventh century of our era with St. Anselm, though the germ of it may perhaps be found in Plato. It is the least popular of the proofs. Even Aquinas seems not to have taken to it : and Bishop Ellicott, in our own day, omits it from his treatment of Theism, remarking : "I must candidly own that, to my own mind, it has never seemed to carry that conviction which, I well know, it carries to many. I have therefore deemed it best to leave it on one side" (*Six Addresses on the Being of God*, p. 27 *n.*). It is, doubtless, one of those arguments that Dr. Thomas Brown, in the passage quoted at the beginning of this lecture, termed "metaphysical" and "*a priori*," and of which he said that they are so laborious and obscure that their tendency is to create doubt in us, instead of confirming faith.[1]

Not so, however, did it appear to St. Anselm, and to many of those tough thinkers, the Scholastics,

---

[1] For an interesting account of the various *a priori* arguments, see lecture ix. of Professor Flint's *Theism*, with the relevant notes in the Appendix: also, Dr. Cazenove's *Historic Aspects of the a priori Argument Concerning the Being and Attributes of God.*

who fed for centuries upon the food with which St.
Anselm and kindred geniuses supplied them. Not
so did it appear to Descartes, who, though throwing out more proofs of the Divine existence than
one, nevertheless gave this as his main proof.
Not so does it appear to a section of philosophers
at the present day who are not afraid of metaphysics,
but who are prepared to speculate with a boldness
to which Descartes's ventures are timidity itself.

1. It was St. Anselm's reasoning, in the *Proslogion*, That, as our idea of God is the idea of the
greatest than whom nothing greater can be conceived, this implies His real as well as His ideal
existence, for a God that had not real existence
would fall short of our idea of God (which includes
real existence), and so our idea of the absolutely
greatest would be met by an idea of a greater
still,—which is absurd.

One suspects that, whatever force this argument
ever possessed lay, not in the reasoning, but in the
philosophical doctrine of Realism, which St. Anselm
and his age accepted. But, certainly, as a logical
argument, it is the merest sophistry. There is no
real proof here, or necessary deduction from
premisses. All that we can say is, that, given God,
and then it follows that He is "that than which
nothing greater can be conceived". But in this

we have simply a *definition* of God, not a demonstration of His existence.[1]

2. Improving upon St. Anselm, Descartes
argued " that we may validly infer the existence
of God from necessary existence being comprised
in the concept we have of Him ".

"When," he said, "the mind afterwards reviews
the different ideas that are in it, it discovers what
is by far the chief among them—that of a Being
omniscient, all-powerful, and absolutely perfect :
and it observes that in this idea there is contained
not only possible and contingent existence, as in
the ideas of all other things which it clearly per-
ceives, but existence absolutely necessary and
eternal. And just as because, for example, the
equality of its three angles to two right angles is
necessarily comprised in the idea of a triangle, the
mind is firmly persuaded that the three angles of
a triangle are equal to two right angles ; so, from
its perceiving necessary and eternal existence to be
comprised in the idea which it has of an all-perfect
Being, it ought manifestly to conclude that this all-
perfect Being exists " (*The Principles of Philosophy,*
Part I., sect. xiv., Professor Veitch's transl.).

---

[1] For a more lucid summary of the *Proslogion* than what is usually
found in histories of philosophy, see Maurice's *Mediæval Philosophy,*
chapter iii. For suggestive criticism of St. Anselm's position, see
Ueberweg's *History of Philosophy,* Eng. transl., vol. i. pp. 381-386.

Now, there does, certainly, seem to be here a leap from subjective to objective existence—an inferring of the real from the ideal ; and then the objection is valid, that we cannot infer from our having the idea of a golden mountain that such a mountain actually exists. All that we can say is, that, *if* God exists, the perfection that is found in my idea of Him must pertain to Him. But that does not prove His existence. No argument from the mere definition of God is valid, until you have first taken for granted His existence (real, and not merely ideal). Once given the existence, you may then, from the definition, argue its character and nature (precisely as is done by Descartes in the example from mathematics of the triangle with its angles) ; but, without the existence being presupposed, your determination of its character and nature, after the analogy of mathematics, is fallacious. No mathematical triangle really exists in our experience : all actual triangles are merely approximations to the ideal. And not Descartes himself ventures to infer the actual existence of the mathematical triangle from our conception of it ; he simply asserts the mind's firm persuasion of the equality of the three angles of a triangle to two right angles, from the fact that this equality is necessarily comprised in the idea of it.

Nor are we greatly helped, if we take the

argument as expressed in another shape. In the *Meditations*, Descartes reasons that whatever reality is in the effect must be also in the cause. But I have in me the idea of God as a perfect Being. This is an effect, which must have a cause. But I myself cannot be the cause of it, for I am finite and imperfect. It follows, therefore, that the cause of it is God. His own words are :—

" By the name God, I understand a substance, infinite, [eternal, immutable], independent, all-knowing, all-powerful, and by which I myself, and every other thing that exists, if any such there be, were created. But these properties are so great and excellent, that the more attentively I consider them the less I feel persuaded that the idea I have of them owes its origin to myself alone. And thus it is absolutely necessary to conclude, from all that I have said before, that God exists : for though the idea of substance be in my mind owing to this, that I myself am a substance, I should not, how-ever, have the idea of an infinite substance, seeing I am a finite being, unless it were given me by some substance in reality infinite. . . . For, as I said before, it is perfectly evident that there must at least be as much reality in the cause as in its effect; and accordingly, since I am a thinking thing, and possess in myself an idea of God, what-ever in the end be the cause of my existence, it

must of necessity be admitted that it is likewise a
thinking being, and that it possesses in itself the
idea and all the perfections I attribute to Deity"
(*Meditation* iii.; see, also, *Discourse on Method,*
part iv.). He said, further: "If we put anything into the idea which is not to be found in
its cause, that would derive its existence from
nothing".

To this John Stuart Mill replies: "Of which
it is scarcely a parody to say, that if there be
pepper in the soup there must be pepper in the
cook who made it, since otherwise the pepper
would be without a cause" (*System of Logic*, 10th
edit., vol. ii., pp. 342-3). This rejoinder, however,
is less than just. For, the efficiency that is in the
cook is only secondary: it consists, not in his
creating the ingredients necessary for the soup, or
their virtues, but in his determining the right combination of them needful to the end in view. He
has, indeed, the "perfection" of the effect in him,
but merely that perfection which is owing to his
culinary skill in adjusting means to ends and producing a certain result. Descartes's argument is
weak, partly because of the assumption that *his*
idea of God is that which is universally entertained, and partly because of his supposing that
this idea must necessarily come from God. Only
on the crudest form of the doctrine of "innate
28

ideas" could such procedure have even the semblance of plausibility.

Taking the ontological argument on the whole, then, we see that it is defective inasmuch as it bases the Divine existence on the mere fact that man has the idea of God, and infers from the mind to reality. Before the conception of God, as found in man, can be of any ontological value, we need first to have it settled that man is driven to this conception *by a necessity of his nature:* [1] not only must we find that he *has* the idea of God, but, also, that *he cannot avoid having it.* But, in that case, the Conception does not "prove" the Reality; it only serves in a manner to *define* it. If this be what Descartes really intended to express, he was on the lines of a great truth; and our objection then has reference, not to the substance of his teaching, but to the infelicitous and misleading form in which he set it forth.

IV.

A word is due on what is regarded by some as a fourth and distinct proof of the Divine Existence, and by others simply as an argument ancillary to the accredited proofs, *viz.,* the argument from the

---

[1] See Lecture v.

CONSENSUS GENTIUM or UNIVERSAL TESTIMONY of mankind.

This argument was a special favourite with ancient Greeks of the type of Plutarch, and was used with much emphasis and insistence by Cicero (speaking as a Stoic), through whom it passed as a commonplace of theistic reasoning into Western Europe. It was also highly prized by the early Christian Apologists and Church Fathers generally (Tertullian, Arnobius, Lactantius, St. Augustine. etc.), and thereby attained a position of eminence in Christian vindications of Religion which it has never lost. Indeed, it has seemed to Protestant apologists to be particularly effective : and great theologians like Hugo Grotius have placed it in the forefront of their polemic with the atheist. " Another Argument," says Grotius, in his *Truth of the Christian Religion* ("another," his second and only other, after the proof from Causality), " for the Proof of a Deity may be drawn from the plain Consent of all Nations, who have any Remains of Reason, any Sense of good Manners, and are not wholly degenerated into Brutishness. For, Humane Inventions, which depend upon the arbitrary Will of Men, are not always the same everywhere, but are often changed ; whereas there is no *Place* where this Notion is not to be found : nor has the Course of Time been able to alter it."

How firmly this argument held its ground may be seen by looking into any philosophico-theological treatise of a century ago—even into Butler; and Bishop Ellicott, in his *Six Addresses on the Being of God*, has recently written it up to date.

But there can be no question that the argument, as usually stated, is very far from convincing, and is liable to serious objections. *Universality* of belief, in the absolutely unqualified form, can hardly be maintained in the face of modern scientific research and of the fuller knowledge of savage races and distant lands that we now possess. Nor will the broadened charity that characterizes the present age permit us to rest satisfied with Grotius's explanation of exceptional cases,—*viz.*, affectation of novelty, bad principle, and distorted reason. Moreover, it is obvious, and (since the days of Carlyle, at least) is generally admitted, that Truth begins in a minority of one; and *Athanasius contra mundum* represents a not uncommon situation.

But replace "universal" by "*general*" consent: and then we see what real force the argument contains. It has no power at first hand, but only indirectly. General consent is not itself sufficient to establish truth; but it is sufficient to give us pause, and to lead us to examine carefully that for which the general consent of mankind is claimed.

Yea, further, it has a wholesome reaction upon conviction. For if Theism be, as is maintained in these Lectures, a Necessity of Human Nature, then we should, *a priori*, expect that men generally would show traces of theistic leanings ; and if, as matter of fact, we actually find these traces, *that*, though no primary proof of theism, is confirmatory or corroborative of it.

LECTURE XII.

WE now reach the last stage of our theistic argument,—that which faces the central difficulties of Theism, and tries to throw light upon them from the side of Philosophy.

"Philosophy" I here use in a special or restricted sense. In the wider signification, Philosophy, of course, includes psychology, and all the other mental sciences; but, in the special sense, in which it is distinguished from psychology, it means the attempt to reach a point of view where facts of experience are explained by having their place assigned them in reference to the whole a whole of which they form parts and are (as it were) organic members. In this sense, Philosophy may be defined as the rational explanation of the universe *as a universe*, or the reasoned interpretation of existence taken in its totality: and it claims to represent the strength of the human intellect, as marked off, on the one hand, from

(438)

cynical despair, which is the bitter acknowledgment of baffled effort and Reason's impotence, and, on the other hand, from that determined negative dogmatism, or dogmatism of negation, into which cynical despair is so apt to crystallize. It is, therefore, pre-eminently the unifying science ; it is that higher discipline and doctrine (for it is both) which looks upon the universe as an ordered organic whole, and which endeavours to show us that only in this way can we rightly understand existence or clearly apprehend Truth.

And this attitude of Philosophy is not confined to one school of thinkers, nor are we restricted by it (as some would have it) to any one shibboleth. Pantheists claim it : Giordano Bruno and Spinoza are typical instances. It is essentially Hegel's position. It is claimed by German mystics and theosophists of the type of Jacob Böhme. But deists, theists, and monotheists, under whatever label you may find them in histories of philosophy, equally lay claim to it. We have Leibniz, on the one side, and, on the other, Bishop Butler ; and between the two, you may place Shaftesbury. Much as these three theorizers differed from each other in vital points, they did, one and all, agree that the rational explanation of existence must rest on a comprehensive survey, and that the seeming exceptions to harmony and order in the world must be seeming only, owing to the fact, as Butler tersely expressed it, that the Divine Government is by us "a scheme or constitution imperfectly comprehended". They all aimed, each in his own way, at concrete, not abstract thinking : and tried to reach the rationale of things through the light of the universal. This is really the meaning of the doctrine a doctrine of the schools, early and late, emphasized by the ancient Stoics, taught by St. Thomas Aquinas, repeated with pietistic setting by Malebranche, re-echoed by Butler that government by general laws is the expression of the highest wisdom, and that such government is clearly discernible in the world taken as a whole.

Note, however, two preliminary cautions.

1. *First:* Philosophy, though aiming at interpreting existence from the side of the whole, must not so be understood as if it pretended to endow the individual philosopher with absolute power to account fully for every single fact in existence and to dovetail all the items into each other with unerring precision. This would require omniscience,— to which not even the philosopher may lay claim. But what is meant is, that philosophy can show us the standpoint from which the true unity of things may be descried, and can help us very materially in the rational attempt to comprehend life and

nature, and also to answer objections drawn
from a partial or one-sided view of things. Philosophical *systems* indeed abound, and there is no such
thing as a finally complete and infallible system :
here, as elsewhere, is writ large, *Humanum est
errare.* But though absolute infallibility is out
of the question, the various systems of philosophy
have value, and the test of value is the number
and suggestiveness of their great and leading ideas:
and that system has the best claim on our allegiance which presents us with the greatest number
and the most illuminative of deep thoughts. This is
what gives perennial worth to the systems of Plato
and Aristotle in days of old, and what marks off as
for all time such philosophies as those of Spinoza,
Leibniz, Berkeley, Kant, and Hegel, in modern
days. You must not expect from any philosophy,
as a system, finality: neither must you expect absolute completeness (though both characteristics have
sometimes been claimed by individual philosophers);
but what you are to expect is an elevated standpoint, stimulating conceptions, and light-giving
ideas, and with this you may rest content.[1]

2. *Next:* Philosophy insists on concrete think-

[1] This has been admirably put by De Quincey in the fifth of his
Letters to a Young Man (see Masson's *De Quincey*, vol. x. pp. 78,
79), and, again, in fewer words, but very pithily, by Mark Pattison in
the "Introductory" of his Clarendon Press Edition of Pope's *Essay
on Man*, p. 6.

ing. But, though it does this,— though it will not rest in abstract thought, but tries to compel you to think things as wholes and as interconnected,—you are not to suppose that abstract thinking is utterly and unreservedly condemned by it. On the contrary, man cannot help thinking in this way; it is necessary for him to break up and isolate phenomena, otherwise he could never advance at all in understanding the universe. But what philosophy insists on is, that, after you have isolated and analyzed, you proceed to synthesize and build up,

that you proceed beyond the logical and analytic stage (still, in light of your analysis), and re-combine your isolated facts, else you cannot grasp the bearings and the meaning of the objects studied. Construction presupposes destruction, speculation rests upon dissection; and the more careful and the more minute your dissection has been, so much the more likely is your theorizing to be both accurate and important. Hence the true place of Logic as the organon of scientific and of philosophic thought alike.

I have just said that the philosophical standpoint is the *unifying* standpoint it is viewing the parts in the light of the whole, or trying to make us keep ever in mind the circumstance that the explanation of a thing is its right location in the universe of thought and of being.

Now, what is Unity; and what is the unifying power that man possesses?

Unity means one of several things. (1) First, it means simply *generalization*; it is the intellectual process (*plus* product, of course) of grouping or classifying objects because of certain points of similarity or agreement between them. Thus, the things we know as mountains are grouped together because of their possessing certain properties in common (denoted by the name), and they are separated from other things known as valleys because of certain differences. Trees, again, constitute a group by themselves because of their fundamental similarities; so do rocks, and fields, and rivers, and so forth. The unity of classification is that of similarity or community of property.

It is but a special aspect of this same generalizing process when we group things together through the category of utility or purpose; so, too, when we sum up units into a total, or when we combine parts into a mechanical whole, as in the aggregation of particles of matter to form a stone, or in a bundle of twigs tied together by a cord.

But, (2) secondly, besides the unity that obtains between related objects, there is the unity that obtains between objects (things not ourselves) and ourselves. Here, we and the objects are not strictly regarded as *one* but as *at one*. And this

unity of *at-oneness* may be of two different kinds.
For, (*a*) first, objects may be separated from us,
may be kept apart from us, because of our *ignorance* of them ; but, whenever we come to know or
understand them, they enter into a new relationship with us ; they and we become *at one*. Or, (*b*)
secondly, we may be kept separate from objects,
more especially human beings, because, for one
reason or another, we are *estranged* from them,
are at feud with them, have come to *hate* them.
Remove this feud, this hatred, this estrangement,
and they and we become *at one*. This is the at-
oneness of reconciliation. If the first form of at-
oneness is the unity of things that have been
apart and kept for a time in isolation by being concealed from each other, this second is the unity of
things that have been in direct conscious antagonism or opposition.

But, (3) thirdly, there is the unity of *assimila-
tion* or *appropriation* ; and this, too, may be of a
twofold character,—it may be intellectual or it
may be emotional. (*a*) When we gain new knowledge and thereby find our mental powers developing and our mental horizon expanding, when we
appropriate it, and make it a part of ourselves, that
may be denominated a unity. (*b*) So is it a unity,
when our affections go forth to a human being and
we two are united in closest friendship ; or when I

form or accept an Ideal and try to work up to it or realize it in practice.

Now, are these different unities also totally distinct unities? Unity of generalization, unity of a person coming to understand an external object, unity of reconciliation between two offended brothers, unity of appropriating or assimilating truth, and unity of my identifying myself with a beloved fellow-mortal or with an ideal: are these, while diverse, also disparate or incompatible? No, although different, they are not disparate or incompatible; and the very fact that the same person possesses and exercises the unifying power represented in each of them proves that they must have a meeting-point in a deeper unity than what any one of themselves can show.

Well, this deeper unity is what we know distinctively by Personality; and in this deeper unity is found, so far as can be found, the explanation of existence. So says Philosophy. And, in saying so, it does not claim to be able to *solve* the long-standing puzzles of metaphysical speculation,—How can mind act on matter?—how can God and Nature meet? –it claims to place you at a point of view where you see that no such questions need be asked, and no solution be required: in other words, where you see that it is you yourself, by your too analytic thought, that have created the difficulty. In the unity of Being, differences indeed exist, but they are completely harmonized; and if you choose to rest upon the logical understanding alone and to make *it* the sole standard of truth, you can only land yourselves in perplexity and enigma. Carlyle caught this, after his own peculiar fashion, and expressed it in his own peculiar phraseology, when he said : " Our professor's method is not, in any case, that of common school Logic, where the truths all stand in a row, each holding by the skirts of the other ; but at best that of practical Reason, proceeding by large Intuition over whole systematic groups and kingdoms; whereby, we might say, a noble complexity, almost like that of Nature, reigns in his Philosophy, or spiritual picture of Nature : a mighty maze, yet, as faith whispers, not without a plan " (*Sartor Resartus*, p. 42).

But, now, if the desiderated Unity be that of the Universal—a unity in which differences' are contained and from which (if I may be allowed the materialistic expression) they emerge, a unity giving both connexion and continuity of members, a living organic unity (like that of the human body), and not the unity of a mere mechanical whole, whose parts are simply in external contact, —it is emphatically the unity of Spirit, or of Conscious Mind. Mind is the interpreting term, for there is no other unity and no other unifier conceivable by us that gives us unity in difference but the Ego ; and it does not require much sagacity to see that the supreme unifier, in the last resort, is, not the mind of any individual finite being, but Mind as gathered up in a centre of conscious being, far greater than the finite, Mind as gathered up in God. "No," you say, "unconscious thought or impersonal mind : *that* is sufficient." " But unconscious thought" and " impersonal mind " are simply meaningless expressions : and philosophers who use these as their ultimate explaining conception are really explaining nothing. They are simply juggling with words, and, while complaining that men are missing the truth through their exaggerated habit of abstract thinking, are themselves dealing in abstractions of the most glaring kind.

Hence, I think, the wisdom of Berkeley beyond that of many, in laying the foundation of his philosophy in a personal Deity, in conscious Active Reason. Whatever improvements it may be possible in this nineteenth century to make upon certain of his words and phrases in *Siris* and *The Minute Philosopher*, and however necessary it may be to drop certain of his arguments and even to recast a great deal of his reasoning, his central position remains intact, and will remain intact, so far as appears, to the very end of time,—and modern criticism has only served to bring it out in clearer light and stronger form.

This being so, it is particularly desirable that we understand exactly what it is that Philosophy can, and what it cannot, do.

In representing the world to us as a manifestation of Mind, in endeavouring to get us to look at things, not as isolated phenomena, but as parts of an organic whole, it saves us in great measure from the perplexities and incompleteness of analytic thought, and shows us that there is a point of view (synthetic in its nature) at which discrepancies disappear and seeming discords are harmonized, and that, if there still remain for us unsolved difficulties and differences unreconciled, this arises from the fact of our limited capacities and of our practical inability to maintain ourselves, without descents, on the higher plane.

But man's powers in this way are certainly limited,—he himself is not omniscient; and this gives us the practical limitations of Philosophy. When Philosophy presents Nature to us as a manifestation of the Deity, it thereby enables us to discover a deep and highly-suggestive meaning in Nature, and, so far, to understand how we ourselves and Nature can come into living contact.

I, being spiritual (it says), can touch my fellow-man—can apprehend him intellectually and go forth to him with the heart,—because we two are of the same nature, we both are spirits. But he and I also can hold communication with outward Nature—can understand it and assimilate it and even love it,—because Nature is only the visible embodiment or sense-manifestation of mind ; and mind, again, is our common property. But how the Universal Mind, or Supreme all-comprehending Spirit, should manifest Himself in this particular form of the *material* remains inexplicable. Spinoza at one time thought he saw light in the fact of the Deity's abundant fulness, which was bound to over-flow in all directions. But that, clearly, though true enough in a sense, solves nothing. The need of an "other," through which self-conscious spirit should realize itself, may indeed be granted ; but why this other should be matter has never been shown, neither has it ever been shown (there is no *a priori* ground for determining it) why the finite manifestations of Spirit are just those they are and no other, and just the number that they are and neither more nor less. This is the ultimate in Philosophy, beyond which it seems impossible to get.

Let us not, then, misunderstand Philosophy ; neither let us prove ourselves ungrateful for its

29

help. When the plain man says to Philosophy, "Explain to me *everything*," Philosophy's only answer can be, —"You make an unreasonable request; I do not know everything, nor do I pretend to. To me, as to you, there comes a point beyond which I cannot go: *I*, too, must stand somewhere, only not quite where you do; and I have fully shown my function and justified my claims when I have driven a shaft through the difficulties of superficial unreflective thought and have touched the fundamental rock, and when, moreover, I have made clear how much farther it is possible to advance than the plain man ever imagines, and what are the necessary limits of man's thought."

Although there have been philosophers who have claimed more for their particular systems than they were justified in doing, and so have exposed themselves to the laugh of the facetious when they have fallen into the well,[1] that must not be allowed to blind us to the fact that philosophy is better than its devotees. The infinite truth and complexity of the universe cannot be comprehended in a single formula, however neat and logically simple it may be. Truth, because living, and to

---

[1] It is recorded by Plato, in the *Theætetus*, that Thales was laughed at by a smart and witty Thracian maid when he fell into a well; for, to her it seemed irresistibly funny that a man should be so absorbed in star-gazing as to be oblivious to the things that lay before him and at his feet.

the extent that we ourselves firmly lay hold upon
it and retain it with entire conviction, is prone to
burst the bonds of formulæ. But formulæ are not,
on that account, useless. On the contrary, they
are indispensable and very helpful, unless awk-
wardly or wrongly handled; and each one of
them, so that it be light-giving, may be gladly
welcomed by us and profitably applied in its utmost range. Philosophy is a standpoint, and,
therefore, a method; and it is, further, the doctrine
that Mind is constitutive of the universe, and gives
it unity and intelligibility. And thus far, surely,
Philosophy is right; and thus far may we heartily
and unhesitatingly embrace it.

But now, the place and function of Philosophy
being such, certain very definite results should be
achieved by it.

1. In the first place, inasmuch as Philosophy
discloses the world as a cosmos and not a chaos,
it shows us the true meaning of what is called
Natural Law. Physicists, impressed by the Uniformity of Nature or the reign of Law in the
material world, have sometimes been tempted to
regard this uniformity as a kind of pagan Necessity, ruling as a sort of independent and inexorable
sovereign supreme over matter and intelligence

alike, and excluding the conception of Divine Mind in the world as both unneeded and impossible. They have pitted Science against Religion, and have maintained that the two are mutually exclusive. But natural law, says Philosophy, is itself but an abstraction; before you can give it meaning, you have to presuppose intelligence, and, unless it bears evidence to an underlying order, it is a pure nonentity. Nay, further: Nature is indeed uniform, and this very fact bespeaks the existence of something supernatural, something rational, something spiritual; and this supernatural, rational, spiritual something is God. Yea, this Uniformity is the very thing that you might *a priori* deduce from God's nature and attributes. If God is, then Nature must be uniform. So reasoned Spinoza, in his *De Deo et Homine;* and so have all others of kindred spirit reasoned, since Spinoza's day.

And this reasoning seems to me to be unimpeachable. Nature, standing by itself, is nothing; and Nature's uniformity is a mere empty phrase, unless it denote a certain mode or aspect under which Divine Intelligence works and makes itself felt. The immanence of Deity is here—*that* is the logical *prius;* and the scientist's attempt (not often made by scientific chiefs, certainly, but often made by those who presume to speak for them) to turn

Nature's uniformity as an argument against the theistic position, simply shows the necessity of guarding against permitting abstract thinking to take the place of concrete thought. "Where Intellect presides," says Berkeley, "there will be method and order, and therefore rules, which if not stated and constant, would cease to be rules. There is therefore a constancy in things, which is styled the Course of Nature" (*Siris*, § 234). It is only another way of stating the same thing when I say, that natural law, as being the perfection of the material world, shows by its very perfection the nature of the Deity, as clearly as does spiritual law ruling and controlling the soul. Hence, the psalmist by a very sound philosophical instinct passes at once (in Psalm xix.) from the heavens as declaring God's glory –from the sun, in especial, with his regular unceasing course and his never-failing impressiveness—to the Law of the Lord which converts the soul, and His commandment which enlightens the eyes. Natural and spiritual are thus far, at any rate, of a piece, that each bespeaks the Divine presence and existence.

"The Vedic poet well understood this when he cried : 'The sun and the moon move in regular succession in order that we may believe, O Indra !' . . . 'It is because of law that we believe in the

gods,' says Euripides ; and the Egyptians went
further still in declaring that 'the gods live by
Maāt'"[1] (Count Goblet d' Alviella, *The Hibbert
Lectures* for 1891).

2. But, next, from the vantage-ground of philosophy, we can take a calm and appreciative view
of Biological Evolution. The Darwinian theory :
why fear it ? It is simply a *method* explanatory,
not of existence, but of the way in which certain
existences have come to be what they are. It is
a way of manipulating given material; but the material itself is not thereby accounted for. No mode of
genesis of finite existences can injuriously affect the
metaphysical presuppositions of philosophy these
remain, being beyond reach of the mutations of
the world in time ; but every mode of genesis
in time, inductively established as a fact, may be
turned to illustrate the philosophical position
of the immanent and all-pervading action of
Mind.

3. Then, thirdly, accepting the attitude of the
philosopher, we see at once the true character

---

[1] "The primitive notion implied by the word *maāt* seems to be
the geometrical one 'right,' as in 'right line.' as opposed to χ^{ab},
'bent,' 'perverse'. *Maāt* as a noun is the 'straight rule,' 'canon'. . . . ."
"*Maāt* is not only Truth and Justice, but Order and Law, in the
physical as well as in the moral world" (P. Le Page Renouf, *The
Hibbert Lectures* for 1879, p. 71 *n.* and p. 120).

of outward Nature (as I have already said), and
are shown how to escape the dilemmas and
antinomies into which an imperfect theory of
knowledge is liable to plunge us.

Underlying Nature, and giving it its meaning,
is Intelligence and Mind. But if so, then Nature,
in all its parts and processes, is but a manifestation
of the Deity. The outward world is not a dead
dull independent mass, set over against the conscious Ego and separated from it *toto caelo*. If
this were so, then Mind and Matter could never
come together ; they would be irreconcilable
opposites. But if Nature be one of the ways in
which the Deity reveals Himself, if it has no
existence apart from Him and in Him alone has
all its signification, then, with Nature thus instinct
with Spirit, the human Ego may well have communication ; for, being itself spiritual, in thus going
forth into Nature it simply finds itself,—or it finds,
albeit dimly and half-consciously, the Divine
Spirit, in whom itself lives and moves and has
its being. And if we must still talk of mind and
matter *meeting*, then they meet because Nature
is the workmanship of the *Erdgeist :*—

> Thus at the whirring loom of Time I ply,
> Weaving the living robe of Deity.

4. Fourthly, we can see how it is unphilosophic

to speak of the *eternity* of matter or of the world. Philosophy objects to regarding matter or the world as eternal because Mind not Matter is the logical *prius,* Spirit not Nature. Given mind, and (as matter is a mode of revealing the Deity) you have given matter also : but not inversely. Moreover, matter is only *one* mode of God's manifestations of Himself : there are countless other modes, possible or actual, conceivable or real ; and Philosophy could regard any one of these modes as eternal only if it bore the special mark of eternity upon it, or if it were the only conceivable mode of Divine manifestation, or even the only mode of our experience. As Substance,[1] apart from manifestation, God is not. An existent God is, also, an eternally manifested God. This is the dictum of philosophy, as well as of the highest theology. But neither philosophy nor theology demands that the *material* mode of manifestation shall itself be eternal.

5. But, fifthly, from the standpoint of philosophy, we can see in a manner how to rebut the arguments of the abstract understanding as to the never-failing problem of moral *evil* and of physical pain, and the difficulties, arising from the ap-

---

[1] That substance is not *substratum*, see Father Rickaby's *General Metaphysics*, Bk. II.

parently untoward circumstances of life and experience, in the way of our fully recognizing the
absolute wisdom and goodness of the Divinity.

(1) An argument against God's Omnipotence,
and, therefore, against the value of the Theistic
conception, is sometimes drawn from the doctrine
of an Overruling Providence. For, this doctrine,
it is said, clearly maintains that God can overrule
moral evil--can control it, can turn it to ultimate
good,—but that He had not the power at first to
prevent its happening or occurring.

If this, in all its literality, were really the
doctrine of an overruling providence, it would be
hard to see how the omnipotence of God could
be effectively saved. For, a power of controlling
or overruling simply would not be sufficient to
establish omnipotence in all its width and significance. Nor would you greatly mend matters by
maintaining that God merely *permits* moral evil--
allows it,—with a view to produce an ultimate good
greater than would otherwise be possible : for, this
very fact of allowing evil that good may come
would cut the character of God in a twofold way.
In the first place, it would be derogatory to His
power, inasmuch as it would imply His inability
or impotence to achieve the highest good without
the instrumentality of evil ; and, in the next place,

it would be destructive of His *righteousness*, inasmuch as it would make God in some measure responsible for the introduction of sin into the world, and would stamp with His sanction the pernicious principle that the end justifies the means.

But rise to the higher point of view—regard the Universe as a great whole, informed by Reason, with its parts interdependent and organic,—and then you see that Evil has its place there through no impotence of the Almighty Author. From the very moment of its entrance into the world, it comes as a conquered factor; and the very day the sons of God came to present themselves before the Lord in fealty and humble submission, "Satan came also among them to present himself before the Lord". It is simply, in philosophic phrase, "the other" which, *under the circumstances*, serves to bring His power into a particular manifestation, and, in one distinct form, to secure its triumph; while having itself no independent existence, and no real efficiency in either restraining or curtailing omnipotence.

Omnipotence is not to be identified with mere superior might or irresistible coercive power; nor is sin to be regarded as a thing *ab extra*, thrust perforce by an alien strength into the world. Sin was in the world from the beginning *potentially* (that is implied in the very idea of finitude); and the mere fact that, at a particular moment of the world's being, it became an *actuality* does not really alter the matter. If the world was to contain man at all, and if man as a spiritual being was to be what he is, sin thereby became a possibility; and its actual occurrence at a given date was no real infringement of the plan and constitution of the world as Divinely established, for this plan or constitution had reference, among other things, to "the realm of persons," with all the possibilities that finite personality implied. The data being such, it is evident that moral evil *might* arise at some time, and *must* and *would* arise if a certain one of the two alternatives equally open to a rational and reflective being were consciously chosen; and, once you clearly see this, there is no difficulty in perceiving that omnipotence is in no way interfered with by the fact of such a choice being made. But if you still ask, Why did God not so endow man that he could not sin? then I answer (with Spinoza), Why did God not endow the circle with the properties of the sphere?

But now, this being so, the argument takes a new turn. For, though the controlling of moral evil, the overruling of it for ultimate good, does not, in the first instance, prove the omnipotence of God, inasmuch as what puzzles us with regard to sin is, not the *counteracting* of it, but its own *existence*,—yet, now that we have seen that its existence is no argument against God's omnipotence, we are in a position to be able to turn the controlling of it into an argument in its favour. For, when potential evil became actual, its tendency was to gain the mastery in the world; and He who subverts that mastery, and makes it, *contrary to its nature*, even instrumental to a higher good, is, without question, possessed of superhuman power, and His controlling and directing agency bespeaks His perfect nature.

Surely, it is a sign of strength, and not of weakness, to have so settled the constitution of the world that, when sin did make its appearance in it, that constitution should not be utterly wrecked and overturned, but should be able to withstand disintegration and to turn the mischief into permanent good. Sin is in the world, but it is *not predominant* there: for, though it is the humour of some to maintain that sin has the supremacy here, we need little reflection to see that, if this were really so, no such thing as Society could exist. As sin is essentially a *disintegrating* force, as its whole tendency is to break up and to pull down, *not* to bind together or cement, does not the very fact of Society prove that good in the world is even more powerful than evil, and that there is, amongst men, more of the preserving salt than of the corrupting leaven ?

(2) In like manner, from the Philosophic stand-point, Pain is seen to be no real evil, and, therefore, no curtailment of Divine Omnipotence. True, if evil be defined as that which is painful, pain must of necessity be an evil. But, in view of the sacred ministry of Pain (bodily and mental) in forming human character and purifying the human soul, in view of its unquestioned efficacy in evoking patience and heroism in man, in training him in the highest moral virtues, in strengthening and bracing his intellectual and moral fibre, it is irrational to suppose that it is a real evil, or that, under our present circumstances, the soul could thrive or grow without it. Omnipotence could, no doubt, put an end to pain ; but it could only do so by annihilating the sensitive organism, or by totally transforming its environment. But given the sensitive organism, and given the present environment, and suscep-tibility to pain is a necessity ; and to demand that God shall (*these conditions remaining*) remove this susceptibility, or destroy pain, is to demand what is self-contradictory,—it is to require that a thing should both be and not be at the same time.

Professor Sidgwick has very well expressed this from the ethical side when, in answering the objection, "that observation of the actual world shows us that the happiness of sentient beings is so imperfectly attained in it, and with so large an admixture of pain and misery, that we cannot reasonably conceive Universal Happiness to be God's end, unless we admit that he is not Omnipotent," he says :—"And no doubt the assertion that God is Omnipotent will require to be understood with some limitation; but perhaps with no greater limitation than has always been implicitly admitted by thoughtful theologians. For these seem always to have allowed that some things are impossible to God: as, for example, to change the past. And perhaps if our knowledge of the Universe were complete, we might discern the *quantum* of happiness ultimately attained in it to be as great as could be attained without the accomplishment of what we should then see to be just as inconceivable and absurd as changing the past" (*The Methods of Ethics*, 4th edition, p. 502).

In fine, our difficulties about Omnipotence arise very much from the fact that we insist on looking upon Omnipotence as an *isolated* attribute of the Deity, whereas it is necessarily conditioned by Wisdom and by Righteousness. We would have it to be unlimited power arbitrarily employed; but this is wholly irrational. "No religious need," as Lotze says, "drives us to seek in God omnipotence devoid of intelligence;" nor does any religious need, we may add, drive us to seek in Him omnipotence devoid of goodness.

(3) Similarly, the fact of suffering among the lower animals is seen, from the philosophical attitude, to afford no sufficient reason for impeaching the Divine Wisdom and Goodness. Pain, as mere suffering, is incidental to a sensitive organism placed in particular surroundings : and, as there is here no question of rightness or wrongness involved (such as there was in the case of moral evil), you cannot legitimately say, from the philosophic platform, either that God is harsh and cruel towards the dumb creatures in permitting them to suffer, or that He is lacking in wisdom in not establishing the world on a different basis so as to preclude the possibility of suffering altogether. For, we must view things in themselves and in their wider relations,—*i.e.*, through the *idea* ; and, doing so, we see that suffering, as mere pain (where no notion of *desert* enters), cannot be either good or bad, but is simply part of that scheme of mundane things which is *necessary* in the given circumstances,— which circumstances, again, must themselves be interpreted in the light of a progressive perfection, working itself out in time. Pain is a mode of realizing the idea under temporal conditions ; and,

if we are prone to regard it as an *imperfection* in the world, this is because we forget that the *perfection* of a thing has no meaning except with reference to the nature of the thing itself and its relations, except with reference to the idea that it is instrumental in realizing. If I make my particular *desire* as to what a thing ought to be the measure of the thing's perfection, then, indeed, many things may appear to me very imperfect, because they do not effect what I desire them to effect, or answer the purpose that I would assign to them. But if we view things in connexion with the whole for which they exist, and not from the individual standpoint of personal desire, then their seeming imperfection at once disappears, and, in the broader light, we discern their function and their place.

Ay, and in this broader light, even the inexorability of Nature and its so-called cruelty, the fact of " Nature red in tooth and claw with ravine," loses its maleficent aspect. Mere superior might, dissociated from the idea of *merit*, cannot be maleficent. The action of natural forces is subservient to general laws; and the ferocity of wild animals preying upon each other could only be condemned as cruel or unjust, if the animals themselves were of a different nature from what they are.

But, now, in order to clearness, I must revert once more to the position that philosophy, with its spiritualistic basis, does not explain to us how Spirit and not-Spirit meet; for, in this matter, there is a great deal of misunderstanding, giving rise to a great deal of irrelevant criticism. When Philosophy sets forth Nature as the "other" of spirit and the translucent garment of the Divinity, it is frequently objected that that explains nothing. There are three distinct realities (it is said) that have to be taken into account,—*viz.*, the human mind or finite Ego, Matter or external Nature, and God; and between these three realities there are three chasms,—*viz.*, between the finite Ego and Nature, between the Infinite Ego and Nature, and between the Infinite and the finite Ego, and not one of these has Philosophy bridged.

To this, we must make answer :—If these three things—Nature, the human Ego, and God—be indeed totally separate realities, then it is true that three chasms exist between them, and these have not been bridged by philosophy; but, then, Philosophy has never pretended to bridge them, and has even made it a great part of its business to point out that it has not done so, and that (in this abstract sense) such bridging is impossible. "Once," it says, "you make the finite and the infinite, and mind and matter, absolute opposites, the possibility of a meeting-point between them is effectually and entirely taken away." But what philosophy does, or claims to do, is to accept the working of the ego as it is found in our own experience, *plus* the rational implications that such experience involves, and to make this the interpreting principle—not, indeed, so as to explain the inexplicable, but so as to set you at a point where you perceive what is inexplicable and why,- and to carry out this principle to its furthest application. The fault lies with the abstract critic, not with philosophy.

It used to be strongly objected to Berkeley that, in denying Matter as a metaphysical substratum, he denied the reality of matter altogether. There could not have been a greater mistake. He simply denied the isolated self-contradictory matter of un-reflective or unsophisticated thought, but left the only matter which has true reality—not the abstraction matter, which is a pure nonentity, but the matter which alone has being because it is in inseparable relation to mind. His work was not that of a constructor of bridges (*that* must be left to the abstraction architect), but that of an interpreter of existence in light of the spiritual ego, which was the best known and the most reliable of all existences. *He* succeeded ; the abstract critic missed the mark.

So has the abstract critic erred, when he has

attacked philosophy on the side of the *unity* of spirit. "Bare unity," he says: "out of *that*, you can never get diversity—not even the various mental and moral attributes of power, wisdom, goodness, and the like." But the unity of personality, with which philosophy deals, is not a bare unity; it is the unity of differences organically connected: spiritual life is an unceasing process, a perpetual activity, not a dead principle, dull, motionless and stationary. In the Ego, there are a variety of unifying processes; but, in each, the soul finds health and expansion,—*realizes* itself,—and, through the never-ceasing rhythm of opposition and the conquering of opposition, of barriers erected and the breaking of them down, widens its horizon and deepens the current of its conscious life. Nay, the various mental attributes of feeling, intellect, and will are differences in a living unity; and, although it suits our convenience to ally power to our voluntary activity, and wisdom to intellect, and goodness to emotion,—yet feeling, intellect, and will are nothing taken separately. The very differences they represent are differences of the living and energizing Self, and not one of them could exist, not one of them have meaning, save as implicating the others and as bound up in the organic whole. Hence, the impulses of our nature—*e.g.*, the impulse to religion and the impulse to knowledge,—though different, are, in principle, one and the same ; and the differences emerge because they are *there*, inherent in the unity, and not alien to it.

One begins to suspect that the abstract critic, in urging his objection, has fallen into confusion—has confounded between a unit and unity. But a unit is simply an individual thing, which difference may break up, may shatter and dissolve ; unity is not individual, but collective or universal, which difference only serves to realize—to further and develop. The essence of the universal is expansion (as we see in altruism and the brotherhood of the race) ; that of the singular is limitation or restriction. If you take a unit for the whole, then unity, in the higher sense, is impossible ; but given unity, and variety is given also— all the variety that is implied in the manifold of experience through which unity is attained. We see the distinction in the human body, every member of which, if taken as a unit, is impotent, but, regarded in relation to the other members and to the whole, finds its meaning and its place. Taken as bare units, the members seem to stand in solitary independence and separation ; but viewed in the light of the body as a unity, not one of them can say to another, " I have no need of thee ".

From all which it follows that the abstract

critic's objection is futile; and that the question, How from mere unity can differences arise? is quite unintelligent and irrelevant.

And now, Ladies and Gentlemen, I must draw these Lectures to a close. For the regular attendance with which so many of you have honoured me (often, as I know, at great personal inconvenience, in the midst of your multifarious duties), I offer you my thanks. Nothing has been more gratifying or more encouraging to me than to find the same faces appearing time after time, and, every time, the same sustained attention accorded me. I thank you heartily; and, while now I bid you Farewell, I do so with pleasant memories, and with the satisfaction of our having meditated together on the greatest and most momentous of the themes that can occupy the thoughts and engage the affections of men. You have now become, as it were, a part of my being; and when, in future, I pursue the subject of Theism, I shall not be able to do so without specially associating it with yourselves.

ABERDEEN UNIVERSITY PRESS.

www.ingramcontent.com/pod-product-compliance
Lightning Source LLC
Chambersburg PA
CBHW032012110726
47901CB00004B/1056